THE FUNCTIONALLY FLUENT TEACHER

STEVE WILLSHAW

Although every effort has been made to ensure that website addresses are correct at time of going to press, Hachette Learning cannot be held responsible for the content of any website mentioned in this book. It is sometimes possible to find a relocated web page by typing in the address of the home page for a website in the URL window of your browser.

Hachette UK's policy is to use papers that are natural, renewable and recyclable products and made from wood grown in well-managed forests and other controlled sources. The logging and manufacturing processes are expected to conform to the environmental regulations of the country of origin.

To order, please visit www.HachetteLearning.com or contact Customer Service at education@hachette.co.uk / +44 (0)1235 827827.

ISBN: 978 1 0360 0753 9

© Steve Willshaw 2026

First published in 2026 by
Hachette Learning (a trading division of Hodder & Stoughton Limited),
An Hachette UK Company
Carmelite House
50 Victoria Embankment
London EC4Y 0DZ

www.HachetteLearning.com

The authorised representative in the EEA is Hachette Ireland, 8 Castlecourt Centre, Dublin 15, D15 XTP3, Ireland (email: info@hbgi.ie)

Impression number 10 9 8 7 6 5 4 3 2 1
Year   2030 2029 2028 2027 2026

Illustrations by DC Graphic Design Ltd.
Typeset in the UK.
Printed in the UK.
A catalogue record for this title is available from the British Library.

*To Ruth, Tom, Joe and Ben –
for the support, love and humour you bring to my life every day.*

ABOUT THE AUTHOR

Steve Willshaw, with a career spanning over 35 years in the education sector, has a wide range of experience to draw upon. He devoted two decades to teaching secondary English, first in Tower Hamlets and later in Nottinghamshire and Lincolnshire, where he was head of English in two large comprehensives. Then, as a senior school-improvement consultant in Lincolnshire, education officer in Guernsey and multi-academy trust subject lead for English, Steve spent an additional 15 years steering educational institutions towards greater achievements and higher standards. He was a trustee of the National Association for Advisers in English, is Chair of the National Baccalaureate Trust and records interviews on a wide range of educational topics for Myatt and Co. Since 2021, he has been the UK Connector for Functional Fluency International, bringing together and growing the network. Steve is a licensed TIFF© provider and trained Get on the Mat© facilitator, has an ILM Level 7 qualification in Executive Coaching and Mentoring and is an accredited Practitioner with EMCC Global. He now works as a freelance educational consultant and executive coach.

ACKNOWLEDGEMENTS

Bringing this book to life has been anything but a solitary task. I am indebted to James Morse, my coach for the last 19 months, for helping me to focus on completing the writing as well as clarifying the key themes that run through all my work.

I hope this book is characterised by radical simplicity. It is an attempt to strip away the noise of modern education and focus on Functional Fluency as an elegant, effective lever that enables both teachers and pupils to thrive.

The book is also the product of a rich community of support and a shared commitment to the professional craft of teaching. In all my various jobs, I have had the pleasure and privilege of working with many inspiring colleagues from whom I have learnt so much.

I am indebted to all the practitioners whose 'stories from the field' exemplify the relational agency that sits at the core of this work. Your insights into how Functional Fluency transforms leadership and classroom dynamics have helped prove that our relational choices are the most powerful tools we possess.

My deepest gratitude goes to Dr Susannah Temple, the creator of the TIFF model. Her measured wisdom and inspirational approach to training in 2011 were the catalysts for my own Functional Fluency journey. I would also like to acknowledge the support I have received firstly from The Fluent Self CIC, and subsequently from Functional Fluency International and its directors, Leona Bishop and Layo Seriki. I particularly want to highlight the team of UK-based Functional Fluency professionals – the challenge and friendship you have provided over the years have driven this project forward.

I would also like to thank those who champion intellectual equity in our schools – ensuring that every pupil and staff member is seen, heard and valued. Special thanks to Mary Myatt for her ongoing support and for providing a platform on Myatt & Co to explore these vital topics. I am also grateful to all those colleagues who have read and commented on drafts of chapters – your feedback helped improve the book immensely. I am particularly indebted to Ben and Sarah Wilkinson for their comments and for their friendship over many years.

To the team at Hachette Learning, thank you for your belief in this project and for navigating the transition from abstract ideas to the physical book you hold today. And to the many educators I've coached – including the 'Rhyses', 'Tinas' and 'Grahams' who appear in these pages – thank you for your vulnerability and for the trust and licence you gave me to join you on your journeys.

REVIEWS

There are many reasons to consider the quality of interactions, ways of working and culture within our settings. One of the most important is that we can have all the results in the world, but if pupils and staff experience conditions as stifling and highly pressurised, then we have to ask ourselves whether it's really worth it. An alternative is to argue that high standards and humane, joyful organisations are not mutually exclusive. Functional Fluency has the potential to be a powerful tool to achieve the latter. Steve Willshaw has written a book that draws together the research and the threads of the TIFF model and shown, through examples and practitioner insights, the difference that such an intentional approach can make. Highly recommend.

Mary Myatt, founder Myatt & Co and The Teachers' Collection

Some books make you think, some books change how you behave; this book does both! Steve weaves anecdotal narrative with the powerful Functional Fluency modelling. It's impossible to read without applying to yourself wholeheartedly. In education there is a tension between doing your best and being your best. As you read and learn more about Functional Fluency and yourself, you can notice, modify and adapt behaviours to form more effective relationships with colleagues and what is arguably the most powerful profession in the world!

Rachel Higginson, keynote speaker, trust and school development facilitator, curriculum designer and the curator of the Finding my Voice approach

What if there is another way? Another way to navigate with energy through the relationships, complexities, uncertainties, stresses and strains and, yes, victories, that are part and parcel of the fabric of life within educational communities? With this book, Steve Willshaw shows us, using classroom 'chalk-face' experiences and examples, that there is another way that works, and how, by using a menu (Functional Fluency) we can heighten our individual and collective awareness and understanding of what's going on in our reality, whether that be as a pupil or principal, and choose behaviours that help us and those around us to thrive, not just survive. This is not just another book!

Ian Dunnett, coach, mediator, trainer, facilitator, owner – Ian Dunnett Coaching

CONTENTS

INTRODUCTION

In the bustling, sometimes chaotic, world of the school on the hill, there was a headteacher named Rhys. Rhys was a good man, dedicated to his school; but, since taking on the role, he had carried a silent, heavy cloak – the burden of imposter syndrome. He felt he had to fight every fire himself, fearing that delegating would make him seem lazy or, worse, reveal his perceived inadequacies. His days were a whirlwind of unmanaged diary commitments, impromptu pop-ins from staff and the constant feeling that he alone was responsible for the school's fortunes. He wrestled with worries, convinced he always needed to provide all the answers and personally address every problem.

Rhys had taken on an underperforming school and, through sheer grit, he had undeniably moved it to a better position. Yet, even with this success, a quiet voice in his head whispered that it wasn't enough, that he hadn't truly earned his place. His PA, Diane, saw his struggles firsthand. He'd **try** to delegate but, often, the job would land back on his plate. His diary was a battlefield of double-bookings – a testament to his struggle to set boundaries.

Then came the turning point. Rhys embarked on a journey of Functional Fluency coaching with me as his guide. It wasn't a quick fix, but a gradual unfolding; a shedding of the old skin. Over three or four years, he began to understand himself and, crucially, his imposter syndrome, not as a weakness to be hidden, but as a part of him that, ironically, had propelled him to do things differently. He started to talk about it openly, even with pride. As his coach, I saw this as a monumental step; a true embracing of his authentic self.

I helped him see the power of Accounting in decision-making – the rational, fact-based approach that wasn't about having all the answers, but about clear, objective thought. He learned to balance Structuring – the organised, planned approach to his day and tasks – with Nurturing – showing genuine care and support for his team. This wasn't about being soft; it was about building trust and creating an environment where others felt empowered. And we discussed the importance of allowing his authentic, Cooperative and Spontaneous strengths to manifest themselves. Every session, I could see the gears turning and the subtle shifts in his perspective this enabled.

Slowly, almost imperceptibly at first, Rhys started to change. Diane noticed it. He began to manage his diary with purpose, encouraging staff to book appointments, creating space for p anned, controlled discussions. The double-bookings became a rarity. More important, he was truly trying to empower others; to delegate 'with purpose' so that the team was truly 'achieving together': the school motto. He continued to l ve up to one of his favourite mantras from New Zealand rugby, that no one is above 'cleaning the sheds', showing humility and solidarity – but the shift was undeniable.

Martin, Rhys's chair of governors, saw it too. Rhys was becoming 'much more chilled'. He was starting to 'apprec ate delegation rather than having to fight every fire himself'. He was trusting his team, becoming 'aware of his strengths and weaknesses' and 'putting trust in others to sort things out'. He was even switching off, finding that crucial balance between work and the rest of life. When Ofsted came knocking, a moment that would once have sent Rhys into a flurry of activity, he was 'fully prepared and organised' and able to 'lead the team with efficiency'. Rhys himself reflected positively on our sessions with Martin, which was incredibly gratifying.

Rhys, at last, was learning to 'recognise his achievements and progress'. The heavy cloak of imposter syndrome hadn't vanished entirely, but it no longer defined him. He had found a new way of leading; one rooted in collaboration, trust and a deep understanding of his own contribution within the collective. The school on the hill, once underperforming, was now thriving: not because Rhys was working harder, but because he had learned to lead smarter by modelling Functional Fluency. He had learned that true leadership wasn't about having all the answers, but about building a team where everyone contributed, where worries were shared and where delegation wasn't a sign of laziness, but a demonstration of shared purpose and collective strength.

Witnessing Rhys's journey has been a testament to the power of Functional Fluency. It has been a privilege to be his coach, seeing him evolve into a more confident and effective leader. When leaders like Rhys consciously model Accounting in decision-making; balance Structuring with Nurturing in their interactions; and utilise Cooperative and Spontaneous modes effectively, they provide a consistent and powerful template for their teams. This lived example is often the most potent catalyst for embedding Functionally Fluent practices throughout the school culture, moving beyond theoretical understanding to tangible behavioural change.

Yet, even with these profound changes, I often found myself with a bittersweet feeling. I am immensely pleased with the progress, but I also know, with absolute certainty, that there is so much more potential for leaders like Rhys to harness within their schools.

Schools are built on communication and are full to bursting point with relationships – not all of them constructive. If a school community – from the leadership to the teachers, teaching assistants, administrative staff, pupils and parents – can become more Functionally Fluent, even just to a small degree, I know that the benefits to the lives of everyone who makes up that community will be enormous. Functional Fluency should be implicit in the way teachers and pupils communicate and how the school encourages pupils to relate to each other. Functional Fluency supports school vision and values and provides a clear way in which these otherwise abstract concepts can be lived out. It also provides a common language with which to talk about relationships, helping to develop congruence between the ways schools and families approach helping their young people to grow up.

This ongoing realisation – this quiet frustration with the untapped possibilities – is precisely why I was compelled to write this book: to share the transformative power of Functional Fluency and empower more teachers and leaders to use it to help themselves and, most important of all, their pupils, to reach their fullest potential.

FUNCTIONAL FLUENCY AND ME

My Functional Fluency journey began in 2011. I was part of a group of school-improvement consultants who were trained by Dr Susannah Temple, the creator of TIFF (the Temple Index of Functional Fluency). I was struck by the model's potent combination of simplicity and complexity. My own TIFF feedback taught me about my tendency towards *placating* and Marshmallowing, which I continue to work on daily. To bring this model to life in this book, I have had to consciously release my *imaginative* and *creative* capacities, such as they are, and try to resist my tendency towards *inhibited* behaviour. The model has played a huge role in my personal development, and I hope I have done it justice.

Learning from Susannah was a privilege. It was remarkable to witness the measured way she talked about Functional Fluency and to experience her inspirational approach to training. Since then, I've worked with headteachers individually, senior leaders, groups of head teachers, heads of departments, department teams, human-resources teams and pastoral and administrative teams, always aiming to replicate the calm yet challenging approach Susannah modelled.

I am confident these individuals and teams have gained insight from this process. However, the full potential benefits of Functional Fluency for teachers and schools, as a fundamental way of understanding human behaviour that can guide us all towards more effective behaviour choices, remains unfulfilled. This book, the next stage in my Functional Fluency journey, is an attempt to explain this potential.

ABOUT THIS BOOK

The book's chapters explore the Functionally Fluent teacher's relationship with the key stakeholders in any school: pupils, other teachers, leadership, parents and carers, governors and other outside agencies. The aim is to demonstrate how Functional Fluency can help teachers to use their finite time and energy more effectively so that all parties benefit. Chapter 1, an introduction to Functional Fluency, is key to understanding the rest of the book, so I would advise all readers to start there.

With the 2025 Ofsted framework placing a renewed emphasis on **inclusion**, school leaders are rightly asking **how** to build a culture where every pupil and staff member feels valued and can thrive. Policies and posters are not enough. True inclusion is forged in the quality of our daily interactions. This book argues that Functional Fluency provides the essential 'operating system' for these interactions – a shared language and a practical toolkit to move beyond well-intentioned ideals to the lived reality of an inclusive community.

The book blends theoretical discussion of the educational application of Functional Fluency with insights from practitioners who are using Functional Fluency in their work in education right now across the UK and beyond. You'll discover, through their experiences, how Functional Fluency has played a role in their own educational journeys and helped them to deal with the dilemmas the profession throws up.

Alongside these insights are practical examples of the model in action, numbered 1 to 21. Based on common classroom situations, these ground the theory in chalkface reality, demonstrating how Functional Fluency provides a clear roadmap to navigate such challenges. Each has a common format, starting with the 'situation', followed by 'immediate thoughts and feelings'. You could stop at this stage and think about what a Functionally Fluent response to this situation might entail. Or you could discuss the example in a team meeting or as an element of your Continuing Professional Development (CPD). Then, compare your ideas with those given in the next two sections of the example: 'pause: choice' and 'Functionally Fluent response'.

Functional Fluency in action is further illustrated through scenarios featuring the fictional Meadowbank Middle School, its headteacher Pat Harrison and other characters, including young teacher Chris Andrews, who is keen to learn about and apply the model.

The journey concludes with audits and other tools that schools can use to gauge their progress towards becoming a Functionally Fluent school.

A NOTE ON THE TEXT

Throughout the book, I reference Functional Fluency itself and the behaviour modes with a capital letter (Accounting), and identify the behavioural descriptors using italics (*alert*). The only exception to this is quotations, where I maintain the original emphasis. The linking of real-world behaviour to descriptors in the model is not an exact science, and you may disagree with my analysis of what is going on in the examples. However, the real benefit is that a discussion about behaviour has started and, by openly discussing our behaviour choices, we can build mutual understanding.

Functional Fluency International trains people to use its tools. Those who complete this training are referred to in this book as licensed TIFF providers or Get on the Mat facilitators. Collectively I refer to both groups as Functional Fluency professionals. Details of all training, including new training programmes to become an accredited user of the Functional Fluency Team Scan, can be found on the Functional Fluency International website at https://functionalfluency.com/training-programs

THE CERTIFIED FUNCTIONALLY FLUENT TEACHER PROGRAMME

It is with an optimistic and ambitious mindset that I present the Certified Functional Fluency Teacher Programme (CFFTP). It is designed as a series of activities that build knowledge of Functional Fluency, which collectively constitute a qualification that teachers can work towards and then carry with them throughout their careers.

Certification by Functional Fluency International involves completing:

- the TIFF questionnaire, including a feedback session with a TIFF provider
- the Introduction to Functional Fluency course
- a Get on the Mat session
- a training session on the use of the 12 Functional Fluency lesson outlines
- a Learning to Question course.

More details on each element are provided in the Appendix.

I hope you find inspiration and insight on your Functional Fluency journey. There is much to gain, and I look forward to meeting you at some point as our Certified Functional Fluency Teacher community grows.

CHAPTER 1
THE BLUEPRINT FOR A THRIVING SCHOOL: AN INTRODUCTION TO FUNCTIONAL FLUENCY

Introducing Chris Andrews, our soon-to-be Functionally Fluent teacher. He is just starting his second year at Meadowbank Middle School since qualifying as a geography teacher. He is keen, but can be quiet and inhibited, which colleagues and pupils can take as inconsiderate or defiant. Before the INSET day at the start of term, he had never heard of Functional Fluency and, as he was feeling quite tired by the time his headteacher, Pat Harrison, started her presentation on it after lunch, his understanding remains hazy. One thing he did remember Pat saying was that we have choices over how we behave, and this struck a chord with Chris.

A model for improving behaviour: understanding Functional Fluency

Relationships determine a school's culture. When you walk into a school building, you soon pick up whether this is a place where people treat each other with care and respect or one characterised by apathy and neglect. You soon know whether results are all that matter there, or whether the development of well-rounded people is how the school judges its success. You know this from how the people in it relate to one another. Functional Fluency is a navigation system that everyone in a school can use to help them to find the best route to improve their relationships and thus the school's culture. And, if a school has a positive culture, the chances of everyone involved being contented and successful are radically increased.

In an article in *Emotional Literacy Update,* Susannah Temple (2004) describes Functional Fluency as follows:

> I mean by this a seamless integration of a wide range of effective ways of behaving that supports the ability to build positive relationships. The 'wide range of effective ways of behaving' are shown in the gold [lightly shaded]

areas of the Functional Fluency model and the 'seamless integration' is what a person does when they move easily between these golden behaviours, choosing the most appropriate ones and blending them effortlessly to facilitate effective communication.

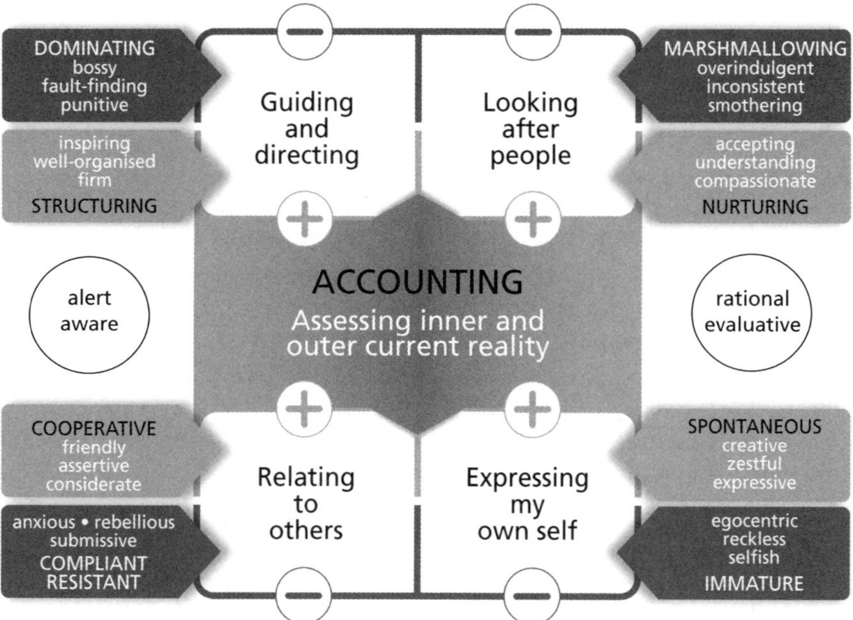

Figure 1 The Functional Fluency model

Temple's article describes Functional Fluency very succinctly:

> The functional fluency model is based on three categories of human existence and functioning. These are: growing up, surviving and raising the next generation. These three categories are divided firstly into five elements and then into the nine modes of behaviour of the full model. These are all shown in the diagram.

The model is constructed in three levels. For example, at level 1 the top third of the diagram relates to 'Being in Charge'. At level 2 this sub-divides into 'Guiding and directing' and 'Looking after people' or control and care. At level 3, these groups of behaviours sub-divide again into more effective behaviour modes (golden or lighter shading) and less effective behaviour modes (purple or darker shading). Within each mode there are six descriptors – three are shown in Figure 1 and others are referred to in the text, as necessary.

To help reinforce understanding of the model, the following nine icons are used throughout the rest of the book to represent the modes of behaviour.

Figure 2 Behaviour modes

The Functional Fluency model is your complete navigation system: your personal GPS or SatNav. It shows you all the possible routes – the effective golden (lightly shaded) paths and the inefficient purple (darkly shaded) pitfalls – allowing you consciously to choose the most fluent combination of behaviours that will enable you to move forwards in any relationship.

The bottom third of the model is our engine for personal growth and connection. It's where we tap into our Spontaneous energy – our *creativity*, *curiosity* and *imagination* – and our Cooperative side, which allows us to build the *resilient*, *friendly* and *adaptable* relationships that make a school thrive. The time and energy we put into these can either be effective (Spontaneous or Cooperative) or less effective (Immature or Compliant / Resistant).

A teacher demonstrating Spontaneous behaviour might use an *imaginative*, unexpected analogy to explain a difficult concept, or a pupil might ask a wonderfully *curious* 'what if?' question that takes the learning in a new direction. We see Cooperative behaviour when pupils work together on a task, respectfully challenging each other's ideas, and when a teacher shows they are adaptable by modifying a plan based on the class's feedback. Schools that encourage and enable their teachers to demonstrate Spontaneous and Cooperative behaviour, by encouraging *imaginative* and *adaptable* approaches to teaching, are great places to work. Furthermore, by exhibiting how to avoid the pitfalls of Immature and Compliant / Resistant behaviour, these schools model effective choices by pupils, thus reinforcing the positive culture.

The central section of the model is all about surviving and reality assessment, and is called Accounting. This is a process teachers should put a great deal of energy into, as they seek to understand the relationships and volatile circumstances of the classes they teach when, on any given day, events in the community or comments made during the previous lesson can have a huge impact on the quality of relationships and the nature of communication. Because you cannot see when someone is using Accounting behaviour, it can be a difficult concept to grasp. The metaphor of a set of tools, such as *alert, aware* or *evaluative* behaviour that a person can choose between to help them make sense of what is going on around and inside themselves, brings this abstract concept to life.

The top third of the model relates to raising the next generation and developing ourselves, and is the most obviously applicable to teaching. It involves looking after ourselves and others, and exerting authority on behalf of ourselves and others. The model captures caring for other people effectively as Nurturing. An example from teaching is providing pupils with genuine encouragement to complete a task well. The model shows effective control as Structuring; an example is establishing a clear set of guidelines around how a task should be completed.

When we make less effective behaviour choices, as we inevitably do, this is represented by the darkly shaded areas of the model. Teachers might fall into Marshmallowing with the best of intentions: a strong desire to help pupils they see as disadvantaged or a wish to show to others the care that they may feel was missing from their own upbringing. But the result remains negative. Pupils feel smothered rather than empowered and the teacher is left tired and frustrated. Alternatively, teachers might over-rely on Dominating to maintain order, leaving students feeling stifled and unheard.

Knowing where the boundaries lie, between Structuring and Dominating on the one hand and Nurturing and Marshmallowing on the other, is a vital first step for teachers. Functional Fluency helps them to make effective behaviour choices that allow both them and their pupils to thrive.

A key to Functional Fluency is realising that effective blending by teachers of the more effective modes of behaviour – Structuring, Nurturing, Cooperative and Spontaneous – creates the psychological safety and inclusive environment that enables pupils to feel empowered to play an active role in their own learning. At its heart, Functional Fluency is inherently inclusive. It moves beyond labels and diagnoses to focus on universal patterns of human behaviour, providing tools that empower every individual – regardless of their background, neurotype or personal history – to make effective choices and build positive relationships.

We should remember that this also applies to how we enable ourselves to grow and, as Temple writes at the end of her article, 'This means that personal development for teachers is synonymous with professional development' (Temple, 2004). Continuing Professional Development (CPD), often seen as a twilight bolt-on, is thus part of the work we need to be doing, all the time, to become better at building relationships and communicating with others. Functional Fluency can play a huge role in this important work.

From friction to flow: solving the people puzzle in schools

On any school day, teachers make countless choices about how to behave. Should we invest this energy in moaning, or in seeking solutions? The answer directly shapes the quality and effectiveness of our communication, both verbal and non-verbal; this, in turn, dictates the nature of our relationships. A chronic complainer, for example, is likely to experience tense and fractured interactions. Seen in totality, the daily tone of our interactions has a profound impact on our school's effectiveness.

Systemic issues make schools volatile and pressurised places. Excessive workload, curriculum changes, new administrative procedures and interminable data collection put teachers and administrators under pressure. Insufficient staffing, budget cuts and a general lack of resources add to this sense of struggle. Accountability measures, including high-stakes testing, place demands on pupils, teachers and their leaders that easily become a downward spiral of negativity. The negative public perception of the profession and a feeling that the government lacks sympathy for your situation adds to the negativity. This toxic combination of factors can be a catalyst for burnout, stress and poor behaviour. In these circumstances, it is not surprising if leaders, teachers and pupils fall into ineffective behaviour patterns that create friction rather than flow.

Given that schools are fundamentally built upon the relationships between adults and young people, Functional Fluency offers a valuable framework to act as a roadmap, showing a route out of this negativity. It promotes conscious behaviour choices; fosters clearer and more effective communication; supports the development of strong relationships; and contributes to the overall effective operation of the school in many ways, including increased collaboration, and helps create a more positive learning environment.

Functional Fluency brings benefits at three distinct levels: individual, institutional and societal.

- Individual benefits:
  - Helping teachers and pupils communicate more effectively, building positive relationships and enhancing their emotional intelligence
  - Helping teachers understand their own behaviour patterns and how they affect their pupils' learning and motivation
  - Enabling teachers to choose the most appropriate and productive ways of responding to different situations and challenges in the classroom
  - Supporting pupils as they develop their self-awareness, self-regulation and social skills, which are essential for academic success and wellbeing.

- Institutional benefits:
  - Creating a safe and supportive learning environment where pupils feel valued, respected and encouraged
  - Developing a collaborative and cooperative culture where pupils work together, share ideas and learn from each other, providing constructive feedback and guidance that helps improve their performance and confidence
  - Encouraging the curiosity, creativity and critical-thinking that fosters pupils' interest and engagement in learning and helps them to address conflicts and challenges in a respectful and constructive way that promotes problem-solving and resolution
  - Recognising and celebrating pupils' achievements and strengths in ways that boost their self-esteem and motivation.

- Societal benefits:
  - Focusing our thinking and feeling on how we get along with each other
  - Addressing the explosion in emotional and mental-health issues
  - Building collective efficacy so that everyone is working towards the achievement of a shared goal – the development of confident, self-regulating young people who can survive and thrive in an unpredictable world.

Using Functional Fluency in these ways helps develop a school culture that fosters self-awareness, emotional resilience and meaningful collaboration among staff. It enhances teachers' wellbeing and strengthens their ability to nurture and inspire the next generation.

While writing this book, I have consciously tried to include examples of professionals outside the UK who are using Functional Fluency in their work in schools. Clearly, the educational context varies between jurisdictions, but the fundamental nature of Functional Fluency is such that it can have a positive impact across the world.

A powerful example of how this works is when schools move from a behaviour-based model to a relationship-based model. Functional Fluency emphasises the Structuring mode. This is the term for constructive Control, which empowers through inspiration and by enabling success. Guidance and help allow the school community to feel safe to explore and learn. Pupils and teachers gain self-confidence. Expectations and limits are clear and consistent. The hidden message is 'you can do it and succeed'. Through blending effective modes of behaviour, those in school learn to manage and improve their relationships. This reframing shows how Functional Fluency underpins a radical rethinking of how schools operate.

To truly grasp the widespread impact of Functional Fluency, let's explore how it addresses other specific challenges schools face today by imagining a year of a fictional school's Functional Fluency journey. Many of these challenges are picked up again in more detail later in the book. While this is an idealised scenario, I hope the essential truth of the narrative comes across.

The Meadowbank journey: a year of working towards becoming a Functionally Fluent school

Welcome to Meadowbank Middle School, where Pat Harrison is headteacher. We've already met Chris Andrews, a geography teacher in his second year in the profession.

September:

Pat Harrison had been looking for a way to transform the school community when she came across Functional Fluency. She completed TIFF with a local provider and found it very insightful, helping her to deal with the stress of her job and issues relating to her aging parents. During discussions with the senior leadership team, they decide to launch their Functional Fluency journey on the September INSET day. When the day arrives, they start with a short explanation and an opportunity for staff to discuss scenarios in groups. The emphasis is on using the model to help everyone to thrive, and the headteacher personally explains her commitment to the model, the ways it has helped her and her ambition to use it to support the school to flourish. She tells staff that the model is about understanding the core parts of being human: how we grow into ourselves, how we look after the next generation and how we manage the day-to-day reality of surviving in between. Staff who have previously found her a little aloof are impressed by the authenticity of the headteacher's explanation. Chris Andrews makes a personal resolution to find out more.

October:

The school decides to focus first on the pastoral care team. They all complete the TIFF questionnaire and have a feedback session with a local provider. This is followed by a meeting of the team facilitated by the provider, who encourages them to think about whether they are using their authority to empower or disempower the pupils. This reveals that some of the team tend to be over-indulgent, and there is agreement to try to focus on cherishing and understanding behaviour that will support the development of strong relationships with the pupils.

November:

The headteacher asks Dave, a well-respected but rather cynical deputy head, to look at the links between the Functional Fluency model and the school's values statement, which was written five years earlier and is rarely referenced. The deputy head puts together a presentation demonstrating the links and explaining how Functional Fluency can integrate the values into daily school life. He delivers it with considerable wit and zest at a whole-staff meeting and this injects energy into the project.

December:

As the mock-exam season kicks off, the pastoral team decide to focus on the importance of Nurturing as a means of alleviating potential mental-health issues. They create a roleplay to demonstrate the difference between Nurturing and Marshmallowing and use Spontaneous mode energy to present it to pupils. The message is that Nurturing is positive care in action, responsive to need, offering the empathy and understanding that enables people to recover, thrive and develop a healthy and positive sense of self. Absence rates during the exam period are noticeably lower than in previous years, as are reports of pupils suffering from debilitating exam-related anxiety.

January:

Having got to know the model well, the staff agree with the headteacher that now is the time to introduce it to the pupils. In PSHE lessons, pupils are encouraged to use phrases such as 'When I use Dominating mode, I'm inclined to do such-and-such' or 'I need to do more Accounting and try out ways to do Structuring effectively' to help them take responsibility for their own behaviour. There is some kick-back from one or two staff members, but colleagues point out that this is perhaps Compliant / Resistant mode behaviour. Early signs that the sessions are helping to develop the pupils' emotional literacy and self-esteem help to re-establish a more Cooperative atmosphere.

February:

The weather is terrible, and the school closes for three snow days. The senior leadership team plan their response using the five 'golden modes', and echo this in their communications with staff and pupils. Engagement with online learning is considerably higher than ever before and complaints about the IT system are noticeable by their absence.

March:

A shocking incident in a midlands city provokes widespread social unrest and demonstrations. Senior leaders discuss this situation and put together an assembly for all year groups. They dissect the event that was the catalyst for the unrest using the Get on the Mat approach. They encourage the pupils to consider how using the 'golden modes' of behaviour could have averted this situation. They then help pupils to use the model to see how they can keep themselves safe by not getting drawn into local demonstrations.

April:

In a training event, teachers in subject teams are asked to think about how Functional Fluency relates to their teaching. The English and history departments get stuck in, reporting that they can see how increasing the pupils' emotional literacy will enable them to speak and write about literary and historical characters with greater sophistication. The science department is sceptical until an assistant headteacher is delegated to work with them. She points out the importance of Accounting to scientific inquiry. She goes on to explain that the model can help the team to develop their pedagogy, which feedback suggests is often inconsistent, punitive and encourages anxious or rebellious responses from pupils.

May:

A recently appointed head of department, Karina Chung, comes to see the headteacher following a meeting with a parent. The head of department had been worried that the mother was going to be irate about a detention given to her son. Karina prepared her explanation using Functional Fluency language, and had an A4 version of the model with her for the meeting. After some defiant behaviour, the mother's mood began to change. She was intrigued by the model and could see how the department had been both consistent and encouraging. She now agreed that the detention was warranted. She took the A4 version of the model away, promising to use it to explain her support for the punishment to her son.

June:

In the end-of-term newsletter, the headteacher briefly charts the school's Functional Fluency journey over the year. She writes that it has been explained to parents of the upcoming intake to help them to understand the school's approach. She is delighted to see that two other articles in the newsletter, one by a PE teacher and one by a science teacher, reference the model in relation to the behaviour of the Year 8 cricket team and the change to mixed prior-attainment level grouping in science, which has been popular with pupils and teachers and delivered the best levels of attainment in Years 7 to 10 that the department has seen in over five years.

July:

The atmosphere during activities week is very positive. It feels as though staff have more energy than in previous years. All the risk assessments are completed on time!

Reflecting, the headteacher recognises the profound impact that Functional Fluency has had on the school community. She recalls the supportive and understanding way in which the staff and pupils responded when a pupil in Year 8 came out as transsexual. She remembers how different the school had been when she was first appointed, when discriminatory language was commonplace. It feels as though the school is now a place where pupils and teachers are increasingly able to do their own thing in their own way. There is clear evidence that everyone involved is getting along with each other just that bit better, and this feels like a powerful vindication of her decision to launch the school on its Functional Fluency journey. She enjoys a brilliant holiday, confident that the pupils are well equipped to make the most of the next phase of their lives.

Functional Fluency practices and benefits

Functional Fluency practices

The Functional Fluency model is supported by several practices that help individuals and teams apply its principles. These include...

TIFF

The Temple Index of Functional Fluency is an *actometric* (a word coined by Functional Fluency professional Rona Rowe), designed to capture a snapshot of your current behaviour choices. Unlike psychometric tests that label you, TIFF is a 'behaviour snapshot' that helps you see what you're *doing* right now, and what you could change. It is based on the fact that our time and energy are finite, and our behaviour is the result of our choices: it is not pre-determined. Through a feedback conversation with a trained TIFF provider, you pick out patterns of effective and less effective behaviour and plan how you are going to change this pattern in the future.

The Functional Fluency Team Scan

An international group of Functional Fluency providers has devised a Functional Fluency Team Scan tool that enables teams to reflect on their behaviour, discern patterns and make plans for ongoing improvements, for the benefit of all. This is a useful tool for senior leadership teams to gain a more honest and objective understanding of how they operate, enabling them to unblock stuck areas, releasing energy and decreasing stress levels.

Get on the Mat

Another useful tool that really brings Functional Fluency to life is the Get on the Mat exercise. Working with a trained Get on the Mat facilitator, this incorporates either a physical vinyl version of the Functional Fluency model that you can walk on and stand on, getting a visceral understanding of the emotions involved in behavioural choices. Alternatively, there s a virtual version of the mat that enables participants to position those playing different roles in a situation in the relevant behaviour spaces and explore how outcomes might be different if other behaviour choices were made. Both versions of the mat allow for and stimulate discussion, enabling scenarios to be explored in a risk-free context. These activities also deepen knowledge and understanding of the Functional Fluency model and its applications.

The school applications of the Get on the Mat exercise are many and various. It could be used as a regular part of CPD sessions to explore issues that have arisen, analyse how they have been approached and teach Functional Fluency lessons about more effective approaches to use in future. The mat could also be used as a tool in class to encourage focused discussion of issues and situations. It enables issues to be externalised so that pupils can analyse them in a more objective way. This helps both to disperse the negativity within social groups that can arise from poor choices of behaviour and has the advantage of increasing understanding of the model, which pupils can deploy to help them make better behaviour choices in the future.

Parents also benefit from attending a well-organised Get on the Mat session, as this gives them a practical insight into how the school approaches behavioural issues while also introducing them to the central concepts of Functional Fluency. It has the additional benefit of bringing the school's and home's approaches to behaviour into closer alignment.

Functional Fluency benefits

So, what are the problems or issues faced by schools that Functional Fluency and its associated tools could help you to fix? Here's a list of some thoughts – there will be many others.

- Completing a TIFF and having a feedback session with a Functional Fluency professional provides school leaders with time to slow down, observe and think objectively about their own behaviour. It is an opportunity to take stock, recognise what is working well and realise how, often with minor changes, they and those they lead could all benefit from more Functionally Fluent behaviour.

- Senior teams become more open, trusting and understanding following the honest, thoughtful discussions that completing the Functional Fluency Team Scan tool elicits. Behaviours that have drained energy from the team diminish and new, more Functionally Fluent, behaviour choices that encourage mutual thriving take over.

- Teachers, through the increased understanding gained from being part of or running Get on the Mat sessions, have an increased understanding of Functional Fluency and the many ways in which they can use it to inform and support their behaviour choices, leading to more effective relationships with both colleagues and pupils.

- Pupils' understanding of Functional Fluency gradually grows. They see links between it and the school's values and the ethical teachings of major world religions. They are able to apply it to their own daily lives – to solve disputes and to help them make better minute-by-minute behaviour choices.

- Parents and carers gain an increased understanding of the Functional Fluency principles that underlie the school's approach to behaviour and begin to use these same principles at home, bringing a valuable continuity to pupils' lives.

- All those connected with the school gain an increased sense of congruence, through the application of shared vocabulary and approaches. Time and energy, once lost to misunderstandings and disputes, are regained.

The power of the pause: how Accounting fuels better choices

At the heart of Functional Fluency is Accounting, a rich concept metaphorically connected with weighing up, recounting and balancing the books. It is all about considering what is going on around us and within us and deciding, on a moment-by-moment basis, how best to blend the Structuring, Nurturing, Cooperative and Spontaneous options that are always available to us all. Insufficient Accounting may well cause us to **react** in situations rather than **respond** to them, resulting in less effective behaviour choices, such as choosing to Dominate or Marshmallow others or behave in Compliant / Resistant or Immature ways.

What is happening during this process is shown in Figure 3. We experience an event or situation, and this provokes both thoughts (head) and feelings (heart and guts). Valerie Fawcett and Stefan Graebe describe this as 'noticing and evaluating reality in any situation, inside ourselves and others, checking things out, thinking with emotional intelligence, and rationalizing about consequences and needs' (Fawcett, 2023, p.12).

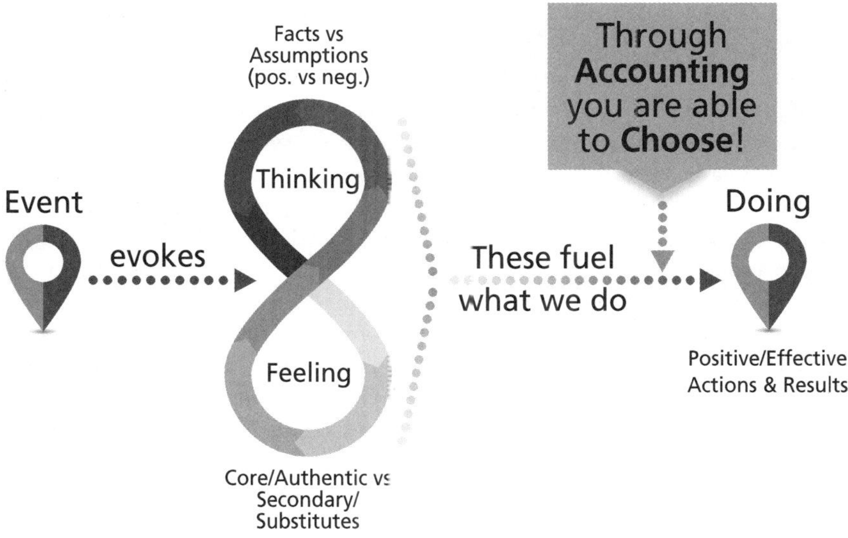

Figure 3 The Power of Choice (Functional Fluency International)

There are useful parallels between this diagram and Caviglioli's depiction of memory from Sherrington's book on *Rosenshine's Principles* (Sherrington, 2019) – both involve an external stimulus and an internal reaction process.

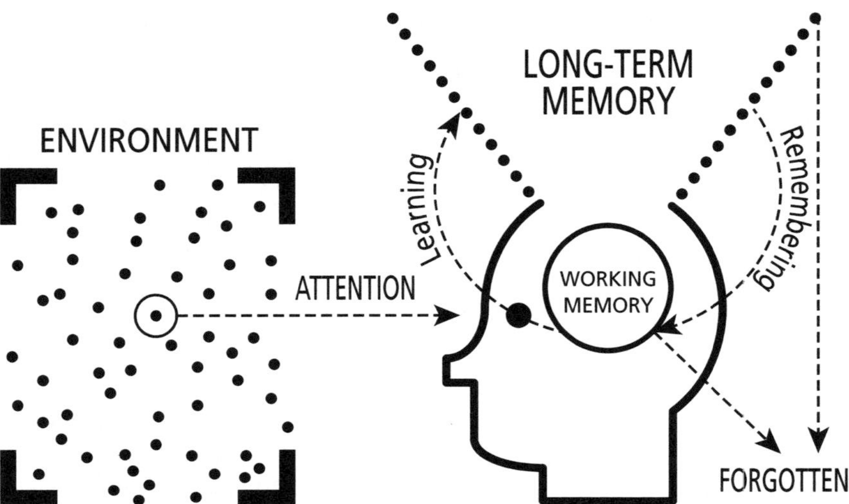

Figure 4 Memory (Sherrington, 2019 / O. Caviglioli)

The key difference is that, in the 'memory' process, everything takes place within the head, whereas in the Power of Choice depiction of Accounting, the locus of the process is not defined. This allows for the process to be co-located in the 'head, heart and guts', in a way that fits with what we know about how the somatic nervous system links up our sensory receptors with our central nervous system. When our behavioural decisions are informed by appropriate Accounting, our responses are frictionless and easy – we know we are doing the right thing because it feels right throughout our body. If we think back to Rhys's story in the Introduction, we can easily imagine the frustration he must have felt when he first became a headteacher, feeling responsible for everything, constantly engaging with colleagues who demanded his attention and unable to focus on his own work. Contrast this with the much calmer version of Rhys later in the account, who has a clear vision of what his responsibility is and what he can entrust to others, allowing him to focus on the high-level tasks he had been employed to oversee.

Accounting and balance

The educational wellbeing of pupils relies on teachers effectively balancing Structuring and Nurturing. Their behaviour choices really matter. The school and individuals all suffer if too much energy goes into Dominating or Marshmallowing (excessive or inappropriate caring). Equally, the individual and, by extension, the institution they serve, fail to thrive if teachers are not able to put a sufficient proportion of their time and energy into Cooperative and Spontaneous behaviour. And it is through Accounting that these balances emerge.

This emphasis on balance highlights the importance of the Functional Fluency model as a mechanism for helping leaders to maintain and develop their own wellbeing. By thinking about the model and holding it in their heads at moments of stress or key decision-making, there is a good chance of teachers making better decisions. With this comes an increased sense both of the wellbeing and the being well that are so necessary for effective functioning, and that our current Ofsted accountability system is so far from encouraging (for more details on this, see 'Chapter 13: The house of inspection' in Morrish, 2025).

Accounting is particularly important for helping us to deal with uncertainty. Schools, and education in general, are riven with uncertainty, and this is a massive contributor to increased stress levels. As a teacher, it is all too easy to allow this to lead to reactions that are not thought through and that make the situation worse. Opening the Accounting toolbox and choosing the appropriate tool enables us to slow down. We can recognise our primeval tendency to **react** and, instead, utilise our higher executive functions to formulate a more considered **response**. There is then a much greater likelihood that we and others will benefit.

I recall times when, as head of department, I would receive the news that a colleague was ill. This meant I would need to make plans for their classes. This could have caused me to panic as I worried about how to complete my existing list of jobs without this additional complication. Instead, by consciously using what Susannah Temple calls 'response-ability' I was able to *evaluate* and prioritise, ensuring that the urgent tasks were addressed first. This avoided crises. Often, the less-urgent matters I had been busying myself with solved themselves or I was able to delegate them to colleagues: a clear example of the value of the Accounting toolbox.

Another process that could result in teachers making less effective behaviour choices is the Transactional Analysis (TA) concept of 'discounting'. Bishop and van den Blink (2023) define this as 'an internal mechanism which involves people minimizing or ignoring some aspect of themselves, others, or the reality of the situation'. Imagine a senior leader who downplays their role in a school's success and refuses to recognise that they would make a highly effective headteacher. By Accounting, we can become aware of this discounting and thus make, or help other to make, more effective behaviour choices.

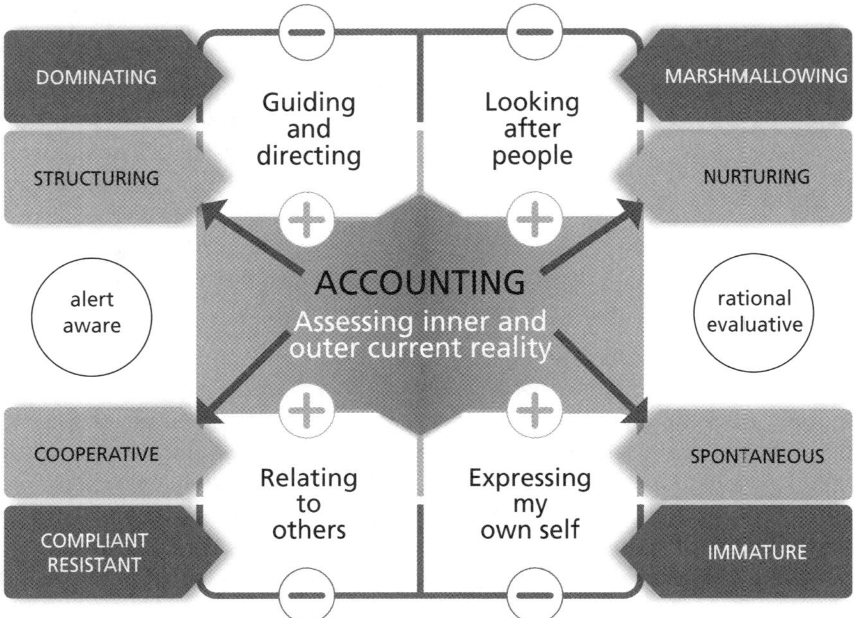

Figure 5 Accounting

A lot of the time, we use our energy effectively; it is during times of stress and anxiety that we are more likely to use ineffective behaviour, and this is when it is important to put energy into Accounting: to figure out what is going on and what to do next. It is useful to think of Accounting as like a toolbox that we can open when we need it.

The Accounting Framework

To extend our toolbox analogy, some household tasks require just one tool, while others, for example putting up a shelf, involve deploying several (spirit level, drill, screwdriver, and so on) in the correct order to achieve the desired result. The Accounting Framework organises the six essential Accounting tools (*grounded, aware, alert, enquiring, evaluative* and *rational*) into a clear, step-by-step process. This moves Accounting from a collection of tools into a powerful and repeatable procedure that help us address complex issues. By using all or part of the Framework to ask questions about situations we find ourselves in, or about information we are presented with, we can go on to make more thoughtful decisions about how to act.

Table 1 The Accounting Framework

Step	Accounting tool	Suggested questions
1.	Get *grounded*:	What are the simple facts of the situation? What is my emotional state right now? Why?
2.	Use *aware* behaviour:	What is my immediate emotional reaction to the stimulus? What is this content trying to make me feel?
3.	Use *alert* behaviour:	What patterns can I notice here? What is the bigger picture?
4.	Use *enquiring* behaviour:	Who created this and why? What is their perspective? What crucial information might be missing?
5.	Use *evaluative* behaviour:	What is being presented? Is it credible? Can it be verified? Does the evidence support the main claim?
6.	Use *rational* behaviour:	What is the most logical interpretation? Are there alternative, equally valid interpretations?

Just as Bloom's *Taxonomy* (1956) provides a hierarchical framework for cognitive skills in learning, the Accounting Framework provides a structure for the critical skills of reflection and response. Its application is twofold: as a tool for pupils to navigate their world, and as a mechanism for teachers to refine their professional practice.

1. **For Pupils: a tool for critical citizenship.** In an era of misinformation and complex social dynamics, pupils need a mental model for questioning what they see, read and feel. We can teach the Accounting Framework explicitly as a procedure for analysing a news article, evaluating a social-media post or deconstructing a personal disagreement. It moves pupils beyond a simple emotional reaction to a structured, thoughtful response.

2. **For Teachers: a structure for professional evaluation.** The same framework is an invaluable tool for professional growth. Teachers can use the six steps to deconstruct a challenging lesson, prepare for a difficult conversation with a parent or evaluate the potential impact of a new school policy. It provides a common language and a consistent process for the deep, reflective work that underpins expert teaching. The Accounting Framework is a powerful tool for inclusive practice. It prompts us to pause and move beyond our assumptions, encouraging us to be genuinely *curious* about a pupil's or colleague's reality, which is the first step towards equitable and empathic interaction. (For more on Pedagogical Accounting, see Chapter 8.)

Account-ability

No teacher or school leader is going to be able to put the necessary amount of time and energy into Accounting to enable them to make the most effective behaviour choices all the time. But this should not put anyone off trying to increase their Account-ability gradually as they learn from each problematic situation they encounter. The alternative is continuing to repeat the same old mistakes, time and again, ensuring that nothing gets better, that educational gaps are never reduced and pupils' life chances are forever negatively impacted. And nor should the difficulty of the process deter anyone in education from teaching Accounting and Functional Fluency to pupils and parents at every opportunity. It is the repetition that builds awareness of shared vocabulary, develops conceptual familiarity and helps to counteract confusion by spreading clarity and shared understanding. This, in turn, gradually fuels more effective behaviour choices across the institution, unlocking previously wasted potential.

Hollis writes about the 'fallacy of overgeneralization', whereby 'what was true then, or apparently true, is repeatedly ratified, reinforced by what is re-experienced – and unwillingly re-created in each new venue' (Hollis, 2009). In this way, our mistakes and prejudices are destined to be repeated and possibly even magnified in an endless cycle of reinforcement. The way out of this trap inevitably involves Accounting. It is only by assessing the situation, using our *alertness* and *awareness* to *evaluate* the situation, that we can possibly seek to **respond** to situations rather than simply **reacting** to them in ways that engrain negative, less effective ways of behaving.

Hollis also proposes that we have a duty to work towards maximising our potential. 'We do not serve our children, our friends and partners, our society by living partial lives, and being secretly depressed and resentful' (Hollis, 2009). We need to ask ourselves, when opportunities present themselves, 'Does this choice diminish me, or enlarge me?'

Functional Fluency helps us to consider, understand and ultimately to overcome the shortcomings of extremism and fundamentalism, of whatever form. Hollis beautifully describes this need for nuanced acceptance of the fundamental ambiguity of life:

> The putative fixity of definitions of race, gender, sexual preference or orientation, Western hegemony, trust in government probity, and many other presumptive truisms have been challenged, and largely overthrown, although many millions cling to the slope side of history in service to their psychological security.

Hollis (2009)

He goes on to explain why Accounting is both so difficult and so necessary for human beings if we are to progress: 'As a species, we ill tolerate ambiguity, contradiction, or whatever proves uncomfortable, and that is what makes the anxiety-fuelled "fundamentalist" in each of us take over from time to time. When that nervous part prevails, we violate the complexity of life, serve regressive strategies, narrow and diminish the journey life asks of us' (Hollis 2009). This description of the complexity of the human condition demonstrates the importance of having tools to support us in this difficult task – Accounting is just such a tool.

Beyond posters on the wall: living your school's values

In their chapter 'The Inspirational Leader: Providing Vision and Purpose' in Fawcett (2023), Jutta Kreyenberg and Hannah Titilayo Seriki explain how leaders can use Functional Fluency to create vision and purpose for their organisation:

> If, as a senior leader, you talk about what you want to achieve, you will attract others with the same or similar desires. Those you work with will then not actually be sacrificing their energy for you as someone external to them, but for a shared purpose, which they are passionate about. This can make a big difference to people's motivation, and sense of responsibility and, consequently, influence people's ability and willingness to use the Golden Five (effective) behaviours described in the Functional Fluency model.

> **Fawcett, 2023**

Kreyenberg and Seriki then expand on what exactly this will look like:

> Using the authoritative behaviour, which is part of effective Structuring, you as a senior leader share what you know and do not know, your expertise and experience, developing trust through your authenticity. ... You play with ideas, dream, allow your creativity to flow freely (Spontaneous). You talk about your dreams, experiments, insights, hypotheses, ... others, whose interest is aroused, listen. They add their own thoughts, opinions and experiences. You, interested in this as an addition to what you have come up with, listen (Cooperative), and a collaborative, innovative process has begun. This needs to be structured so as to continue and bear fruit in the long term. Structuring behaviours (in contrast to Dominating) will help you communicate the framework ... with clarity, authority and recognition of each party's ability to contribute – as opposed to just telling people what to do 'because I say so'. The collaborative approach and your own knowledge and enthusiasm will help to inspire others.

> **Fawcett, 2023**

The blending of the effective modes of behaviour from the Functional Fluency model thus creates a compelling case for the direction of travel you have decided on.

In *The Kindness Principle*, Dave Whitaker references a description of the thinking of the educationalist Carl Rogers that also comes very close to being a definition of Functional Fluency:

> For a person to 'grow' they need an environment that provides them with genuineness (openness and self-disclosure), acceptance (being seen with unconditional positive regard), and empathy (being listened to and understood). Without these, relationships and healthy personalities will not develop as they should, much like a tree will not grow without sunlight and water.

> **Whitaker, 2021**

For this growth to occur, for both the school and the individuals who constitute it, there needs to be agreement on these principles of genuineness, acceptance and empathy as, without them, it is impossible to establish trust. And many schools have sets of values that are very close to these. Choosing five schools randomly, a quick internet search collected the following values from their websites: respect, *resilience*, kindness, *creativity*, *curiosity*, *empathy*, integrity, positivity, responsibility, self-belief, commitment, opportunity, respect, excellence, trust, fairness, teamwork.

Some of these (shown in italics) exist as identified descriptors of positive behaviour within the Functional Fluency model, thus making the link very easy to make. We might call these **explicit** values within the model. Others – the **implicit** values – can be formed from a combination of behaviours from across the model. For example, we could describe kindness as a combination of *cherishing* from the Nurturing mode, *considerate* from the Cooperative mode and *helpful* from the Structuring mode. Integrity is perhaps more complex, but we could see it as being made up of *aware* and *grounded* from the Accounting mode, *expressive* from the Spontaneous mode and *consistent* from the Structuring mode.

These **implicit** values are perfect examples of the fluent aspect of Functional Fluency, as these highly beneficial ways of engaging with others draw freely from several different modes of effective behaviour. Thus, the model provides a way in which schools can explain their values to their school community, conveying the 'what' that makes the vision for their school different. But because Functional Fluency is all about behaviour and relationships, this linkage also makes clear to staff, pupils and parents 'how' everyone should live out these values as they go about their normal day-to-day activities within the school. This helps to give real substance to what is otherwise an abstract set of nouns and provides congruence between the school's values and those of the individuals within it.

By making the behavioural expectations more explicit, this process also points out where there is a lack of congruence between the school and specific individuals, encouraging them either to rethink their approach to behaviour and relationships or to seek employment in another school where they are a better fit, thus reducing stress and wasted time and energy all round.

In contrast to 'warm-strict' and 'zero tolerance' approaches to behaviour that are increasingly advocated for use in schools, a Functional Fluency-based approach to values and behaviour has the advantage of being both clear and easy to understand and subtle and complex in ways that mirror the complexity of humans. As Whitaker puts it:

> The problem is that children are complex; therefore, managing their behaviour with simplistic approaches will not work in every case and the system will inevitably fail for the most complicated, and often the most vulnerable, children – and there are a surprisingly high number of these in every school.

Whitaker, 2021

Approaches that recognise and embrace complexity are always going to be more successful than those that deny it, as complexity is a fundamental feature of human life. Functional Fluency is, in a sense, a container that helps to make sense of this complexity by focusing on and systematising its essential, underlying principles.

A useful task that a leadership team could complete is to identify the proportion of each of the five golden behaviours that would contribute to the achievement of each of their values, thus bringing the Functional Fluency model to life in the context of their institution.

Building character, forging a vision

Lemov et al., (2023) cite the US psychologist Angela Duckworth, the author of *Grit* (2016), who has completed work on what she calls 'virtues'. She describes these as 'ways of thinking, feeling and acting that we [can] habitually do that are good for others and good for ourselves'. This links with Functional Fluency in two very clear and important ways:

1. *The Functional Fluency starter pack* (Functional Fluency International, 2022) defines Functionally Fluent behaviour as 'most effective when it helps us achieve our short and long-term objectives and benefits ourselves and others'. This links directly with Duckworth's notion of virtues as doing good both for ourselves and others.

2. If we continue to make our behavioural choices by directly reacting to stimuli, we rapidly descend into self-serving, short-term, instant gratification that damages others and, very soon, us too. The key feature of Accounting is that it is central to Functional Fluency, such that it becomes a key part of how we respond, all day every day. This habituates the process of Accounting, ensuring that, more often than not, we make thoughtful behavioural choices from which both we and others can benefit, just as Duckworth describes.

It is worth mentioning here that Angela Duckworth is a research colleague of David Yeager, whose work on Wise Feedback is explored in Chapter 3.

As Peps McCrea, cited in Lemov et al., (2023), points out in his very carefully named book *Motivating Teaching*, the biggest influence on how we behave is our perception of what the behavioural norms are within our society. The habituation of Accounting, described above, thus becomes central to helping pupils in our schools to understand how they should behave. The Certified Functional Fluency Teacher Programme (CFFTP) supports schools in taking this further. By setting up repeated teaching sessions at the start of each new key stage that emphasise the type of behavioural choices that are most likely to enable us and others to benefit, schools are helping to establish these social norms. By exploring behavioural choices through regular Get on the Mat sessions, schools open real behavioural choices for examination, clarifying how benefits can be shared and, again, helping to cement positive behavioural norms.

In the post-Covid scenario we find ourselves in, where social expectations have been eroded or have simply dissolved, concerted effort to re-establish norms that benefit everyone is vital. In this context, it is worth acknowledging how previous social norms were often seriously lacking because they were predicated on only a small slice (generally a white, male, well-educated, middle- and upper-class slice) of the population benefiting while many others suffered. Thus, Functional Fluency can become an important force in the movement for improved equality, diversity and inclusion (EDI) and a key tool that schools can use to inform their work in these areas.

Lemov et al., (2023) highlight the work of the Jubilee Centre on Character Education. Their Framework for Character Education in Schools persuasively makes the case for an approach very like the one espoused here. The congruence around the 'educable' nature of character education is clear.

So, let's listen in to an imagined conversation at the fictional Meadowbank Middle School senior leadership meeting. Pat, the headteacher, is well versed in Functional Fluency. She has asked Dave, a deputy head, to find out more about the Framework for Character Education in Schools so that they can discuss how the two approaches relate to each other. Also present are their assistant headteacher colleagues, Phil and Jen.

Dave: OK, the first principle is that **character is fundamental: it is the basis for human and societal flourishing**. I think that fits well with Functional Fluency, don't you, Pat?

Pat: Absolutely. Functional Fluency is all about relationships, and character determines the nature and quality of our relationships.

Jen: Yes. If we can't foster good relationships on the small scale within a family, class or school, we have no chance of doing so at the national or global level

Phil, slightly startled, takes a sip of tea.

Pat: Good start. What's next. Dave?

Dave: Point 2: **character is largely caught through role-modelling and emotional contagion: committed leadership, school culture and ethos are therefore central**.

Pat: That puts a lot of emphasis on us as a leadership team, doesn't it?

Jen: Yes, if schools opt out of this area as too complex, other less scrupulous elements will ensure the role is taken and the results will not be positive.

Phil: That reminds me, have you seen the latest resources on County Lines? Shocking.

Pat: That's a great example, Phil, that shows just how serious this is.

Phil sits up a little.

Dave: The next point is quite similar **character should also be taught: direct teaching of character provides the rationale, language and tools to use in developing character elsewhere in and out of school**. I think that could link with what you have been telling us about the draft lessons in the Certified Functional Fluency Teacher Programme.

Pat: Yep, the idea is we teach the 12 lessons at the start of each key stage, so sixth formers will have gone through them three times when they leave. What's next, Dave?

Dave: *Rifling through papers.* Sorry, lost my place. Ah yes, **character is sought freely to pursue a better life**. Not sure I get that...

Jen: Well, I think it chimes with that phrase you keep using, Pat – that Functional Fluency can help you to 'thrive at life'.

All nod or mutter agreement.

Dave: Next, they say **character is educable: it is not fixed and the virtues can be developed. Its progress can be measured holistically, not only through self-reports but also more objective research methods**.

Phil: Well, I know that Functional Fluency is based on the idea that we can all change and that our behaviour is the result of choice, not character type.

Pat: Yes, it is about shining a light on current behavioural choices and thinking about the advantages and drawbacks of this pattern so future change can be planned. Dave?

Dave: OK, **character depends on building Virtue Literacy**. Well, I know Functional Fluency has helped to develop a shared vocabulary. Since the launch in September, I keep hearing staff talking about Marshmallowing. If we could extend this to the pupils, it might help the Year 9s stop grunting at each other.

Jen: Now, is that *blaming* or *fault-finding* behaviour, Dave?

Dave: Good point! Next, they say **good character is the foundation for improved attainment, better behaviour and increased employability, but most importantly, flourishing societies**.

Phil: Well, if it's going to improve behaviour I'm all in favour!

Jen: Always the behaviour lead! But seriously, if less energy is wasted in less effective forms of behaviour, there will be much more left for both teachers and pupils to focus on the learning process, to everyone's benefit.

Pat: That's a great point, Jen. OK, let's move on, Dave; I've got tai chi tonight.

Dave: Right, number eight: **character should be developed in partnership with parents, families, employers and other community organisations.**

Pat: I really want to work together with parents, so that they understand where we are coming from much better. And they might even start to use some Functional Fluency ideas themselves: win–win!

Dave: Nearly there now. **Each child has a right to character education.** I don't think any of us are going to argue with that.

Phil: *Muttering.* Certainly not at this time!

Pat: Absolutely, and the 12 craft lessons at the start of Years 7, 10 and 12 would enable us to deliver this in a manageable way.

Phil: And finally...

Dave: *With an annoyed glance at Phil.* And finally, **the development of character empowers pupils and is liberating.**

Jen: That's really important, and surely what all education should be about: empowering young people and liberating their minds.

Pat: Yes, Jen, I love your idealism. If we can give pupils the vocabulary they need and model how to use it to interpret their own and others' behavioural choices, we will be giving them a gift that will stay with them long after they leave here. OK, Jen and Phil, can I ask you to think about the next stage of Functional Fluency implementation and report back next Monday?

Jen: On it!

Phil: Oh, OK then.

They all start to pack up.

Hopefully this dramatised situation shows the connections between the Framework for Character and Functional Fluency. And it is a short step from there to see that Functional Fluency could be utilised in schools as a mechanism for developing the positive character traits featured in the Framework in a systematic and systemic way across an institution such as a school. The Jubilee Centre and the University of Birmingham (2022) provide brief details on 70 character-education teaching strategies that anyone seeking to develop this kind of work could usefully consult.

What I am presenting here is a coherent vision of how a set of approaches can be used across a school to help all its key stakeholders to use their time and energy more effectively and affectively. In this way, the school's values and the character virtues that it espouses become built into the way people within the school behave and the nature of the relationships they create that, in turn, govern the effectiveness of the teaching and learning that take place there.

As Lemov et al., (2023) point out, character education is not without its critics: 'to some people the idea smacks of paternalism – how can one person say what characteristics are virtuous? To others it smacks of politicization – character virtues will be a vehicle for proselytizing values in an agenda that is not their own' (Lemov et al., 2023). The benefit of the Functional Fluency model in this context is that it is not about character virtues really, despite everything I have written above; it is actually about behaviour, communication and relationships. The model is not about people's innate character; it is about the behaviours they choose to employ. The distinction may seem an arcane one, but it is a central philosophical point that helps to protect the model from the criticisms outlined above. Temple (2015) explains it very clearly:

> To understand the model, and functional fluency itself, it is vital to remember that it is about behaviour, not about the person. Basically, Functional Fluency refers to the natural way that human beings get along well together. People are being functionally fluent when they relate to others in ways that are fit for purpose, with flexibility, flow, and mutual benefit.

> **Temple, 2015**

There is a fundamental, utilitarian simplicity to the model that protects it from accusations of political bias or moral favouritism. In this way, it can be accepted and used by people and institutions of widely varying political and religious stances or, as we will see in the *akrasia* section in Chapter 8, none at all.

> It means taking responsibility for one's own wellbeing and, when in charge of others, taking responsibility appropriately for them too. It means using one's full capacity for assessing and reflecting on situations moment by moment, taking all relevant factors into account. It means using energy on one's own behalf by relating effectively to others, warmly, heart to heart, and openly, and being willing to express one's own unique, creative individuality. Becoming more functionally fluent is about turning survive into thrive and converting stress and frustration into effectiveness and satisfaction.

> **Temple, 2015**

Temple's phrase 'taking responsibility appropriately' is so carefully considered, so balanced and so thoughtful, that it is very difficult to take offence at. The model was developed because of such precise thinking in the course of Temple's doctoral research (Temple, 2015), so that:

> the research process produced a TA model of human functioning that is valid and reliable as a basis both for behavioural diagnosis and for use as a tool for personal development.
>
> **Temple 2015**

So, the model has rigour, is valid and reliable and as free from ethical and political biases as any human construction is likely to be. This does not mean it could not be misused in thoughtless or malign hands, but it does give it as good a chance of success as possible.

Another point Lemov et al., (2023) raise is that, when seeking to build community within a school, 'we should seek out traits that the greatest number of parents (and hopefully pupils) place value on and that we have reason to believe will really help pupils'. There are problems with this approach. Firstly, how do we find out what the greatest number of parents place value on, without a very time-consuming consultation process? Even then, gaining anything like a 100% response rate, and developing a process to whittle the myriad suggestions down to something usefully concise, is extremely difficult. Furthermore, what do we do if the character traits that a proportion of parents favour, even if not a majority, are not those that the school feels are likely to further the effective development of the school community? Surely it is far better to start from an already existing model, which has been thoroughly researched and found to have reliability and validity? The Functional Fluency model provides this template, enabling pupils, staff and parents to work together to develop into the Functionally Fluent people who habitually make the effective behaviour choices that the model outlines, and experience the benefits and positive feelings that come with this.

Vision

In a conversation that I recorded with him for Myatt and Co, Daryl Sinclair (Sinclair, 2024) explained that, for a strong idea to gain traction with a school leadership team, it must be clear how it relates to the school's central vision. Schools spend a lot of time and energy coming up with and agreeing on their vision statement, and it is very difficult to get any initiative going that does not directly relate to this. As the Functional Fluency model is so fundamental to human relationships, it seems unlikely that a school will develop a vision statement that does not align with it, but it is worth checking this out. Chris Drew (Drew, 2023) has pulled together a useful list of the best school-vision statements, from which the following are taken:

> Our vision is to forge strong, positive connections with students so they can achieve independence, build confidence, and gain academic knowledge.

Here, the word 'connections' makes a clear link with the Functional Fluency focus on relationships and its background in TA, which is very explicitly concerned with interpersonal connections. The emphasis on building independence also relates closely to Functional Fluency: the top third of the model is all about growing and developing so that people can become effective and interdependent. And *confidence* is also fundamental to Functional Fluency, sitting explicitly in the Cooperative mode, but also more implicitly being one of the key aims of Functional Fluency as an individual gains an understanding of how to blend the behavioural modes with *zest*. The fundamental nature of Functional Fluency comes through very clearly here.

> We aim to develop well-rounded and thoughtful students prepared to cope with a changing post-modern and globalized world.

In this vision statement, the focus on developing 'well-rounded' young people links very clearly with the notion of balance within Functional Fluency. Structuring and Nurturing behaviours need to be in balance for us to operate effectively and develop effective relationships. Similarly, Cooperative and Spontaneous behaviours need to be in balance if we are fully and effectively to develop ourselves and show up as defined individuals in the world. *Thoughtful* links closely with Accounting behaviour, and the forward-looking element of the last few words of the vision links with Functional Fluency's emphasis on the development of the self and the next generation, the model placing importance on growing and becoming.

These two vision statements were the first two in Drew's piece (Drew, 2023), and the ease with which it is possible to draw conclusive links with Functional Fluency demonstrates the fundamental nature of the model. In this way, we can see that it supports any worthwhile work that a school is involved in. It is not a new fad or the latest innovation: it is an ageless, unchanging model of human behaviour that provides an anchor for schools, helping them to understand what really matters in these complex times.

Rebuilding connection in a disconnected world

In their book *Reconnect: Building School Culture for Meaning, Purpose, and Belonging* (Lemov et al., 2023), Lemov, Lewis, Williams and Frazier focus in on the post-pandemic problem of teenage loneliness. There are several ways in which Functional Fluency helps to address the issues that they raise.

The authors reference psychologist Sherry Turkle's suggestion that, due to technology, we are now 'forever elsewhere'. They go on to point out the issues that young people have with attention, saying that 'to learn well you must be able to maintain self-discipline about what you pay attention to'. As we have already seen earlier in this chapter when discussing the importance of Accounting, Functional Fluency places a very strong emphasis on where we focus our attention. The process of Accounting makes this explicit, encouraging us to think through what we have experienced, separate out the important things and then choose carefully how to respond to these things. This is 'paying attention' made less abstract, given a set of procedures that we can follow that should make it easier to be intentional with our attention.

The Get on the Mat sessions encourage an embodied form of engagement with issues. When discussing a situation on the mat, the physicality of the mat makes it much easier to be in the present, sharing ideas with the group and working with them to find better behavioural choices.

An even more serious issue that Lemov, Lewis, Williams and Frazier (Lemov et al., 2023) suggest may be affecting us in our increasingly technological age is the trend to distrust institutions and their ability to solve problems. They suggest that people increasingly think of institutions as incompetent and, even worse, 'ethically suspect'. Clearly, society is in a great deal of trouble if the population views its schools and the wider educational establishment in this way. The transparent and objective aspects of Functional Fluency, which everyone can easily understand and apply, provide this ethical underpinning that is in danger of being eroded. This, connected with a school that teaches Functional Fluency, hopefully enables pupils and parents to see it in action in the behavioural choices that the school's teachers and leaders make. They also witness it in their interactions with the school and are able to use it themselves when discussing issues with the institution. They are thus able to hold the school to account, using its own behavioural code, and this process helps to rebuild confidence in the ethical nature of the institution.

The authors go on to highlight other approaches that fit beautifully with Functional Fluency. They quote W.H. Auden's writing that language is the mother, not the handmaiden, of thought; and suggest that having words for things conjures them into being (Lemov et al., 2023). This is exactly how Functional Fluency works. It provides a shared language with which all those in a school can talk about situations, enabling them to address and examine behavioural choices with a previously impossible precision.

They also reference psychologist Martin Seligman's formulation for happiness, which involves combining pleasure, engagement and meaning (Lemov et al., 2023). It is my contention that Functional Fluency, when a school implements it effectively and coherently, has a clear and beneficial impact on behaviour, helping to create more connected, engaged and meaningful relationships across the school community, thus contributing to the creation of a radically happier place.

Social norms

As we have seen, we live in an age when social norms have become much less clearcut. There is no single moral code to which the majority of our pupils and their parents adhere. The UK government, in a post-Brexit push, has tried to establish the notion of British Values, but there is little about:

- democracy

- the rule of law

- individual liberty

- mutual respect

- tolerance of those of different faiths and beliefs

that most British people would recognise as being distinctly British or something to rally around. Indeed, 'individual liberty' is precisely the opposite. It encourages citizens to pursue their own whims, legitimised by the idea that their own freedom to make money at the expense of others' happiness and security is built into the fabric of our society.

In the absence of an agreed set of social norms, Functional Fluency represents a model that is sufficiently sophisticated to capture the complexities of life and relationships in all their maddening glory, while also being simple enough for most people to understand. And it can build the connections that we must have if we are to thrive as individuals, communities and societies.

Now it will be useful to hear about the experiences of Viv Grant, who brings much of this theory to life.

Functional Fluency in Action

Viv Grant

In the course of some work I have been doing with the educational consultant Mary Myatt, I was lucky enough to record an interview with the ex-headteacher, now CEO of the coaching company Integrity Coaching, Viv Grant (Grant, 2024a). I had contacted her with a view to recording a piece about her work as a black school leader, and subsequently as someone working with and encouraging other black teachers to take on leadership roles.

What I did not know when I first approached Viv (Grant, 2024b) was that she had been diagnosed with cancer a few months earlier, had had a hysterectomy and was enduring ongoing post-operative cancer treatment. This had caused her to think very deeply about the wellbeing of educational professionals and the way in which school leaders deal both with themselves and with their colleagues.

The fundamental reality of the situation, which her experience of cancer diagnosis had made particularly clear, was that we are all real people; individuals with inner lives that are important and require nourishing. During her treatment, Viv experienced responses from medical professionals that failed to acknowledge her individuality. They ignored her knowledge of the specifics of her rare type of cancer, which primarily affects black women and is therefore, shockingly, not widely known about or researched. This has left her with trauma, on top of the original trauma of the diagnosis. But it has also sharpened her own understanding of the need, as a school leader and a human being, to listen to the experiences of other people, particularly when their intersectional identity means that this is very different from your own. She describes her own experience at the hands of the medical establishment as leaving her feeling 'bent out of shape'; this has encouraged her to think carefully about how school leaders can ensure that they are not contributing, through their use of the power and status that comes with their position, to bending others out of shape themselves.

Schools require systems in order to operate. What Viv's thinking has led her to question is how these systems can be developed in ways that do not distort those who have to operate within them. Given the way in which Ofsted dominates the educational system in England, the pressures of which distort many school leaders 'out of shape', it is all too easy for school leaders to replicate this misshaping process in the systems that they set up and manage in their schools, in an attempt to ensure the highest possible grading. If this happens, and social media is awash with anecdotes that suggest it is far from rare, the result is trauma. School leaders need to be aware of this possibility and recognise the superficial nature of many of the wellbeing projects (yoga sessions or bowling evenings, for example) that schools sometimes put in place, as being wholly inadequate in the face of these experiences.

In *My Grandmother's Hands*, Resmaa Menakem makes it clear that trauma, as we saw earlier with Accounting, is a bodily experience, not an emotional reaction. 'Trauma is the body's protective response to an event – or series of events – that it perceives as potentially dangerous' (Menakem, 2017). This trauma response happens at 'lightning speed' and is likely to trigger behaviour in the purple modes of Functional Fluency, largely because of the speed of the reaction. This activates what Menakem describes as our 'lizard brain', and this is likely to result in Compliant / Resistant, Immature or Dominating behaviour. Being aware of this situation is the first step towards being able to remedy it. We need to understand this process so that we can work with people who are making reactive behaviour choices due to trauma. We also need to think about our own behaviour and the possible sources of trauma that may lead us to react to situations rather than respond to them.

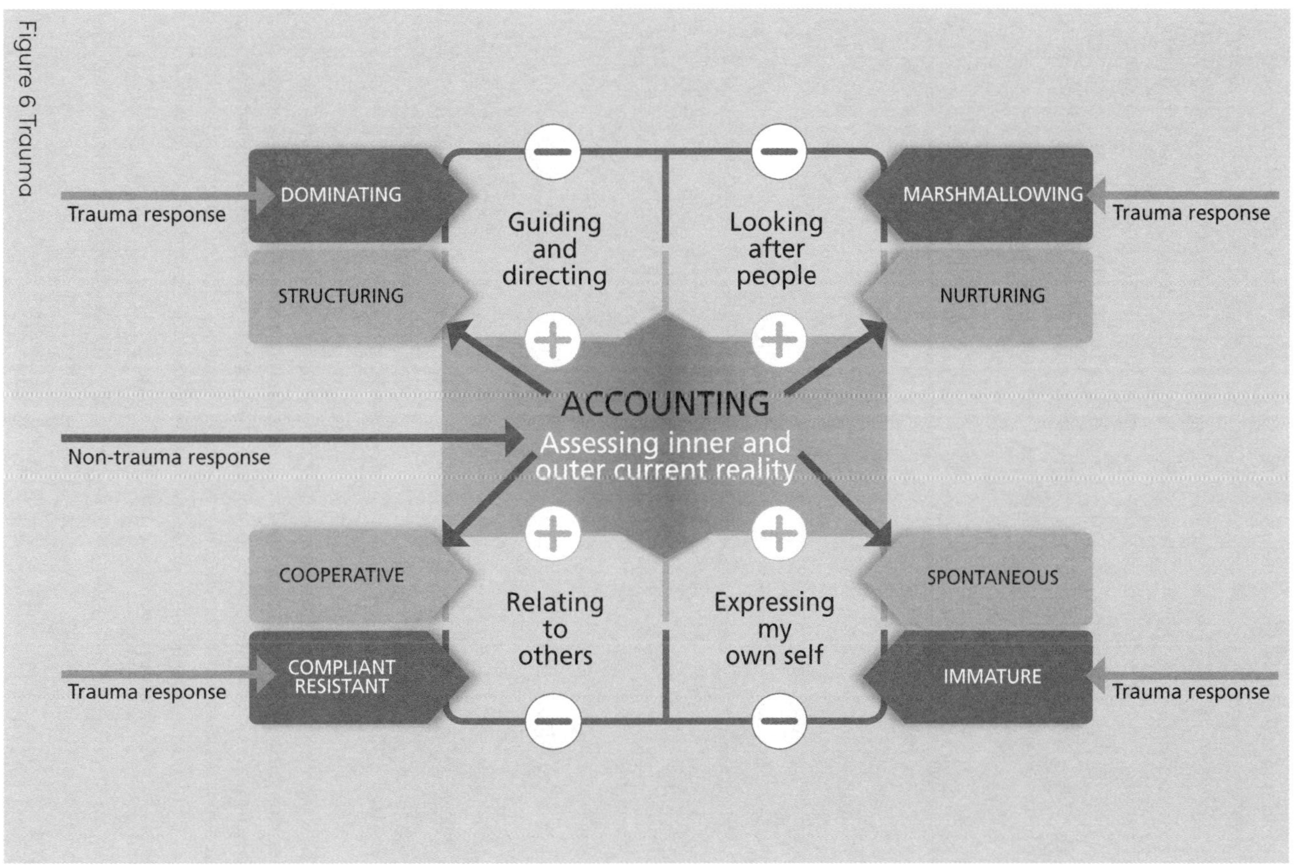

Figure 6 Trauma

How can we attempt to develop a response to this trauma that many school staff struggle to deal with every day? Clearly, there is no simple answer. Viv herself found that the route to exploring her own response to her situation involved art therapy. With the support of one of her daughter's friends (her hospital, an outstanding London institution that is a world leader in cancer care, hadn't employed an art therapist for the previous 18 months), she explored the ways in which 'a cancer diagnosis changes you' in an attempt to come to an understanding of the post-traumatic stress disorder (PTSD) and delayed shock that she has gone through.

School leaders need to think in a profound way about how they can empathise with the community they lead to give them insight into the various physical, social, emotional and economic traumas that 'bend out of shape' many of the individuals that make up the community. Functional Fluency, particularly the Accounting mode, is a model that helps school leaders to do this.

Accounting is characterised by *grounded, alert* and *aware* behaviour, as well as *evaluative* behaviour, all of which enable school leaders to formulate considered and considerate responses to circumstances, avoiding the reactions that might serve to add to communal trauma. Additionally, the *empathic* and *considerate* behaviours within Nurturing provide further encouragement for the compassionate leadership that – when blended with the requisite Structuring elements, such as *firm* and *inspiring* behaviour – characterise Functionally Fluent leadership. Add to this the model's focus on self-care and self-development through the Cooperative and Spontaneous modes – the space where art therapy would fit – and we have the basis of a sustainable approach to difficult circumstances that enables leaders to lead in ways that diminish communal and individual trauma, rather than add to it.

Viv Grant's journey is a powerful testament to the deep need for the inclusive leadership this book advocates for: leadership rooted in empathy and self-awareness, and the courage to see the profound human challenges our colleagues and pupils navigate every day. Her story is a call to action, reminding us that the principles of Functional Fluency are not abstract concepts but vital tools for our most profound human challenges.

As we now turn to the heart of every school – the relationship between teacher and pupil – let's carry with us the understanding that the most impactful work begins within, by becoming more aware, more responsive and more fully ourselves.

CHAPTER 2
THE HEART OF THE MATTER: BUILDING THE RELATIONSHIPS THAT TRANSFORM LEARNING

During breaktime at Meadowbank Middle School, a disagreement erupts between two Year 7 pupils about whose football to use for their breaktime kickabout. Chris Andrews, who has been thinking about what Pat Harrison said on the INSET day about Functional Fluency and choice, speaks to them, listens to both sides and points out to the pupils that there are other behaviour choices they could have picked, other than arguing and almost starting a fight, that would have enabled them both to be happy. He guides them towards an agreed way forward, involving using the balls on alternate days.

Observing all this from a discrete distance, headteacher Pat Harrison is delighted and joins the discussion, praising everyone for using Cooperative and Structuring behaviour to prevent a serious incident.

How would a Functionally Fluent teacher engage with pupils?

The most important relationships in any school are those between the teachers and the pupils. They set the tone and determine the quality of learning. Too often, teachers and leaders spend their time and energy managing behavioural issues that undermine these crucial connections. Redirecting that energy towards learning helps a school thrive and makes life less stressful for everyone involved. The stakes could not be higher.

Cracking the code: understanding the teenage brain through Functional Fluency

Recent neuroscience, powerfully summarised by Sarah-Jane Blakemore in *Inventing Ourselves* (2018), reveals that the adolescent brain undergoes far more change than previously understood. It actively prunes synapses and shifts the balance of its grey and white matter. These changes help explain behaviours common to teenagers: intense self-consciousness and self-concern, increased risk-taking and a remarkable capacity for new learning. Blakemore argues these traits are not flaws, but necessary parts of the journey to adulthood.

Does this distinct neurological phase require a different behavioural model? No. Functional Fluency remains the ideal framework. It describes a state where a person responds effectively to their environment, making well-judged choices that benefit themselves and others. While no one achieves this state perfectly all the time, the model provides an unwavering ideal to strive for. An adolescent's tendency towards risky behaviour doesn't invalidate the model any more than an adult's tendency to be judgemental does.

Functional Fluency acts as a Rosetta Stone, creating a common language for different generations to discuss behaviour. It serves as an objective reference point from which mutual understanding and personal growth can emerge. The model provides a map for self-regulation, helping both adults and adolescents negotiate the fine line between effective and ineffective choices. We can explicitly teach young people to use the Accounting Framework to make thoughtful decisions, improving their self-regulation, resulting in better academic outcomes and strengthening the community.

As Laurence Steinberg notes in *Age of Opportunity* (2014), 'we should pay less attention to trying to change teenagers and more to try and change the settings in which they spend their time'. Functional Fluency provides the tool to structure those settings. Steinberg points out that adolescents need authoritative parenting (and teaching) that is warm, firm and supportive – precisely the approaches the model champions. Promoting self-regulation does more to reduce substance abuse, unprotected sex and reckless driving than conventional education on those topics. It also equips students with the skills to succeed in higher education, where adult supervision is minimal.

Adolescence is a time of peak brain plasticity. It is a unique opportunity to establish the behavioural practices that enable young people to become Functionally Fluent adults. To do this effectively, we must first understand a core human need that is especially acute during these years: the need for recognition and connection. This fundamental drive for social validation is the psychological currency of the classroom. Transactional Analysis (TA) gives us a powerful term for this unit of recognition: the 'stroke'.

Strokes: the unseen currency of the classroom

Functional Fluency has developed from TA, which posits that human beings *'need* to relate to people in order to become fully human' (Temple, 2016). In TA, the unit of this relational attention is the *strcke*. Educationalist Geoff Barton has often cited his concern about pupils who can go through a whole school day without having any interaction with an adult, receiving zero strokes. Such pupils, whether they are avoiding interaction or simply being overlooked, will struggle to develop into well-adjusted adults.

Strokes break down into four types.

Table 2 Stroke types

	Conditional	Unconditional
Positive	Approval + 'That was a great answer because...'	Acceptance ++ 'Good to see ycu today'
Negative	Disapproval – 'You need to read the text mɔre carefully'	Rejection – – 'You are the wcrst class I've ever taught'

All people need strokes to survive. Many get a lot of positive strokes at home, but others do not and arrive in school 'stroke starved'. If, during the school day, they continue to be ignored, they soon demand attention by acting in ways that elicit negative strokes. This, as Temple (2015) points out, is not a trivial matter but actually all about survival, going back to prehistory when 'if a child wasn't noticed at all, if no one had an eye on it, then it might have actually got eaten up or left behind'.

Observe any classroom, and the stroke-starved pupils quickly become apparent. They are the ones demanding attention by arriving late, shouting out or disrupting others. As their Functionally Fluent teacher, you must find ways to satisfy their need for strokes without derailing the lesson. A simple greeting by name at the door (an unconditional positive stroke) is a s⁻art. If this is backed up by conditional, positive strokes, such as 'I hear you worked really hard in science yesterday', which acknowledge the pupil's effort and demonstrate that the school values it, this has an ever stronger impact.

As Karen Pratt (2021) points out, the behaviour that receives strokes is the behaviour you encourage. If you provide mainly unconditional negative strokes, your classes quickly become discouraged, and their behaviour worsens. This is why practices such as the 'meet and greet' are so effective: they ensure that all pupils start off the lesson with a positive, unconditional stroke, encouraging the kind of cooperative behaviour from which learning flows.

As they grow up, people 'develop a stroke filter which will filter out the types of strokes that don't fit their accustomed ratio' (Pratt, 2021). This explains why some pupils respond badly to praise. We must know our pupils well enough to 'package strokes in a way that will impact them' (Pratt, 2021). In Functional Fluency terms, we could think about strokes in relation to the five golden modes of behaviour. Positive strokes are likely to involve Structuring and Nurturing, though, if used to excess, this could fall into Marshmallowing behaviour, when pupils see through too many insincere or 'plastic' strokes (Pratt, 2021). Negative strokes are likely to be Dominating mode behaviour.

As teachers, we must use Accounting behaviour to determine the diet of strokes that our classes need to survive and thrive. Getting this right encourages the Spontaneous and Cooperative mode responses that establish a productive learning atmosphere. As Temple (2016) writes, 'It is hard for anyone to feel motivated and benevolent without enough positive strokes'. Just as teachers need to consider the stroke economy for their pupils, so leaders need to think about the one they create for their teachers. In both cases, they must avoid 'game playing', where people seek negative strokes to gain attention. The stroke provider needs to resist being pulled into negativity by carefully evaluating the situation and by judiciously using the tools in the Accounting toolbox (see pages 16–17 for details). As groups, teachers and pupils need to develop a healthy stroke economy as a vital step towards creating a Functionally Fluent community.

Beyond disruption: understanding the unmet need

Example 1 Coping with a disruptive pupil

Situation

The behaviour of a specific pupil is really annoying you. He talks incessently while you are trying to explain things to the class; he fidgets and disrupts your flow of thought and asks annoying questions all the time (*immature*). You are finding it increasingly difficult not to lose your temper as soon as you see this pupil (*anxious, rebellious*).

Pupil:

▼

Immediate thoughts and feelings

This situation is making you dread these lessons. Your teaching is beginning to suffer and the rest of the class are starting to notice and become resentful.

You:

▼

Pause: choice

You realise that this is probably all about strokes. The pupil is not receiving enough positive strokes at home, perhaps because his parents work long hours. This lack of attention drives the pupil to demand attention, and the easiest way to do this is to behave badly – he has learned how to do this because he has had a lot of practice!

You:

▼

Functionally Fluent response

You consider (Accounting) a range of strategies (warm personal greeting, front-row seat, attention from a TA, several check-ins each lesson) that will ensure that this pupil gets attention without having to behave badly (*encouraging*). You explain to the child that you want him to learn and that you know he can achieve (*encouraging*) but that there are limits to what you will tolerate (*firm*). You may decide to refer the pupil to his form teacher who can talk to him about strategies to reduce disruptive behaviour. The relationship begins to improve as the pupil realises there are productive ways to gain the attention he needs.

You:

Pupil:

▼

Key learning

This scenario demonstrates how using Accounting to understand a pupil's need for strokes can prevent reactive behaviour and lead to a more constructive outcome.

From classroom to community: building a culture of safety and trust

Just as managing the stroke economy is vital for individual relationships, the collective trust within a school is crucial for learning. This brings us to the importance of building a Functionally Fluent community – a concept powerfully underscored by trauma expert Bessel van der Kolk.

In his seminal work *The Body Keeps the Score*, van der Kolk (2014) writes: 'People can learn to control and change their behaviour, but only if they feel safe enough to experiment with new solutions'. Functional Fluency is built on this very idea: because our behaviour is a choice, we can learn to change it. The model provides a road map for positive change and a safe structure that encourages community members to try new ways of behaving, giving them the strength to resist peer pressure or established norms.

Van der Kolk argues that, for traumatised children, we must not cut the very activities that build safety and help them escape fight-or-flight states: 'chorus, physical education, recess, and anything else that involves movement, play, and other forms of joyful engagement'. Schools are full of anxious pupils (and teachers). The Functional Fluency model and the TIFF profile make this anxiety visible, bringing it into the open for discussion. While telling an anxious person not to be anxious is useless, so is hiding the feeling. Through its physicality – for example the act of standing on a mode on a floor mat – Functional Fluency connects the head, heart and gut. It validates our feelings as the first step towards understanding the behaviours that stem from them.

Van der Kolk captures the reality of the English educational landscape when he asks what our schools would look like if they cultivated 'cooperation, self regulation, perseverance, and concentration (as opposed to focusing on passing tests)'. Functional Fluency champions exactly these behaviours:

- Accounting is a synonym for self-regulation.

- Cooperation is a key positive mode.

- *Curiosity*, part of the Spontaneous mode, is the foundation of learning.

- Perseverance and concentration emerge from a healthy balance of Structuring and Nurturing within the environment.

In recent years, school leaders have sometimes neglected community building because external agencies cannot easily measure it. Yet, the metrics these agencies *can* measure – such as test scores – depend on these ineffable qualities. Pupils and teachers who belong to a supportive community, one they trust to treat them fairly, focus more effectively on their work. As van der Kolk (2014) puts it, 'Children and adults will do anything for people they trust'. The trust that a Functional Fluency approach fosters may be hard to quantify, but that makes it all the more important to cultivate. It yields far-reaching benefits for everything from academic achievement to diversity and inclusion.

Safety first: how the nervous system shapes learning (the polyvagal connection)

In *Our Polyvagal World*, Stephen and Seth Porges (2023) define polyvagal theory (PVT) in a single sentence: 'How safe we feel is crucial to our physical and mental health and happiness.'

PVT centres on the vagus nerve, named from the Latin for 'wandering' because it connects to our major organs. This extensive network allows our entire body to feel and respond to threats. When our environment signals safety, we enter a receptive state, ready to learn. In Functional Fluency terms, we can use Spontaneous and Cooperative behaviour to socialise productively.

Our sense of safety matters deeply. Unfortunately, school safeguarding practices, such as high railings, can, ironically, increase feelings of threat. PVT suggests we absorb these signals automatically through a process called **neuroception**. If our body senses a threat – using ancient predator-evasion circuits – our autonomic nervous system can trigger a **fight-or-flight** state, making learning difficult. It can also send us into a **shutdown** state: an echo of our ancestors playing dead to survive. PVT posits we have no conscious control over these states; our autonomic nervous system chooses for us.

Table 3 The Polyvagal Ladder (Dana, 2018)

State	PVT term	Behaviour
Top (green)	Ventral vagal	Safe, social and able to learn (homeostasis)
Middle (yellow)	Sympathetic	Fight or flight; focused on safety not learning
Bottom (red)	Dorsal vagal	Shutdown; frozen and unresponsive

Our state directly impacts our ability to respond. In fight-or-flight or shutdown, we cannot think as clearly as when we are in a calm state of homeostasis. In shutdown, tiny muscles in our ears even adapt to filter out the pitch of human speech, making us more attuned to low, threatening sounds. The pupil with their head on the desk may literally not be able to hear you properly.

A Functionally Fluent teacher must use Accounting to assess a pupil's state. By asking 'Is this defiance, or a "fight" response triggered by feeling unsafe?', the teacher can choose behaviours that help guide the pupil back to homeostasis. One key tool is prosody: the sing-song, varied tone of voice that calms our nervous system. A stressed trainee teacher often defaults to a flat monotone, which pupils can neuroceptively register as a threat, undermining learning. Again, the Functionally Fluent teacher uses Accounting to become conscious of their own state and its impact on the class.

This process of using our own calm state to soothe another person is called 'co-regulation'. It is how we form the productive social bonds essential for human functioning. A teacher who remains calm when facing a dysregulated pupil can initiate co-regulation, using 'golden' mode behaviours, including Accounting, to de-escalate the situation rather than inflame it.

Here lies the crucial link between the two models. PVT describes the autonomic nervous system, where unconscious **neuroception** determines our state. Functional Fluency addresses the somatic nervous system, where conscious *Accounting* has the ability, if we choose to use it, to determine our voluntary behaviour. This is a crucial distinction with important implications for educators.

A Functionally Fluent teacher can use their knowledge of PVT as a critical factor in their Accounting process. This understanding helps them to distinguish between pupils who are wilfully misbehaving and those who are in an uncontrollable vagal state. This helps teachers by informing a more compassionate and effective response. We must remember that the foundation of learning is safety. None of us can accurately predict how we will react in traumatic situations until we experience them, and this should encourage us to think carefully about the causes of dysregulated pupil behaviour and how to reduce it. By using the Accounting Framework to co-regulate with pupils, teachers can create an environment where everyone feels secure enough to learn, connect and thrive.

Tools for every learner: adapting your approach for neurodiversity

A key test of any school's commitment to inclusion is how it supports its neurodivergent pupils. The strategies in Table 4 demonstrate how the Functional Fluency model can be adapted to create a truly inclusive classroom where every learning style is understood and valued. Practices that support neurodivergent students often benefit everyone and, here, the Functional Fluency mat is a particularly powerful tool. By making thinking visual and providing a common language for behaviour, it helps people articulate differing perspectives, build empathy and resolve conflict.

Table 4 outlines practical strategies for using Functional Fluency and TIFF effectively with neurodivergent individuals.

Table 4 Functional Fluency and neurodiversity

Factors	Considerations
Sensory needs	Consult the school's SENDCo about pupils' specific sensory needs in advance. Discuss allowances for helpful behaviours, such as using fidget tools, to ensure they don't interfere with others' concentration.
Contracting	Establish a strong bond of trust before the session. All parties must know what will happen and why. Clearly define the rules of confidentiality to create psychological safety.
Language	Use concise, literal language, avoiding metaphors that could confuse. Check for understanding by asking in multiple ways, such as 'How have you understood this?' or 'How is this working for you?' Using the term 'neurotypical' can be useful, as it indicates that everyone has a label.
Tailored feedback	Tailor all feedback to the pupils' specific needs and communication styles. Discuss these preferences during the initial contracting phase.
Attention span	Recognise that this work can be draining, especially for neurodivergent pupils. Timetable sessions thoughtfully – perhaps at the end of the day – to avoid leaving pupils unable to focus in their next lesson.
Co-creation	Ensure all parties are fully present and focused. Functional Fluency is a co-creative process where everyone contributes their Accounting energy to make the session productive.
Environment	Create an environment that is 'safe enough' for everyone. Small actions such as doodling or fidgeting may aid focus, even if they look like inattention. Allow for movement and provide such sensory objects as velvet cushions, visual timers or stress balls. Meet the person where they are.
Signals	Establish pre-arranged, simple signals that a pupil can use to communicate their needs without having to find complex words. Examples include a physical gesture (closing a book or moving an object) to show they feel unsafe, or a phrase such as 'Too many words' if they feel overwhelmed.
Pupil perspective	Actively seek feedback from neurodivergent pupils about their experience with Functional Fluency. Use their insights to improve and adapt future sessions.

Case study: using the Functional Fluency mat

To see Functional Fluency in action, let's look at a case study from TIFF provider Beatrijs Dijkman. In a 2024 *Transactional Analysis podcast*, she described using the Functional Fluency mat to help her 15-year-old son navigate a difficult relationship with a teacher. Example 2 breaks down the situation and the successful outcome.

Example 2 A breakthrough on the mat: a case study in communication

Situation

A 15-year-old Dutch school pupil is struggling with one particular course and teacher.

Pupil:

▼

Immediate thoughts and feelings

The boy feels the teacher doesn't respect him, and his first impulse is to quit the course.

Pupil:

▼

Pause: choice

As his mother is a Functional Fluency professional, she has a Functional Fluency model mat on the floor in her office. She persuades him to use the mat to explore his feelings. Together, they discuss which behaviours he could use to address the situation constructively with his teacher.

Mother:

Pupil:

▼

Functionally Fluent response

Having talked it through with his mother, the boy approaches his teacher and uses the 'golden modes' to communicate his feelings. In response, the teacher changes her behaviour. Their relationship improves, and the boy succeeds in the class.

Pupil:

▼

Key learning

In this scenario, we see a young person beginning to understand that confronting issues in a mature manner can result in much better outcomes for everyone.

The principles of adapting Functional Fluency for different needs, including neurodiversity, are best understood through real-world application. The following insights from practitioners Simphiwe Mahlanyana and Liz Jackson provide powerful case studies of how to use these concepts to improve pupils' lives in diverse educational settings.

Functional Fluency in Action

Simphiwe Mahlanyana: Functional Fluency in a South African school

Functional Fluency, comprehensive sexuality education and gender-based violence programmes

Simphiwe Mahlanyana, also known as Sim, is from Kwa-Langa, Cape Town's first township in South Africa. Sim is a coach and youth facilitator. Since becoming a licensed Functional Fluency professional in September 2019, he has been an integral part of Functional Fluency International, providing support in administration, marketing and web services. Sim is a passionate believer in the efficacy of Functional Fluency and TIFF in both his personal and professional life. His current focuses include working with teenagers to understand their behaviour and helping rehabilitated drug and alcohol abusers reintegrate into their communities.

Sim presented a plan to start using Functional Fluency in a school in South Africa, where he was already working as a freelancer delivering comprehensive sexuality-education courses and programmes to counter gender-based violence. He had observed the pupils' behaviour in this school, which was set up to cater for young people who had been expelled from other mainstream schools. He felt that there was a clear need for Functional Fluency education to help them to think about and moderate their behaviour. He was already using Functional Fluency language and approaches in an implicit way within these programmes, and the headteacher had noticed a clear behavioural improvement in the pupils, especially the boys, and so asked for a more direct approach. The headteacher had big plans for Functional Fluency, including wanting to set aside a Functional Fluency room where pupils who were sent out of classes could come to discuss their behaviour with Sim. Unfortunately, at the time, the school did not have the finances to make this happen. However,

Sim went into the school for three hours a week on a voluntary basis to work with pupils and help them to see that the golden behaviours of the Functional Fluency model could help everyone to thrive.

As a result of hearing about Sim's work and about Functional Fluency through Sim's cousin, a parent approached Sim to see whether he would be willing to work directly with her 16-year-old daughter whose behaviour was causing the mother increasing concern. This gave rise to the idea of individual interventions with young people using Functional Fluency. The daughter had become increasingly depressed, silent and isolated at home, and there were also issues of bullying at school that had led to a change of schools.

Sim spent about 45 minutes talking to the girl, exploring her situation; then he explained the Functional Fluency model and how completing a TIFF might be beneficial. She responded well to this pitch (which was clearly very different in tone and approach from a Functional Fluency pitch to an adult CEO, for example). After she had completed the 108-item TIFF questionnaire, Sim held a feedback session, which lasted two hours, where he made it clear that he is not a counsellor. The girl had already had several negative experiences of counsellors who, she felt, were all siding with her mother. During the feedback session, two major root causes of the girl's depression became clear through Sim's coaching approach, which was to allow the discussion to follow a course dictated by the girl's own curiosities about the TIFF profile results. Using the Get on the Mat approach, the girl was able to explore her own behavioural choices and begin to consider the impact of these on others. These approaches revealed that the girl had not spoken to her mother properly for around four years. The mother was both shocked and delighted to receive a letter of apology from her daughter – testament to the impact of Sim's work.

It is clear that Functional Fluency and TIFF provided a route through to the problems at the heart of this girl's behaviour, suggesting that there is huge potential for using TIFF in one-to-one interventions with pupils who are experiencing a range of difficulties. In particular, the feedback session enabled the girl to unpick her relationship with her mother and the actions that she was taking that contributed to the issues. The girl was also able to use the model to interpret both her own and her mother's behaviour in insightful ways. The relationship between the mother and daughter improved as a direct result, to the extent that the mother offered to pay Sim double for his work.

Sim also worked with another 16-year-old girl from a very privileged background. The focus here was on helping both the mother and daughter to break out of a pattern of Marshmallowing behaviour that had established a damaging degree of dependence between them. They realised that this situation needed to change if the daughter was going to be able to transition successfully to university. Together, Sim and the girl spent a lot of time focusing on increasing Accounting behaviour to help her become more in touch with reality.

The common factor in both situations was the way in which Marshmallowing on the part of the mother made it difficult for her child to grow up in appropriate ways, leaving both girls incapable of coping properly with the adult world to which they were increasingly being exposed. In a South African context there are a range of additional issues, with parents who live in the cities unwilling to allow their children to visit their relatives in the townships, even though the parents themselves were born and brought up there.

As he talked about the gender-based violence project work, it became clear that the situations Sim was hearing about and attempting to address were perhaps more extreme than those facing most UK schools. There is, nevertheless, a distinct similarity in the attitudes of the boys that he described and the toxic masculinity exhibited by many boys in the UK. Sim referenced how Susannah Temple, the author of TIFF, created the model to understand better the behaviour of young people in schools; this is a strong justification for his use of the model with groups to investigate and then break the cycle of bullying. He has been working with them to develop roleplays that explore, in a safe and structured way, the behaviours involved in bullying, then helping them to examine the behaviours through the lens of the Functional Fluency model. Group members who have taken on the role of observers use the model to suggest which types of behaviour would have resulted in better outcomes for all concerned, in a direct parallel with the example situations of this book. This is particularly useful as a means of exploring issues around sexual consent; a difficult area within current gender politics.

When the adolescent boys Sim was working with saw the model, they expressed the idea that, to have a successful relationship, men needed to use Dominating behaviour towards women, as opposed to the golden behaviour modes. This clearly demonstrates the amount of work that still needs to be done in this area. While Functional Fluency has not solved this issue, it has at least brought it out into the open, providing everyone with some shared language to use when talking about it and forcing these young men to see the reality of their beliefs laid bare. Hopefully, this is a necessary first stage on the path towards developing more equal relationships between the sexes.

A colleague of Sim's runs the comprehensive sexuality-education programme with groups of teenage girls. When individual girls in this group outline specific problems, this colleague often refers them on to Sim for one-to-one work using Functional Fluency. Sometimes, this involves working with the parents to explore the behaviour of both the parents and the child, and to explore complex issues that include abuse, pornography, sex addiction and gambling. Where appropriate, referrals are made to specialist therapists.

Finally, Sim reported on the way the teachers in the school he works in see him as a calming influence. What is clear is the need for Functional Fluency training for teachers so that they can begin to move away from the reactive way in which they are tending to behave, and towards the more thoughtful and responsive type of behaviour that Sim exemplifies. Hopefully we will soon have a cohort of Certified Functional Fluency Teachers in South Africa to take this work forward.

Functional Fluency in Action

Liz Jackson: Functional Fluency in English schools

Liz Jackson is a teacher, coach and counsellor who has used Functional Fluency in all elements of her professional life.

In her classroom-teaching role, Liz has taught Year 9 pupils personal, social, health and economic education (PSHE) modules on TA, which have included the teaching of Functional Fluency. The work has included practical elements, such as giving groups of pupils laminated versions of the Functional Fluency model, cut up into sections which they discuss and use to re-create the model. This activity generates much useful discussion about the thinking that lies behind it.

Liz facilitates exploration of the three top-level concepts of the model:

- How we use our behaviour on behalf of ourselves to realise our own individuality
- How we take on responsibility for others and ourselves by being in charge
- How we notice and evaluate reality in ourselves and others, in the moment, so that we can make effective behaviour choices through a process we call Accounting.

With this understanding of the model, Liz presents scenarios to Year 11 pupils for them to consider in pairs. These are situations that relate to their own experiences, such as dealing with conflict around option choices, when the pupil and their parents or carers have different ideas about the best way forward. The task is to decide which blend of the golden modes they would use to handle a particular situation. This generates a lot of high-level discussion as they begin to recognise that there isn't a 'one size fits all' answer and that it depends on each person's unique situation and the different personalities involved.

Liz explains:

'In working in one-to-one situations, I particularly use the Control and Care elements of the model to help students reflect on how best to manage themselves, as well as when they are in a role of being in charge of others. For example, one A-level student had a coping strategy of staying off school whenever things got difficult in life and when she felt overwhelmed by all the revision she needed to do. She led a chaotic lifestyle and felt a real failure. Using Accounting mode, I invited her to think about how her current strategy was helping her achieve success in her exams and whether we could explore alternatives. She began experimenting with the Structuring mode, and came up with a plan to create a revision timetable, which was realistic and incorporated regular breaks (Nurturing herself) and doing fun activities such as going outdoors for a run (Spontaneous mode). Fuelled by this success, she went on to use Functional Fluency to change her eating habits and sleep habits too. It was clear from comments she made that she was finding the framework of the model useful, for example she said "Liz, I set my alarm and started work early today. I wanted to stay under my duvet, but I didn't Marshmallow myself like I used to!" I was delighted when she messaged me months later, thanking me and letting me know about her exam success and university offer.'

The pupils consider ways in which Functional Fluency can help individuals make behavioural choices from which everyone can benefit. This approach demonstrates to pupils how Functional Fluency can have practical implications in their own lives, helping them to navigate some of the issues they inevitably face as they grow up. It also functions as a reinforcement of their understanding of the model, helping them to remember and internalise it more fully so that they begin to apply it in their own lives without having to consult a copy of the model. This approach, with its emphasis on repeatedly returning to the model so that pupils may forget it and then be reminded of it again – thus gaining a deeper understanding – fits with what we know from Ebbinghaus (1913) about the role of forgetting in learning.

Liz has also used Functional Fluency in one-to-one work with a school refuser and her mother. An extensive series of sessions involved both mother and daughter completing a TIFF questionnaire. Liz helped the pupil to see the need to engage in a higher level of Accounting to develop greater awareness of the reality of her own situation and to recognise that social anxiety rather than physical illness was at the root of her school refusal. In parallel, the mother came to realise that she was putting too much of her time and energy into Marshmallowing behaviour, when what her daughter needed was Structuring and more effective use of strokes as a means of demonstrating love and deepening the mother–daughter relationship. Subsequently, the pupil was able to increase her school attendance considerably and go on to take up a place in the local sixth-form college.

In a school for pupils with moderate learning difficulties, Liz used Functional Fluency with the staff team. All the staff were taught the Functional Fluency model as part of their work on an introductory TA course (TA101), and all went on to complete their own TIFF and to have a feedback session to explore their results with Liz. Here, contracting was particularly important to counter defensive ideas on the part of some staff who were concerned about issues of confidentiality. Once this clarity had been established, staff were pleased to have the chance to focus on themselves for a block of time. Many of them took up the opportunity to engage in a follow-up telephone consultation with Liz to check in on progress against the action plan they had co-created during the original feedback session. This work highlighted how exhausted many of the staff were. They were devoting too much of their time and energy to doing things for the pupils, and did not know when to stop and instead direct their energy into appropriate levels of self-care. Again, reassurance around privacy was required during the contracting phase, but the staff took the process as a huge positive stroke. It encouraged an increased emphasis on Spontaneous behaviour, freeing up the staff to enjoy playing with the pupils without feeling guilty about it, as well as encouraging more Spontaneous behaviour in their lives outside school. Figure 7 is an attempt to capture some of this complexity diagrammatically.

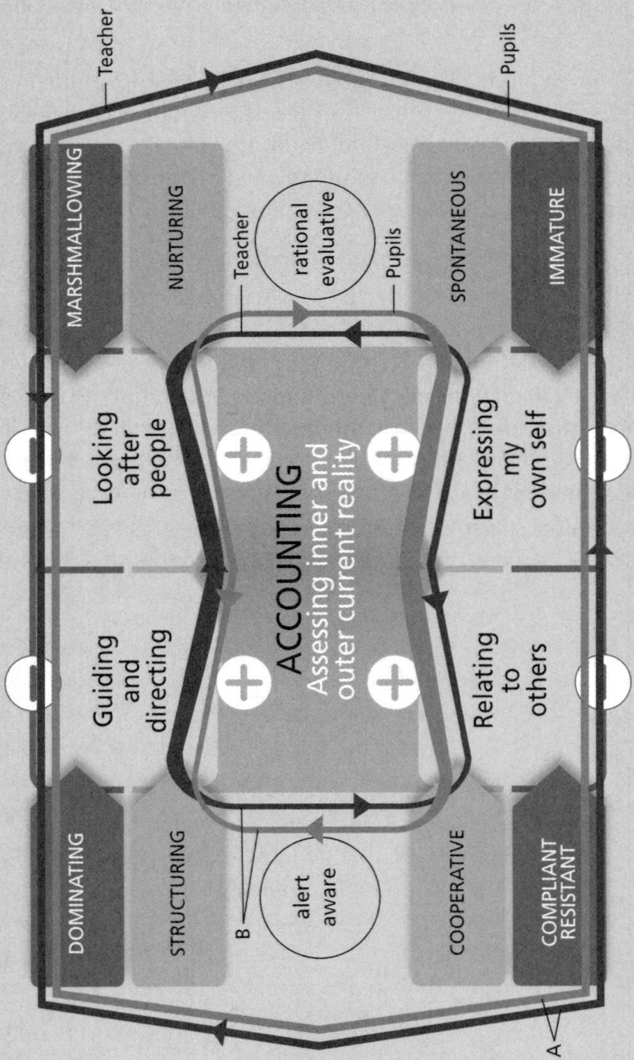

Figure 7 Non-Functionally Fluent (A) and Functionally Fluent (B) teaching and learning

In her school-governor role, Liz has introduced her governor colleagues to Functional Fluency with an emphasis on wellbeing. She has run Get on the Mat sessions for the school's staff so that teachers gain an understanding of the model and how it can help guide them towards making behaviour decisions from which everyone can benefit

This case study shows the wide range of ways in which one person can use Functional Fluency across their professional work to help in a variety of situations: as a teaching resource to help pupils regulate their behaviour and build a sense of community; as a targeted intervention with individual pupils with specific behaviour issues; and as an approach to address wider staff wellbeing issues across a school.

To illustrate how the concepts covered in this chapter are relevant, let's explore some common situations in schools.

The art of balance: combining care and control

One of the key insights of Functional Fluency is that, for our behaviour to be effective, we need to have a balance between the amount of time and energy we put into guiding and directing ourselves and others and the amount of time and energy we put into looking after ourselves and others.

A key question is 'How do I manifest authority when I am in charge?' (Temple, 2015). There is a very clear link here with the profession of teaching: the quintessential 'role that carries authority'. And at this top level, before we get into the value-laden aspect of what constitutes effective and less effective behaviour, it is important to realise that, to be effective in the implementation of authority to help others to grow (such a fundamental aspect of any teacher's role), we need to find an effective balance between controlling others and caring for others.

In terms of the effective modes of Functionally Fluent behaviour, this means that we need to balance the energy that we are putting into Structuring things for ourselves and others and Nurturing ourselves and others. If this key balance is missing, we find that our teaching work becomes far more difficult. If we set ourselves harsh limitations and do not allow time for rest and recuperation, we are in danger of burning out before we get to the end of term. By worrying too much about things, we are wasting energy questioning ourselves and judging ourselves and others in unhelpful ways, draining away energy that we could use more positively for supporting and nurturing ourselves and others.

Equally, if we put all our efforts into trying to look after our form group and do not provide them with enough structure and clarity, we soon find that they are taking advantage of this situation. This is because too much Nurturing, without a counter-balancing quantity of Structuring, is perceived as Marshmallowing. We have all witnessed teachers who focus too much on providing support for their classes without clear rules. This frequently descends into chaos. Nurturing intent has tipped over into Marshmallowing reality. Similarly, too much Structuring, whether for self or others, without an equivalent focus on Nurturing, often creates an impression of Dominating, and the result is often a Compliant / Resistant or Immature reaction. We have all worked for leaders who dictate tasks without sufficient acknowledgement of team needs. The result is often resentment – what is intended as Structuring is experienced as Dominating behaviour.

Finding the right balance between care and control is rarely easy. The following examples explore how the Functional Fluency model can help us understand and resolve the situations where that balance is lost.

Example 3 Nurturing without Structuring

Situation

The class is not listening to you. You cannot understand this as, since you met them, you have been keen to encourage them, listen to their issues and make it clear that you are interested in them as individuals. What more do you have to do?

You:

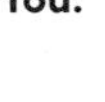

Pupils:

Immediate thoughts and feelings

You are frustrated because you are putting a great deal of time and effort into Nurturing, in the form of *encouragement*, *understanding* and *cherishing*. But the more you try to Nurture this group, the more they take advantage of your good nature.
The class feel that you are not Structuring things for them sufficiently and thus that your behaviour is Marshmallowing rather than Nurturing.
You feel upset that all this positive energy on your part is being met by negativity. You feel as though you will soon snap and resort to shouting at them (*blaming, punitive*) as you blame them for the deterioration of the teaching relationship.

Pupils' perception:

Your perception:

You:

You: 

Pause: choice

You pause and ask yourself some key questions (*enquiring*). Using the Accounting toolbox, you become *aware* and acknowledge what is happening, internally. You realise that you are caring for this class in ways that aren't working. As a result, you are putting up with too much and your patience is wearing very thin

What you perceive to be Nurturing behaviour is taken by the class as a sign of weakness. They want you to Care about them, but they also need you to Structure learning for them so that they understand where the boundaries are and can feel confident that you are in control. Through Accounting, you realise that you need a more effective balance between Nurturing and Structuring.

You: 

Pupils: 

Functionally Fluent response

You clarify with the class that you want the best for them (*encouraging*), that you are interested in them (*empathic*) but that **you** are in control and will set consistent boundaries (*firm*) and implement them fairly (*consistent*).

Because you are now balancing Nurturing with Structuring, the class learn that you are in control. They no longer feel that you are Marshmallowing them and they are comfortable to learn. Through Accounting, you have ensured that your own internal theatre does not take over.

Key learning

Here we see that effective relationships with classes depend on the balance between the time and energy we put into Nurturing and Structuring.

Example 4 Structuring but no Nurturing

Situation

The class are not responding to you. You cannot understand this, as you have established a set of very strict behaviour expectations that have ensured a calm atmosphere in the classroom. Why are they still so reluctant to contribute the thoughtful, expressive responses that you are looking for?

Your perception:

Pupils' perception:

Pupils:

Immediate thoughts and feelings

Your main emotion when you took on this class was fear (*anxious*). You wanted to appear strong and in control and so you established very tight rules about how they should enter the class and where and how they should sit during your lessons (*punitive*). Now you feel that the lessons are difficult to manage because the pupils are unresponsive and lack enthusiasm for your subject (Compliant / Resistant).

You:

You: 

You pause and ask yourself some questions (*enquiring*). Why did you come into teaching in the first place? You recall it was because of your love for your subject and because of a couple of inspirational teachers when you were at school. You then realise that, because of your fear of being perceived by your colleagues or school leadership as weak or lacking in control, you have implemented a classroom-management approach that lacks basic humanity. You have established a pattern of alternating between Compliant / Resistant and Dominating behaviour, which is draining your energy and not working. You thought that the strict systems you insisted on would provide a structure where your pupils could flourish but, by using the Accounting toolbox, you now realise that they experience this approach as Dominating. You begin to understand that what is required here, as in all effective human interactions, is an effective balance of Structuring and Nurturing behaviour. You also recognise the underlying fear of being seen as weak or ineffective by others that has driven you to these choices.

Pause: choice

▼

You: 

You clarify with the class that you want the best for them (*encouraging*), that you are interested in them and that you value their contributions (*empathic*), as it is through trying out ideas that the whole class will make progress. You suggest a method that will incentivise pupils to answer questions thoughtfully, such as 'no hands up' or using a random name generator, and ask them for their ideas on how to make this work. You continue this dialogue over the coming weeks to demonstrate that you are serious. Because you are now balancing Structuring with Nurturing, the class learn that you want the best for them. They no longer perceive you as using Dominating behaviour towards them, and they feel comfortable to contribute thoughtfully to the lessons.

Functionally Fluent response

Pupils: 

▼

Key learning

Again, we see that effective relationships with classes depend on a balance between the time and energy we put into Structuring and into Nurturing.

Example 5 The Functionally Fluent form teacher

Situation

Leadership has initiated a new policy that has an impact on your form group.

You:

▼

Immediate thoughts and feelings

You can see that there are implications of this change that the class are likely to dislike. You really don't want to have to tell them about it as you are worried about how they will react (anxious).

You:

Pupils:

▼

Pause: choice

As you arrive at the classroom, you employ your Accounting energy to be alert to the group's mood. They are unsettled about something. You get them in and ask some questions to find out what the problem is (Accounting / Spontaneous). The issue turns out to be about a homework task set by another teacher and a disagreement over the deadline. You tell the class that you will ask the relevant teacher to clear this up when you see her at break time and that you will let them know the outcome after lunch (Structuring).

You:

▼ 

Functionally Fluent response

Using Accounting, rather than reacting, to respond to the group has settled them down well and they are now in a receptive mood to listen to your announcement about the new policy. You explain the implications and the rationale behind the change (Structuring / Nurturing). The class are not pleased but they appreciate the way you have told them about it, and they reciprocate your Cooperative approach. You agree to try out the new policy for two weeks and that you will then discuss it with them and feed back their thoughts to leadership.

You:

Pupils:

▼

> Here, we see the importance of being flexible and not ploughing on with tasks when there are other things going on that need addressing first. Psychological safety is a vital pre-requisite for Cooperative behaviour.

Language

Ultimately, the goal of applying these strategies – from understanding adolescent self-regulation to managing strokes and building community – is to embed Functional Fluency so deeply that it becomes a tool pupils themselves use to navigate their world. When you hear a pupil say 'Stop Marshmallowing me!', you're hearing more than just new vocabulary; you are witnessing a culture shift in real time. You are seeing young people armed not just with academic knowledge, but with the tools for self-awareness, emotional regulation and mutual respect. This shared language transforms the classroom from a simple place of instruction into a community of practice, where every interaction is an opportunity for growth. It is this foundation of relational trust that allows learning itself truly to flow: a dynamic we will explore next.

The teaching of Functional Fluency is addressed directly in the Certified Functional Fluency Teacher Appendix. The Certification involves training to teach the 12 lesson outlines, which are designed to be taught at the start of each key stage. Using repetition in this way builds understanding and recognition. This is further reinforced if teachers and leaders reference the language and concepts of Functional Fluency in their day-to-day encounters with pupils, parents and colleagues. The examples cited in this book give plenty of ideas of how to do this.

CHAPTER 3
MAKING LEARNING FLOW: THE ART AND SCIENCE OF A FUNCTIONALLY FLUENT CLASSROOM

During her regular tours of the school, Pat Harrison, headteacher, rarely enters Clem Watson's science class. Frankly, she is a little afraid of what she might discover. Despite being in his third year in the profession, he still seems to be struggling to build effective relationships with the pupils.

Evaluating the situation, she realises she is being placating and avoidant. So, she taps smartly on his classroom door and enters, to find the class working calmly. Clem is working with Roman, who is finding the task difficult. Pat is delighted to hear Clem saying 'Look, Roman, you are clearly finding this challenging. Let's pick out what you have understood and then we'll break down the rest together.'

At this point, Clem Watson senses Pat Harrison's presence and looks up, blushing slightly. Pat beams back at him, saying 'Well done, carry on'. She is delighted to hear Clem using Structuring phrases from the recent Functional Fluency pedagogy training to encourage cooperation in problem solving, and makes sure she tells him so at the next break.

Later, Clem talks this through with Chris Andrews. Chris tells Clem about how he used Functional Fluency to solve the dispute about footballs. Together, they laugh about how they are now using Accounting to evaluate their successes. If Functional Fluency can have such a positive impact on Clem's teaching, thinks Chris, it really has got potential!

Functional Fluency in action: from pupil comprehension to pedagogical practice

While writing this book, I was keen to check whether the Functional Fluency model could be explained to pupils in a way that would help them to make sense of their school experiences and enhance their learning. Through a contact with a local special school, I was able to teach two lessons to a group of 16 to 19-year-olds with wide-ranging special educational needs, including physical and medical needs, autism spectrum disorders, social communication difficulties and severe and profound learning difficulties. The pupils were very quickly able to grasp the ideas behind the model and to use the terminology to discuss situations and explain the dynamics of scenarios I presented. The precision with which they used the model as a tool to dissect the behaviour involved in bullying situations was impressive, and demonstrated its power to support more effective communication. Teaching the second lesson four weeks after the first showed the importance of returning to the model repeatedly to embed the language into pupils' consciousness.

This chapter covers how we can use Functional Fluency both as a teaching tool and as a model to improve understanding of the complex processes that we call 'teaching and learning'. The chapter also looks at existing models of effective teaching and learning, and deconstructs these using Functional Fluency terminology. The aim is to demonstrate the fundamental qualities of the Functional Fluency model and to show that other models of teaching and learning that may be used in your school could be analysed in a similar way.

Setting the stage for success: the power of contracting

Contracting is a key element of Transactional Analysis (TA), the psychological theory developed by Eric Berne, from which Functional Fluency developed. Nicole Pierre has written about her use of this approach in her work as a teacher in France in her chapter in *Educational Transactional Analysis* (Barrow and Newton, 2016). She explains how she carefully sets up the complex expectations that pupils, teachers and the educational institution in which they all work have of each other. By exploring this three-cornered contract explicitly at the start, she establishes clarity over how she and the class are going to work together over the coming year. She also uses this approach for individual lessons, which gives the pupils a sense of agency in their own learning. There is little sense in demanding that pupils learn in the same way first thing on a Tuesday morning after a library lesson and last lesson on a Friday when they have just come from an exhausting cross-country run: it is just unrealistic.

Having established this approach, she is able to use contracting with individual pupils, working with them to develop improvement plans that are far more specific, tailored and realistic than most self-assessments, which often focus on the superficial. This can be extended, as Pierre explains, to include four-cornered contracting with families, incorporating the expectations and responsibilities of the parents in relation to their child's learning.

This emphasis on contracting increases the pupils' understanding that they are responsible for themselves and for their own behaviour – a central facet of Functional Fluency. Using the Accounting Framework, pupils and teachers have an opportunity to review their situation and make behavioural choices that are considered, not kneejerk. In this way, pupils are encouraged to see that they are in control of themselves and their own behaviour, and this should help to avoid situations spiralling out of control. By enabling students to interact more thoughtfully, Accounting saves the time and energy otherwise spent resolving issues.

The classroom as a system: navigating the teaching and learning feedback loop

My thinking here is indebted to the work of Christian Moore-Anderson, a biology teacher working in an international school in Barcelona. While working on this chapter, I interviewed him for Myatt and Co about his book *Difference Maker* (Moore-Anderson, 2024).

In the early chapters of this book, Moore-Anderson describes the teaching and learning process using terms from cybernetics and feedback loops. 'Likewise, a teacher gives direction to a lesson by constantly responding to the actions of their students' (Moore-Anderson, 2024). Teaching is a feedback loop in action: a teacher acts, the class respond and the teacher takes that response into consideration when deciding on their next action; this whole process is a system.

Moore-Anderson uses the distinction between trivial and nontrivial systems: 'Unlike cars, the classroom is a nontrivial system' (Moore-Anderson, 2024), by which he means that, unlike a car where pressing the accelerator or the brake has a predictable outcome on the vehicle, classes are much less predictable. The range of factors at play within any given classroom is huge, with many of them beyond the control of the teacher. Therefore, you may very often carry out a behavioural act as a teacher that had a positive impact on learning yesterday or last week, but a negative impact today. Moore-Anderson goes on to say: 'This makes steering, regulation, and adaptation the necessary – the endless – process of teaching'.

Thinking about this in Functional Fluency terms, we see an effective teacher as operating constantly within this teaching feedback loop, employing Structuring and Nurturing behaviour to encourage the class. In deciding which of these types of behaviour is required at any given moment of a lesson, the effective teacher needs to return frequently to the Accounting mode. It is only through being alert and aware of the class and their needs, and evaluating the progress that they are making, that the teacher is able to decide whether it is Structuring or Nurturing that they require from minute to minute.

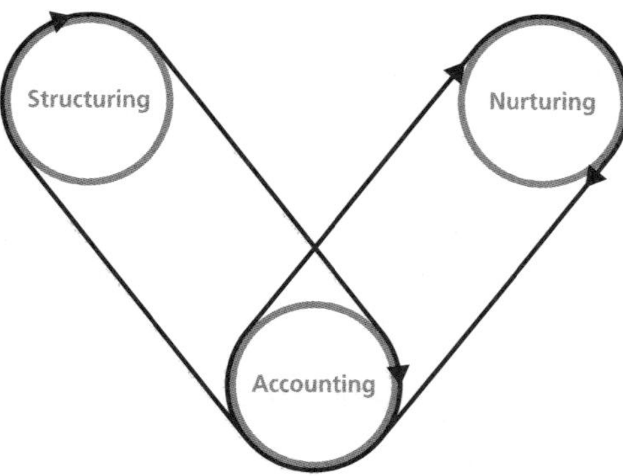

Figure 8 Functionally Fluent teaching feedback loop

Just as Functional Fluency gives us these insights into how to understand the complex, circular patterns of teaching, so it also helps us to engage with the complexities of learning. To engage fully with a lesson, pupils need to utilise their own feedback loop, moving between Cooperative and Spontaneous behaviours as their own Accounting processes suggest is required. More mature pupils utilise this feedback loop more effectively than their less mature colleagues, as the former are more likely to understand and be aligned with the purpose of schooling. Less mature pupils are more easily distracted into Immature or Compliant / Resistant behaviour at times because their Accounting processes are less well developed.

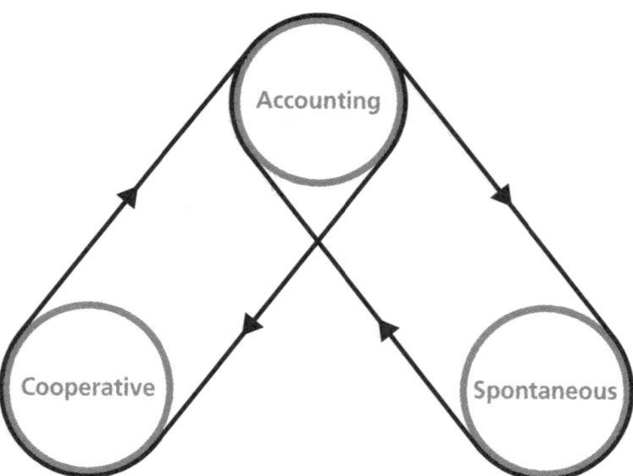

Figure 9 Functionally Fluent learning feedback loop

Making pupils aware of this feedback loop and how it works for effective teachers and engaged pupils provides a shared vocabulary useful for clarifying expectations and making the learning process more explicit.

Some of the sophistication of the teaching and learning process can be captured by superimposing these two loops, as shown in Figure 10.

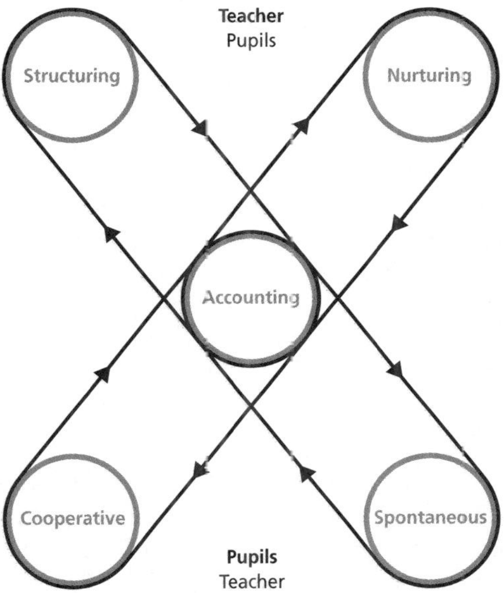

Figure 10 Functionally Fluent teaching and learning feedback loops

Here, we can see that the teacher and the pupils each have their predominant feedback loops, but that, at times, they can swap, with teachers taking a turn at using Cooperative and Spontaneous behaviours and pupils using Structuring and Nurturing behaviours to drive the lesson forward. This sense of there being major and minor feedback loops for both teachers and pupils really begins to capture the complexity of what is happening in a classroom. We can layer on top how pupils in a class do not behave as one. Some use Accounting often, while others do so rarely, resulting in very different behaviour choices. This makes Accounting by teachers all the more important as they have to *evaluate* how best to respond to these complex patterns.

It is important to clarify what we mean by Spontaneous behaviour in this context. For pupils, it means engaging in the learning in an open and energetic manner, asking *imaginative* questions and taking a *curious* and *creative* approach to solving problems. For teachers, it means being highly responsive and willing to change the direction of the lesson, as befits the generative learning taking place, which results from the interaction between the new material being taught and the pupils' prior knowledge. It is not about the teacher aimlessly drifting off topic to follow *egocentric* whims. For example, a teacher could realise (*aware, alert*) that the class have not fully understood the material they have taught and, instead of ploughing on, use a combination of Structuring (*well-organised, helpful*) and Spontaneous (*creative, expressive*) behaviours to devise a recap activity to embed the learning.

This way of thinking about the teaching and learning processes is particularly helpful in the context of teacher training. Inexperienced teachers may often make the mistake of not going back to the Accounting mode frequently enough, with the result that they may put too much of their time and effort into Structuring, not realising that the pupils are perceiving this as Dominating behaviour. As a result, the pupils may begin to utilise Compliant / Resistant behaviour, the teacher starts to lose their grip on the lesson and learning opportunities are lost. The model provides a useful basis for self-evaluation as trainee teachers seek to become more adept at understanding the complexity of the classroom situations they experience.

Thinking in terms of these feedback loops helps us understand the dynamic, responsive nature of teaching. It is a continuous cycle of Accounting, Structuring and Nurturing. But what does this look like moment by moment in a bustling classroom? To see how this theoretical cycle translates into concrete, effective practice, let's turn to one of the most widely respected frameworks available: Rosenshine's Principles of Instruction.

The hidden layer: how Functional Fluency underpins Rosenshine's Principles

For Functional Fluency to be truly relevant to teachers, it needs to link with and inform high-quality teaching practices: what teachers actually do in classrooms and the decisions they make that enable learning to take place. Clearly, teaching is a highly complex and diverse practice that a huge number of teachers carry out worldwide, in many ways and with varying degrees of effectiveness.

One well-established and widely accepted framework for improving teaching is Rosenshine's set of ten Principles (Rosenshine, 2012) that most teachers and researchers would agree underpin effective classroom practice. Let's look at them through the lens of Functional Fluency. If Functional Fluency is fundamental to the creation of strong inter-personal relationships, which in turn are fundamental to effective classroom practice, then it follows that Functional Fluency should surely also be fundamental to classroom practice.

Table 5 captures this using Chris Andrews' persona to draw out the links as he considers his next Year 8 lesson.

Table 5 Rosenshine's Principles and Functional Fluency

Principle	Chris Andrews' thoughts
Begin a lesson with a short review of previous learning.	OK, Year 10 next Ah, this is the lesson where they are coming from PE, and we haven't had a lesson since last Thursday (Accounting, *evaluative, grounded.*) The short quiz I have prepared will remind them of what we covered last lesson (Structuring, *well-organised*). Also, this class contains a number of SEND pupils who struggle with remembering factual details and who get nervous when asked direct questions, so I'll make sure they get a chance to work in small groups with pupils who are more confident (Nurturing, *compassionate, empathic*).
Present new material in small steps with pupil practice after each step.	As it is the last lesson of the day, it will be best to maintain a steady pace today and not introduce too many new concepts (Accounting, *alert, aware*). It will be important to give the class opportunities to watch me work through an example, then try it several times in groups before giving it a go individually (Structuring, *firm, inspiring*, Nurturing, *understanding, empathic*).
Ask a large number of questions and check the responses of all pupils.	I will think about a range of questions of varying levels of complexity that I can ask that will enable me to check whether the pupils have grasped the key concepts. I can then target the more straightforward ones at the pupils who struggle, making sure they know they can ask a friend to help them (Structuring, *well-organised*, Nurturing, *understanding*). I'll add the best ones to the scheme of work after the lesson so that colleagues can use them and so they are available for me next time I teach this topic (Accounting, *evaluative*).
Provide models.	It is important that I find a balance between showing pupils how to complete the task (Structuring, *authoritative, consistent*) and encouraging them to give it a try without becoming exasperated or sarcastic (Nurturing, *helpful, encouraging*). That Numicon that I borrowed from the maths department could be really useful for some pupils (Spontaneous, *imaginative*).
Guide pupil practice.	Although it is the last lesson of the day, I will need to be proactive to ensure that the pupils get on with the task well. I know sometimes my instructions are too vague, so I'll need to avoid that (Structuring, *inspiring, firm*), but I will also need to show them that I know it is difficult (Nurturing, *understanding*) and that I value their effort (Cooperative, *friendly*).

Principle	Chris Andrews' thoughts
Check for pupil understanding.	I will need to have a clear list in my head of the pupils I need to check in on to make sure they have understood the content of the lesson (Accounting, *enquiring*). I'll do this by asking questions, listening to group discussions, checking facial expressions for signs of puzzlement and looking at written work as I circulate (Spontaneous, *curious*).
Obtain a high success rate.	I know it is important that pupils experience success so that they feel they are making progress. So, I have created tasks that start off in a very straightforward way (Nurturing, *understanding*). When the pupils do well with these tasks, I will be *encouraging* and *inspiring*, and this should build their *resilience* to try harder tasks.
Provide scaffolds for difficult tasks.	I will need to use Accounting behaviour (*alert, evaluative*) to assess where the difficulty lies and which pupils are experiencing it. Then I will blend Structuring (*well-organised*), Nurturing (*compassionate*) and Cooperative (*adaptable*) to ensure that the various types of support I can provide (TA assistance, writing frames, additional explanations) are targeted effectively.
Require and monitor independent practice.	Those three pupils on the second row tend to rely too much on me, so I'll need to use Structuring (*firm, authoritative*) and Nurturing (*encouraging*) to ensure they give it a go on their own. Then it's all about Accounting (*alert, evaluative, enquiring*) as I check how they get on.
Engage pupils in weekly and monthly review.	Finally, I'll make sure I round off the lesson with plenty of time for a full review of the new material we have covered in the last four lessons (Accounting, *aware*) Structuring (*well-organised*). This will help to embed what they know and give them *confidence* that they are making progress.

This gives some indication of the complexity of the teacher's role. It is a direct application of the Accounting Framework as the teacher moves through the steps of getting *grounded* in the classroom reality, being *aware* of pupil needs and *evaluating* their understanding before making a rational pedagogical choice. Rosenshine's Principles sound relatively straightforward but, when they are unpicked in this way and the underlying behaviours laid bare, it becomes all too clear what a profoundly involved and sophisticated set of behavioural patterns are embedded in them. In turn, this has the effect of demonstrating the fundamental nature of Functional Fluency, as the model represents these complex procedures with subtlety and fidelity. This may well give practitioners greater understanding of the complex nature of the work they are involved in and increased respect for the profession they are part of.

A third column could of course be added to the table, showing the pupil behaviours that the Principles require if they are to result in effective learning. These would be blends of all the different behavioural modes. Pupils need to practise Accounting to be aware of what they already know and to *evaluate* the impact of new learning. Cooperative behaviour is key to success, as pupils need confidence and adaptability to try out new things. Spontaneous behaviour is important too, as *expressive* behaviour helps them to construct questions and seek further guidance. This complex, pattern-forming approach to behaviour makes very clear the need for pupils to be taught the Functional Fluency model, so that teachers can explicitly refer to the model and the types of behaviour required from pupils for learning to take place. Functional Fluency is as fundamental to effective learning as it is to effective teaching.

Beyond judgement: a new model for lesson observation

One of the greatest sources of stress for teachers is the dreaded lesson observation. A senior leader, multi-academy trust (MAT) director or local-authority adviser comes into your lesson, watches it and makes a judgement about you as a professional. Their criteria for making this judgement are often not at all clear, and they rarely have enough information about the background to the class or the circumstances in which the lesson is taking place to make constructive comments. Also, they may not be knowledgeable about your subject, which adds a further level of inconsistency and potential confusion to the exchange. The experience is often a dispiriting one that takes up huge quantities of time and energy, with no guarantee that it will improve anything.

As lessons are based on relationships between people – teachers and pupils, pupils and other pupils – basing the observation process on Functional Fluency offers a logical structure that can help. Firstly, your observer can use the model as a prompt to encourage evaluation of the way in which you constructed the balance of guiding and nurturing required for an effective teacher–class relationship. Were you helpful and inspiring, encouraging and empathic, or did your structuring become at times bossy and punitive and, if so, what were the pupil behaviours that invited you to react in this way? Looking back, how could you have been more responsive and less reactive, and how might this have been beneficial?

This approach, which peer observers could also use, places the emphasis of the observation on how effectively the teacher–pupil relationship is fostered during the lesson. It provides common language for talking about this relationship. The discussion after the lesson, whether with oneself or with a colleague, deepens understanding of the ways to create relationships effectively in the classroom. It simultaneously strengthens understanding of the Functional Fluency model and its application. The potential benefits of this approach – which, through its co-constructed and positive nature, also embodies Functional Fluency – are considerable, as suggestions for improvement emerge through dialogue rather than diktat.

A second, alternative, way to incorporate the model into lesson observation uses a version of the Functional Fluency model (see Figure 11) as the actual observation form and, instead of focusing solely on the teacher's behaviour, concentrates on the behaviour of both the teacher and the pupils and the relationship between the two. Teaching and learning is a two-way transaction, and the behaviours of both parties are inter-dependent. The observer can write their commentary in the centre of the page, using arrows to link with elements of the model, as required. By using the Functional Fluency model when observing the complex interactions that take place within a lesson, we can begin to see this inter-dependence in action. Do the pupils react in that Compliant / Resistant manner because they perceive the teacher's behaviour to be too dominating? Is the over-tolerant approach of the teacher feeding the Immature responses of the pupils? These are the kinds of patterns that may become more obvious when using this observation tool. This can support and augment more subject-specific approaches to teaching development, while further embedding understanding of the Functional Fluency model in ways that have positive impacts for the teaching and learning relationship well beyond the end of the lesson.

The Functional Fluency lesson observation form makes it easy to map out patterns of behaviour that can be related to the Functional Fluency teaching and learning feedback loops diagram (Figure 10) to identify productive patterns that can be built upon and strengthened and destructive patterns that need to be discouraged.

Teacher

Dominating	Marshmallowing
fault-finding	over-protective
judgemental	over-tolerant
punitive	smothering
Structuring	**Nurturing**
authoritative	accepting
consistent	empathic
firm	encouraging
Accounting	
aware	
grounded	
rational	
Cooperative	**Spontaneous**
adaptable	creative
assertive	expressive
confident	zestful
Compliant / Resistant	**Immature**
defiant	egocentric
placating	inconsiderate
submissive	unorganised

Observer's comments

Pupils

Dominating	Marshmallowing
blaming	over-tolerant
bossy	self-denying
knows-better	smothering
Structuring	**Nurturing**
helpful	cherishing
inspiring	compassionate
well-organised	understanding
Accounting	
alert	
enquiring	
evaluative	
Cooperative	**Spontaneous**
adaptable	creative
considerate	curious
resilient	playful
Compliant / Resistant	**Immature**
defiant	egocentric
placating	inconsiderate
submissive	unorganised

Figure 11 Functional Fluency lesson observation form

Using the Functional Fluency classroom behaviour observation form

The framework we have explored in this chapter is not just a theoretical model; it is a practical tool for capturing the live, dynamic reality of a lesson. This observation form is designed to move beyond simple checklists and help map the actual interactions – the behavioural transactions – that create the climate of the classroom.

How to use this tool during an observation:

- **Map the Interactions:** The grid is laid out with Teacher behaviours on the left and Pupil behaviours on the right. As the lesson unfolds, use the blank central space to draw arrows linking a teacher's actions to the pupils' responses (or vice versa).

- **Record the Evidence:** Use the central space to jot down verbatim quotes, tally the frequency of specific modes or note the exact time a shift in behaviour occurs.

- **Spot the Loops:** Look for cause-and-effect patterns. For example, you might draw an arrow showing how a teacher's shift into the Structuring mode (being *firm* and *consistent*) successfully moved a pupil from Immature to Cooperative. Conversely, you might track how a pupil's Dominating behaviour triggered a Marshmallowing response from the teacher.

By tracking these behavioural loops in real-time, you will build a clear, evidence-based picture of the classroom dynamic, providing incredibly rich and specific feedback for professional development.

You will notice that in some cases the descriptors included are identical for both the teacher and pupils while in other modes they are different. These choices have been carefully considered to ensure the focus is on observable behaviour rather than internal states such as *anxious*. Of course, this does not mean these cannot be discussed in the feedback following the observation. A very useful exercise that schools could carry out would entail collecting examples of all the behaviours shown on the chart. This discussion could involve groups of teachers and pupils so that everyone is clear about how their behaviour in lessons can contribute to Functionally Fluent teaching and learning.

Here are some examples of the kind of comments that an observer could write when watching a lesson. Observers could link the comments with the descriptors of the behaviours they witness either by inserting them in brackets, as below, or by adding lines or arrows to the relevant areas on the Teacher and Pupils copies of the Functional Fluency model.

10:15: Pupil shouting across room. [*egocentric*] Teacher uses calm, non-verbal hand signal and waits. [*authoritative*] Pupil stops talking, apologises and opens book. [*considerate*] Excellent de-escalation.

10:30: Pupil forgets ruler. [*unorganised*] Teacher immediately issues a detention and criticises them in front of the class. [*punitive*] Pupil crosses arms, refuses to do any work for the rest of the lesson, mutters 'I don't care'. [*defiant*] Consequence was disproportionate and broke rapport.

10:37: Pupil says 'I don't get it.' [*submissive*] Teacher spends 5 minutes practically writing the opening paragraph for them. [*over tolerant*] Pupil nods, smiles and copies it down without actually engaging with the cognitive process. The teacher worked harder than the pupil here.

10:48: Teacher scanning room during independent task, notices a pupil hesitating at the back and approaches quietly. [*grounded*] Pupil asks a highly specific question about where they lost a mark on the previous task. [*curious*] Teacher provides a factual, step-by-step breakdown. [*adaptable*] Highly focused interaction.

I am indebted to Stephanie Carlin, who has usefully pointed out that this form can be used in conjunction with the target-setting form (Table 6), which enables the teacher to work with their observer to agree on a series of actions to develop their teaching. This form was originally created to capture action planning decisions following a TIFF feedback session.

Table 6 Functional Fluency teaching targets: confidential

Teacher	
Observer	
Organisation	
Date of observation	
Role	
Big-picture objective	

Effective mode strengths to celebrate and use	Progress Q1	Progress Q2	Progress Q3	Progress Q4

Effective mode low scores to use more	Progress Q1	Progress Q2	Progress Q3	Progress Q4

Ineffective mode high scores to reduce and transform	Progress Q1	Progress Q2	Progress Q3	Progress Q4

Action plan: Action 1

What do you want to achieve?					
What is the underlying desire?					
Who will benefit?					
How will you and others know you are making progress?					
	Baseline %	Progress Q1	Progress Q2	Progress Q3	Progress Q4
Progress					
Benefits					
Evidence					

By focusing first on celebrating effective teaching behaviours, this approach is inherently positive. It picks out effective behaviours that the teacher could use more, before looking at less effective behaviours that they could reduce. These can be turned into a set of actions, using the action-plan template, which can be copied as required, to ensure the teacher achieves the targets outlined. The discussion required to complete this process reveals any training requirements, and should set in train the improvement that quality-assurance procedures are intended to deliver but seldom achieve. The inclusion of periodic review windows emphasises the long-term nature of school improvement and ensures that developmental priorities are personal to each teacher and are not replaced as soon as the next pedagogical fashion comes along.

Finally, if return on investment and the demonstration of impact is important (and, in my experience, it always is), the observer and teacher can complete a more public form of record that pulls together evidence of the impact of this work and records it in a way that can be shared with senior leaders. Here, the emphasis is not just on capturing the personal impact of the observation and subsequent discussions, but also the impact on the teacher in terms of increasing their understanding of the model, any personal gains they have made as a result of implementing the action plan and how the pupils and the school have benefited too, in line with Guskey's model (Guskey, 2000) of effective evaluation.

Table 7 Functional Fluency teaching-observation impact statement: public

Teacher	
Observer	
Organisation	
Period covered	

Action 1

Increase in understanding of teaching	
Understanding of Functional Fluency model	
Personal gains	
Benefits to the pupils and school	

Action 2

Increase in understanding of teaching	
Understanding of Functional Fluency model	
Personal gains	
Benefits to the pupils and school	

Next steps

Having explored the theoretical underpinnings and practical applications of Functional Fluency in teaching and observation, we now turn to the real-world experiences of educators who have embraced this model.

Functional Fluency in Action

Dr Sean Warren

Dr Sean Warren began his career in education in 1984, working with primary children in play centres in Tower Hamlets, East London. He went on to work with young people in Papua New Guinea, Romania and the United States. His wide-ranging experience spans many roles in education, from supply teacher to keynote speaker at national and regional educational events.

Sean served as a secondary-school head of department for 14 years, an advanced skills teacher (AST), a behaviour consultant for the local authority and a university lecturer.

After qualifying with a B.Ed (Hons), Sean embraced the role of practitioner-researcher, critically reflecting on his dual role as teacher and authority figure. He subsequently earned a Diploma and a master's degree, and completed a PhD. His six-year part-time doctoral study examined classroom dynamics in 16 of his own classes and applied those findings to support six colleagues managing challenging groups. He captured the essence of this research in his book *Living Contradiction* (Warren and Bigger, 2017).

Sean now works alongside educators who are navigating complex classroom dynamics. Opportunities to collaborate with him or explore his innovative tools are available at <u>teachersreflect.online</u>

As an ex-teacher, Sean has been working with Functional Fluency for many years. In his book *Living Contradiction* (Warren and Bigger, 2017), he writes about what he learned from completing his TIFF and then talking it through with Susannah Temple. The title of the book was inspired by a realisation for Sean that grew directly out of this experience, namely that *schooling* does not equal *education*. What he came to understand, from the reading and studying about complexity theory that he completed for his master's and then his PhD, was that education is a *complex* phenomenon – a matter that is subject to an infinite number of variables and is inherently unpredictable. The problems arise when politicians, educational writers and school leaders try to reduce it to something that is merely *complicated* – a matter with many variables that can be understood if sufficient effort is expended.

One of the realisations for Sean that emerged from his discussions with Susannah was the distinction between compliance and cooperation. This is clear in the Functional Fluency model in the names of the modes, with Cooperative and Compliant / Resistant being respectively the more effective and less effective manifestations of the socialised aspect of relating to and getting on with others. Sean realised that, in school, his Dominating form of Control was resulting in Compliant behaviour from pupils, which he was mistaking for Cooperation. Through discussion about the need for a counter-balancing amount of time and energy going into the Care mode to match the energy he was putting into Control, Sean began to realise that he had become successful professionally by being Dominating towards himself. He describes himself as operating professionally while wearing an 'inauthentic mask'.

This 'mask' had seemingly beneficial effects. In his school, pupils behaved as he wanted them to and, on the back of this, he was seconded to the role of behaviour lead for the local authority. What he discovered then was that the 'mask' he had worked so hard to fashion carried little weight with pupils who did not know him and his reputation: his 'status' as a disciplinarian did not travel with him.

There were other problems. Sean began to realise that the creation of the mask had cost him dearly. He had become a perfectionist and a workaholic, Dominating himself as well as his pupils in his pursuit of improved behaviour. This situation worsened when he worked in other schools where he was not well known, and he found himself endlessly replaying incidents to try to understand why the pupils' behaviour was not as he wanted and expected. This resulted in mounting exhaustion and an increasing reliance on yet more Dominating (*blaming*) and Compliant / Resistant (*moaning*) behaviour to explain the situation.

The discussions with Susannah Temple helped Sean to understand himself and his situation much more clearly. He realised he was using Accounting behaviour excessively to try to work out why things had not gone to plan and, as a result, was not living in the present.

Additionally, he came to understand his previous need to Dominate his classes, and the negative impact this was having on both them and him. He made a conscious plan to try to be more patient and understanding in his approach to classes – behaviours he had previously seen as signs of weakness. He set himself the task of avoiding **reacting** to pupils and classes and, instead, sought to train himself to **respond** to their needs. By seeking to balance Control and Care in his approach, he came to enjoy the company of young people again, as he built the authentically Cooperative relationships with them from which true learning flows. He gave himself permission to be himself in the classroom, and this enabled a rebalancing of his approach, which released a lot of strain and wasted energy that had been stored up by his previous, inauthentic approach.

Functional Fluency in Action

Martian Slagter: Functional Fluency within an MBA course

The scope of Functional Fluency as a teaching tool does not stop with school-age pupils, as the work of Martian Slagter shows. She is a certified TIFF provider from the Netherlands who uses Functional Fluency in her teaching of the MBA course at a business school. She uses *The Fluent Leader* (Fawcett, 2023) as a course book, and the individual students each complete a TIFF profile. They then work in groups, looking at the Functional Fluency model and considering its application in a variety of scenarios, using a tabletop version of the model with suitably sized objects representing the different people or groups within the scenario. They also complete an assignment in which they reflect more personally on their own TIFF profile, and what they have learned about themselves from this process and the implications of this learning for their approach to leadership. The MBA students, who are used to a great deal of managerial training, find the model refreshingly new, straightforward and inspirational.

They particularly like the simplicity of the model, which facilitates deep and complex reflection about the nature of relationships and communication. A buddy system is used to open up discussion between students.

Additionally, Martian uses the Functional Fluency model when working with teams, to encourage team members to discuss their patterns of behaviour and vulnerabilities. The advantage is that Functional Fluency provides a common language with which to talk about behaviour. The power of this way of working is in the permissive nature of the model, which does not use language linked to 'rights' and 'wrongs'.

Martian has written a book in Dutch about her use of Functional Fluency within schools, where she used Functional Fluency as a tool for individual coaching of school leaders and teachers, as well as with other coaching clients outside education.

Martian feels that Functional Fluency is useful in schools for helping teachers to avoid burnout. A way of visualising this is shown in Figure 12.

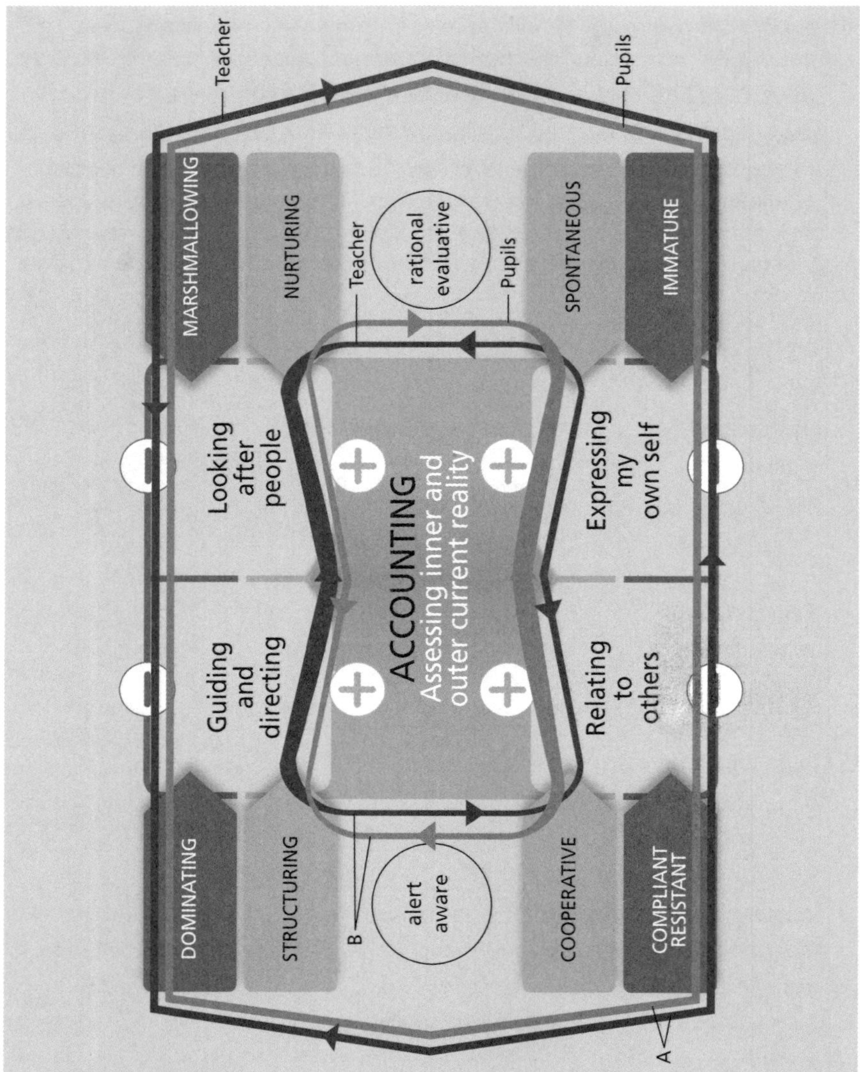

Figure 12 Functionally Fluent Teacher–Pupil engagement

The flowing, curved inner pair of lines that pass through the gold (lightly shaded) areas of the model show the easy nature of the interaction between teacher and pupils when the relationship is truly Functionally Fluent. The outer, straight, angular pair of lines show a teacher–pupil's relationship that is characterised by a lack of Functional Fluency, and the longer length of these lines captures the more effortful, tiring nature of working in this way that can quickly lead to burnout. As Martian says, it is all about 'how you manage the in-between' so that energy, which is finite, is not pointlessly dissipated in ineffective communication and relationships that do not allow either party to thrive.

In the Functionally Fluent relationship between teacher and pupils, shown in the flowing, curved inner pair of lines, an educational experience is co-created in a way that does not waste energy and effort, but is energising in its creativity. Only a proportion of lessons are ever going to be like this but, if leaders and teachers can work towards creating the circumstances that encourage this situation, the proportion can increase. This visualisation helps to explain why some teachers get to the end of the week and still have some vigour left, while others are completely exhausted.

Putting Functional Fluency into practice: classroom scenarios

To solidify the practical implications of Functional Fluency in diverse classroom scenarios, let's investigate some detailed examples that demonstrate how these principles can be applied.

Example 6 uses Functional Fluency to make sense of a common teaching situation that could confound a teacher. It links back to the examples of neurodiverse pupils' behaviour in the previous chapter. Hopefully, teachers will see ways in which the analysis helps to explain the behaviour of classes they have known. It is not my intention to suggest that neurodiversity is a source of major difficulties in schools – the idea is to demonstrate how Functional Fluency could potentially bring increased understanding and better communication between teachers and pupils where previously these have been lacking.

Example 6 Teaching a neurodiverse class

Situation

A particular class is posing you several issues. They seem to find it very difficult to settle (*defiant*).

Pupils:

▼

Immediate thoughts and feelings

You feel that the class's response to you is a rejection of you as a teacher and of the way you plan and deliver your lessons (*egocentric*). This is beginning to make you depressed and to dread teaching the class (*anxious*). Your approach to the class is becoming increasingly defensive and tetchy and you are starting to raise your voice too often (Compliant / Resistant, Dominating).

You:

▼

Pause: choice

You do some reading about neurodiversity, speak to the SENDCo and come to the realisation that every class you teach is neurodiverse. Through Accounting, you realise that a substantial minority of your pupils are struggling with different aspects of being in school and that it is not surprising therefore if their behaviour is less than perfect. You realise that you need to reserve judgement (Accounting) and, instead of picking out things they can't do, spend time looking for capabilities where you can find them. You realise that it is important to introduce and reaffirm the Functional Fluency model so that pupils know you are acknowledging neurodivergence.

You:

▼

You: 

Pupils: 

Functionally Fluent response

You go back to the meet-and-greet activity at the start of the lesson, which you dropped a few months ago, to ensure every pupil feels seen. Using *firm* (Structuring) behaviour, you explain that you cannot put up with behaviour that is damaging to the class's learning. Then, using *empathy* (Nurturing), you explain that you realise that some pupils in the class may find aspects of it challenging and that you are committed to working with them to find solutions. You propose introducing visual lesson schedules and transition warnings, adaptations that you have discussed and agreed with the SENDCo, and you invite individuals to propose additional ways in which learning could be organised to suit them. The lesson is a considerable improvement, and you dismiss the class feeling better about teaching than you have for weeks.

▼

Key learning

It is important not to take things personally in teaching, but to be open and talk to experienced colleagues who can help you develop more effective approaches to challenging scenarios

This example is designed to give an indication of ways in which teachers can consciously use the Functional Fluency model to address some of the issues surrounding neurodivergence in the classroom. This is a complex area, and the example is not intended to minimise this complexity in any way. It is designed to indicate how the Functional Fluency model can help individuals and institutions to navigate issues and situations as they arise. Neurodiversity was not widely discussed in schools 30 or 40 years ago, and we do not know what the key topics will be in education in 2050, but, whatever they are, because Functional Fluency is a valid and reliable model of human behaviour, we will be able to use it to try to find solutions to whatever issues arise in the future.

The Functionally Fluent teacher observation

The following example is taken from the Ofsted report *Moving English Forward* (Ofsted, 2012). The inspector's description and thoughts are direct quotations, and are followed by a commentary. The imagined thought processes of the teacher and pupils in the scenario described are then presented, as understood through a Functional Fluency lens. Then, an alternative, more Functionally Fluent scenario is described, along with how the teacher, the pupils and, finally, the inspector would experience it.

The inspector's description of the lesson

The lesson involved a Year 9 class working on techniques of persuasive writing. The lesson was planned in detail. The first phase involved an explanation of the learning objectives and a starter activity where pupils worked in groups to complete a card-sort activity. In the next phase of the lesson, pupils used a grid to identify persuasive devices on mini whiteboards. The teacher then took them quickly through the criteria for assessment at Levels 5–7 and gave pupils examples of extracts from two essays on capital punishment. Pupils were asked to choose the more effective piece, linking it to the assessment criteria. They were then asked to produce at least one paragraph of writing on the topic of capital punishment. In the final part of the lesson, pupils were asked to peer mark two other pupils' work, then to look at and review their own work and check the comments. One further activity was introduced before pupils were asked to say what they had learnt in the lesson. The lesson closed with a final activity where pupils revised persuasive techniques on the board.

Ofsted, 2012

The inspector's thoughts on the lesson

There were many positive elements in this lesson. Pupils were fully engaged and certainly learnt more about persuasive techniques. However, several things struck the inspector. First, the person who worked hardest in this lesson was the teacher! The lesson involved seven or eight activities completed at speed. It was as though the teacher felt that the more she did, the better the lesson would be. During the lesson, the teacher managed a number of potentially interesting tasks effectively. However, the sheer quantity of activities limited pupils' learning since they had insufficient time to complete tasks or consolidate their understanding. Attempting to understand the assessment criteria for three different Levels in five minutes was unrealistic, as was the time allowed to analyse the two extracts of writing. Only 10 minutes were provided for the pupils' writing. As a result, few were able to complete the task. The teacher in this lesson concentrated on the pace of activities rather than the pace of learning. The centre of this lesson should have been the opportunity for pupils to show what they had learnt about persuasive techniques by producing a piece of their own writing. The desire to complete all elements of the planned lesson meant that the writing task could not be completed and the fast movement from one activity to another limited pupils' development of new learning or their consolidation of existing learning. This pattern is noted regularly by inspectors.

Ofsted 2012

Commentary

It seems clear that, in the inspector's view, the teacher put a lot of energy into Structuring behaviour (*authoritative, well-organised*) but that there is also an element of Compliant / Resistant behaviour (*anxious*), probably as a direct result of being observed in this high-stakes manner. The implication of the inspector's description is that the pupils' behaviour is *submissive* and that opportunities for learning are lost.

The teacher's perspective (imagined)

I am going to be inspected by the Ofsted lead inspector for English, a subject in which I am an expert. So, I need to show what I can do, by planning the lesson meticulously. The class are generally well behaved but can get a little silly at times, so I will keep moving the activities on so that they do not have time to relax (*knows-better*). I will show the inspector and my school leadership team that I am in command of the class by relentlessly introducing new activities to ensure I cannot be criticised for the lesson lacking pace (Structuring).

A pupil's perspective (imagined)

Not sure what got into Miss today. I know there was that bloke there in a blue suit but there was no need for her to be quite so manic (*curious*). We did one activity after another and, thinking about it now, I'm not sure what the lesson was about or what I was supposed to be learning (*anxious*). What I do know though is that I was knackered afterwards! It was a good job we had PE next – if it had been science, I think there would have been a rict (Compliant / Resistant)!

The Functionally Fluent teacher's perspective (imagined)

Well, I suppose I should be pleased I've been chosen to demonstrate a lesson for the Ofsted lead inspector for English – the school clearly values my professionalism and subject knowledge (Accounting). I will try to ensure the lesson is as close to normal as possible (balancing Structuring and Nurturing behaviour to encourage a Spontaneous and Cooperative response from the class). I will plan a lesson that incorporates time for discussion of persuasive devices so that the inspector can witness the high level of speaking and listening of which the class are capable. Then I will ensure there is a substantial period in the lesson when, after the discussion, the pupils can focus on a serious piece of persuasive writing so that the inspector has an opportunity to see what they can do. I will make sure there is time for several pupils to read their work out before the end of the lesson and encourage thoughtful discussion (Accounting, *evaluation*) of these responses. Just a normal lesson really!

A pupil's feedback on this Functionally Fluent lesson (imagined)

It was really clear what we were working on. It was great that we got to have a discussion at the start of the lesson as this helped me to get my ideas straightened out (Cooperative, *evaluative*). When we started writing, I knew what I was aiming to achieve and I really focused on it – the time passed very quickly. It was good to hear several examples read out at the end of the lesson – other people had tackled things slightly differently from me, but contributing to the critique activity and getting positive oral feedback from the teacher gave me the confidence that my piece was good too. PE now, great!

The inspector's response to this more Functionally Fluent lesson (imagined)

The lesson involved a Year 9 class working on techniques of persuasive writing. The lesson was planned in detail (Structuring). The first phase involved discussion of what the pupils already know about this topic (*evaluative*). The teacher helped the class to recall key points with careful questioning (*encouraging*). She then read a piece of persuasive text to the class. She asked them to think about the techniques the writer had employed and the impact that this had on them. She then reread the passage before giving the class time to discuss their answers in small groups. After this, she asked each group to feed back one new thing they had learned about persuasive writing from this activity. The class were then allowed a substantial amount of time to try out the techniques they had been discussing. The lesson ended with carefully chosen pupils reading out their pieces, and the class critiqued the effectiveness of the persuasive techniques they used (*evaluative*).

'I know you can meet these high standards': the secret of feedback that works

David Yeager's notion of Wise Feedback (Yeager and Duckworth, 2024) is a powerful one that deserves to be better known. It is research-based and, I feel, exemplifies how a Functionally Fluent teacher could respond to the work of their pupils in a way that maximises the chances of it having a positive impact and therefore being time well spent.

Wise Feedback is a great example of the Functionally Fluent teacher effectively balancing Structuring and Nurturing in such a way as to maximise the likelihood of a positive response from the pupils.

The key phrase used in Wise Feedback is 'I'm giving you these comments because I have high standards and I know that you can meet them' – a perfect balance of Structuring and Nurturing.

Example 7 Wise Feedback

Situation

You spend many hours laboriously reading and annotating your pupils' written responses to tasks (Marshmallowing).

You:  

▼

Immediate thoughts and feelings

You find this work tedious and depressing. It takes up a great deal of your time, which you could spend with your family (*self-denying*). Also, the pupils do not seem to value or sometimes even to understand the comments that you carefully consider and write on their work. Certainly, they do not seem to be making the progress that you feel they ought to, given the amount of time and effort you are putting into providing them with personalised feedback.
The pupils perceive you to be picky and over-critical. You write lengthy, detailed comments on their work, which leave them feeling demoralised. It feels as though you inhabit a different world, and the feedback you provide just seems to emphasise how different and unattainable your world is for them.

You: 

Pupils: 

▼

Pause: choice

After considering the Wise Feedback research and watching the video (www.youtube.com/watch?v=YyX6hf8Q9So), you realise that you have been attempting to care for your pupils in an inappropriate way (Marshmallowing) by *over-indulging* them with excessively detailed help. You also realise that the pupils have perceived your efforts differently – they have seen them as Dominating, in the form of *knows-better* comments that serve mainly to drive a wedge between you and them, rather than supporting them to progress.

You: 

▼

Functionally Fluent response

You begin to use the key phrase 'I'm giving you these comments because I have high standards and I know that you can meet them' and variations of it in both written and oral feedback. You begin to make your written comments on essays and assignments shorter and more direct so as not to be overwhelming. These comments begin to elicit specific actions by the pupils that result in improved work. You gain some time to spend with your family and become a little less *anxious* about how your classes will perform in public examinations.
The pupils gradually start to see that you are aiming to develop their skills incrementally and they appreciate your efforts and the way you are now balancing Caring and Controlling energy in your approach to feedback.

▼

Key learning

No one likes constant criticism. Be kind to yourself and your pupils by limiting the comments you make on their work to a couple of things you want to praise and one specific improvement they can make straight away.

As the examples of teaching neurodiverse classes, observing lessons and providing Wise Feedback demonstrate, Functional Fluency provides a powerful lens for refining a teacher's practice and building stronger relationships. The model clarifies the interpersonal dynamics that drive effective learning. However, the application of Functional Fluency is not limited to teacher–pupil interaction and pedagogical strategy; it can also be embedded directly into the curriculum. As we will now explore, it offers a robust framework for analysing the very subject matter of our lessons, particularly in subjects that deal with human behaviour, such as literature.

Beyond behaviour management: weaving Functional Fluency into your curriculum

In the curriculum subjects where human behaviour and relationships are studied – the humanities, English literature, PSHE and the arts, for example – knowledge and understanding of Functional Fluency provide a useful set of reference points for teachers and pupils.

As an English teacher, I have been interested in the possibilities that Functional Fluency provides in relation to literary analysis ever since I first heard about it.

Literary texts are necessarily about human behaviour, and pupils generally do not have the language to describe this in a subtle and effective manner. Even more important, unless they have a religious background (see the section on *akrasia* in Chapter 8), they probably do not have a developed model of human behaviour that enables them to describe or analyse the behaviour of fictional characters with any finesse.

Well-known picture books such as *Where The Wild Things Are* (Maurice Sendak, 1963) can be used to explain Functional Fluency concepts to younger pupils or to explain them to older pupils efficiently by referencing a text they may already know, or that can quickly be read to them. You can discuss with the class whether the child's behaviour is Immature and whether the mother's response demonstrates Dominating or Structuring behaviour. Towards the end of the story, you can talk about whether the child and the mother are both using Accounting behaviour to evaluate their situations and respond in ways that result in harmony, in contrast to the earlier chaos.

An Inspector Calls (J.B. Priestley, 1945) is widely taught in UK GCSE English literature courses. In the play, both Birling parents demonstrate Dominating behaviour: Arthur in his treatment of Eva for her role in demanding a wage rise for the workers in his factory, and Sybil, when she refuses to provide help to the now pregnant and destitute Eva through the charity she runs.

The younger generation of Birlings feel that they have more open-minded attitudes, but the play reveals that they too have treated Eva in a similarly Dominating manner. The Inspector's questioning encourages the characters to do some Accounting. However, just when it seems that the characters are awakening to a new understanding of the impact of their behaviour and may be able to develop ways of living that incorporate more Nurturing and Cooperative responses, they begin to wonder whether the whole police investigation is real.

Using the Functional Fluency model in this way or, even better, moving representative figures around on a copy of the model, is a great way to open up a text for pupils. The model provides a range of words to describe the behaviour of the characters. The model also, through its clear colour coding, encourages pupils to begin to group characters by their behaviour choices, classifying in ways that make it easier for them to write analytically. Furthermore, once pupils understand the model, they can use it as a planning tool for their own writing, helping them to construct conflicts between characters that give life and drama to their own texts and further embed the model into school life.

This use of the model within English literature can be mimicked in other subjects where human behaviour and moral dilemmas are studied. This further embeds the language of the model into school life and pupil consciousness while also providing pupils with a sound basis for analysis, helping to make their lived experience of school genuinely values-based, as explored in Chapter 1.

The classroom is a complex feedback loop; a dynamic dance between teaching and learning. What the principles of Rosenshine and the stories of practitioners including Sean Warren and Martian Slagter show us is that Functional Fluency is the human operating system that powers effective pedagogy. It is the art of connection that fuels the science of instruction. Mastering this moves a teacher from merely managing a room to orchestrating a thriving learning environment. Yet, this ecosystem does not exist in a vacuum; its health is deeply connected to the culture of the staffroom – the very world beyond the classroom door we will now enter.

CHAPTER 4
BEYOND THE CLASSROOM DOOR: CREATING A THRIVING STAFF CULTURE

Following the whole-school training on Functional Fluency, a suggestion box is set up in the staff room. Pat Harrison was initially a little wary, concerned that it would allow staff to give voice to their Compliant / Resistant or Immature ideas. But, when Dave put out the box, along with a notice encouraging colleagues to use it as an opportunity to share Spontaneous and Cooperative ideas, her fears began to subside.

In the first three weeks, several constructive ideas are suggested and these are now well on the way to being implemented: incorporating more vegetables into school meals; reducing the school's energy consumption by ensuring all lights are turned off at night; and an idea from Chris Andrews to print the Functional Fluency model into the school planner so it is always available. The ideas are so good that Pat and Dave are now planning to install suggestion boxes for pupils to use too.

In a meeting with his mentor (deputy headteacher Dave), Chris mentions how he used Functional Fluency to resolve the dispute over footballs. Knowing Dave, Chris half expects him to roll his eyes but, in fact, he listens carefully to Chris's account and jots a quick note in his planner. Somehow Chris has the feeling that they had both just increased their professional capital a little.

While getting a coffee before the leadership meeting that evening, Dave says 'You know, Pat, I thought this Functional Fluency thing was just another initiative, but seeing how it's changed the way Chris and Clem are teaching... I'm sold'.

How would a Functionally Fluent teacher engage with colleagues?

Sometimes it is relationships between teachers and those they teach that makes life difficult in schools, but often it is relationships between members of staff that lack effectiveness, wasting valuable time and energy that could be much better used on teaching or relaxation. Functional Fluency provides a key to unlock what is going on when these circumstances arise. It enables those involved to examine their past behaviour, question their own motivation and consider how they could best adapt their behaviour in the future to make better use of their time and energy, so that they and others benefit.

'We teach who we are'

Parker J. Palmer (2007) writes that 'Teaching, like any truly human activity, emerges from one's inwardness, for better or worse' (page 102). This truth helps to explain why Functional Fluency can have such efficacy for teachers. One of the insights that often emerges from a TIFF feedback discussion with a teacher is that the whole process of thinking about their behaviour choices does not relate solely to their professional life, but in fact covers all aspects of their existence. So, we often end up discussing a teacher's relationship with their own children or behaviours that are triggered by something their spouse says just as much or more than that troublesome Year 9 class they teach on a Thursday afternoon. This is because, as Palmer (2007) says, 'The entanglements I experience in the classroom are often no more or less than the convolutions of my inner life'.

Palmer goes further. He suggests that, without self-knowledge, which is exactly what Functionally Fluency and TIFF help to develop, you cannot be an effective teacher. 'When I do not know myself, I cannot know who my students are. I will see them through a glass darkly, in the shadows of my unexamined life – and when I cannot see them clearly I cannot teach them well' (Palmer, 2007). It is through the improved understanding of ourselves that Functional Fluency can help to develop that we gain increased understanding of human behaviour in general, the nature of behaviour choices and the way human beings function, both optimally and sub-optimally. It is only through developing this understanding that we can have any hope of connecting with our pupils in ways that support learning.

This is because teaching is not just an intellectual pursuit. If we attempt to explain surds to pupils who are distracted by a fight at break or whose parents are suffering from mental-health issues or who are too hungry to concentrate, without addressing these needs, we are unlikely to be successful. Teaching involves not just the intellectual but also the emotional and spiritual realms. All three of these aspects are required if teaching is to be sufficiently related to the real world, sufficiently inspiring and sufficiently sustaining to make sense to pupils. As teachers, we need to consider all these aspects, and Functional Fluency, with its emphasis on the head (intellectual), gut (emotional) and heart (spiritual), can help teachers to build their awareness of all these realms and thus build the connection with individuals and classes that supports effective, continued learning.

Palmer's formulation of teacher quality is not formulaic, like Hargreaves and Fullan's idea of professional capita, covered in the next section, but it comes down to much the same thing. Palmer writes 'good teaching cannot be reduced to techniques; good teaching comes from the identity and integrity of the teacher' (Palmer, 2007). There are plenty of approaches to Continuing Professional Development (CPD) that focus on developing a teacher's techniques, but very few that have identity and integrity at the heart in the way that Functional Fluency does. Completing a TIFF and engaging in the ensuing feedback session, interacting in a Get on the Mat session or being involved in ongoing Functional Fluency coaching are all ways in which teachers can work on developing their identity and integrity. This work requires honesty and openness and helps individuals to gain greater understanding of the behavioural patterns that create their current identity. It also enables them to take charge of their future behaviour, so that they can control the development of their own identity in ways that have powerful professional benefits. Because Functional Fluency is all about truth, it enables teachers to develop themselves in ways that are in line with their own beliefs and values and thus endorses and sustains their identity, making them more engaging professionals who consistently inspire pupils to learn.

Palmer sums up the frustrations of CPD that jumps on the latest educational fad:

> If good teaching cannot be reduced to technique, I no longer need suffer the pain of having my peculiar gift as a teacher crammed into the Procrustean bed of someone else's method and the standards prescribed by it. That pain is felt throughout education today as we insist upon the method *du jour* – leaving people who teach differently feeling devalued, forcing them to measure up to norms not their own.

Palmer, 2007

Functional Fluency instead provides a 'bed' that has the flexibility to adapt to the infinitely varying skills of the teaching workforce, allowing and encouraging each teacher to fulfil their pedagogical potential by being fully themselves in the classroom. This acceptance of different approaches promotes greater understanding between colleagues as they witness and learn from each other's integrity. Building on this understanding of the teacher's inner life and its impact on their effectiveness, we can explore how Functional Fluency also supports the development of professional capital, a concept that further elucidates teacher development.

Investing in your greatest asset: building professional capital together

Hargreaves and Fullan (2012) define their concept of professional capital in their book of the same name using the formula: PC = f{HC, SC, DC}. Professional capital is a function of human capital, social capital and decisional capital. Let's look at each of these terms in turn in relation to Functional Fluency.

Human capital

Hargreaves and Fullan (2012) define human capital as something very individual: 'It is about possessing the passion and the moral commitment to serve all children and to want to keep getting better in how you provide that service.' This links with the values-based aspects of Functional Fluency that are explored in Chapter 1. Both human capital and Functional Fluency are self-improvement concepts that have, at their heart, continual striving to be better.

Social capital

'*Social capital* refers to how the quantity and quality of interactions and social relationships among people affects their access to knowledge and information' and, as such, 'Social capital increases your knowledge – it gives you access to other people's *human capital*' (Hargreaves and Fullan, 2012). The link here with Functional Fluency could hardly be clearer: both are centrally concerned with the quality of interactions and social relationships.

Decisional capital

'Decisional capital here is the capital that professionals acquire and accumulate through structured and unstructured experience, practice and reflection – capital that enables them to make wise judgments in circumstances where there is no fixed rule or piece of incontrovertible evidence to guide them' (Hargreaves and Fullan, 2012). Again, the link with Functional Fluency is clear, where the emphasis on Accounting as a process to improve decision-making is central. It is through repeated exercising of Accounting that we get better at Accounting, making increasingly mature and effective decisions when faced with complex behavioural choices.

Professional capital

Given that Functional Fluency is so intimately interwoven with each of its constituent elements, Functional Fluency must be vitally important in the development of professional capital. However, both are complex concepts that cannot be reduced to easy checklists or mandated actions. Both could easily be distorted out of recognition, and the effective essence that could transform a school community could be too easily lost with superficial, imposed implementation. Functional Fluency is a school-improvement process, and schools must continually strive to be worthy of it. A means of achieving this is the nurturing of true collaboration between colleagues within the school community. As Hargreaves and Fullan write in relation to professional capital, 'Strong and positive collaboration is not about whether everyone has a word wall, or a set of posted standards, or not. It's about whether teachers are committed to, are inquisitive about, and increasingly knowledgeable and well informed about becoming better practitioners together' (Hargreaves and Fullan, 2012).

In the final chapter of their book, Hargreaves and Fullan (2012) offer ten 'Guidelines for Teachers', along with similar lists for school and district leaders and state, national and international organisations. All three lists link closely with Functional Fluency, but I will focus on the list for teachers. All their proposals could link to Functional Fluency, but number 2 'Start with yourself: examine your own experience' is particularly apposite. Functional Fluency is all about self-reflection, looking carefully at the behavioural choices you have made in the past, evaluating their effectiveness and resolving to make more effective decisions in the future. There is a strong focus on taking control for yourself, of your own development as a teacher and as a person. Proposal 3, 'Be a mindful teacher', also resonates deeply with the Accounting concept in Functional Fluency, while Proposal 4, 'Build your human capital through social capital', links directly with the behaviours in the Cooperative mode of Functional Fluency.

I could go on and outline the multiple other ways in which the other proposals link to the model, but I think the message s clear. Functional Fluency provides a coherent basis for school-improvement processes. It can make sense of otherwise diverse initiatives and give school leaders a touchstone against which to evaluate any new ideas, allowing school values and the concept of professional capital to remain uppermost in planning and thinking. Above all, Functional Fluency helps to improve the quality of relationships between colleagues, providing the circumstances in which the trusting collaboration and co-creation upon which effective education is based can be built. If a school embarks on the process of developing Functional Fluency within its staff body, the benefits will be hard to identify because they will be deep and profound and evolutionary, incrementally helping to build professional capital and create a more effective school culture. What could be more vital.

A practical approach to fostering such positive behavioural change and thereby enhancing professional capital can be found in the 'as if' principle, which posits that acting out desired qualities can help in embodying them. We will discuss it shortly.

Functional Fluency coaching and professional capital

To illustrate how Functional Fluency coaching directly builds the forms of capital that Hargreaves and Fullan (2012) discuss, let's consider a recent case study from my own practice. I have completed some Functional Fluency coaching with headteachers who work for an independent organisation that runs a number of special schools and care homes across the UK. The action-planning sessions that form part of the feedback meeting following their completion of the TIFF survey identify targets and developmental aims that tie in closely with professional capital.

The action plan that the headteacher (we'll call Tina) and I co-constructed focused strongly on the idea of becoming a more authentic version of herself in her role as headteacher. Her TIFF results indicated some golden modes where her behaviour was strong, including *considerate, inspiring, understanding* and *rational* behaviour. However, her scores in the Spontaneous mode were low, especially those for *creativity, playful* and *expressive* behaviours. Tina recognised that the way she behaved at work was not her true self – she felt inhibited by the role she had recently taken over, and over-shadowed by the reputation of her predecessor. She was wasting lots of time and energy on Marshmallowing behaviour and the result was a feeling of exhaustion.

In the eight months following the feedback meeting, Tina consciously and actively worked to reduce the time and energy she put into Marshmallowing behaviour, and she felt that her life was now completely different and that the coaching 'worked wonders'.

One of Tina's actions related to how she engaged with her son. Following the coaching session, she actively treated him in a grown-up way, and he responded positively to this by taking on more responsibility for his younger brother. By moving from Marshmallowing to Nurturing, Tina felt that their relationship improved, and her *anxiety* reduced. She now arrived at school with an increased capacity to be truly herself. This boosted Tina's **human capital** and increased her confidence levels, leaving her feeling more energetic. This also had a direct impact on Tina's **social capital**, giving her more energy to focus on creating effective working relationships at school.

Tina took a consciously Structuring approach to her work within the school. She tackled anyone who mentioned her predecessor by saying 'this is my school now', and implemented clear rules for both staff and pupils to follow, using *firm* and *authoritative* behaviour. In a follow-up discussion, she told me 'I feel a lot stronger', and this gave her the confidence to reduce her own teaching load to ensure she had the time to complete all the many tasks expected of a headteacher, rather than Marshmallowing her colleagues by continuing to teach a full timetable. The coaching and the way in which Tina actively worked to implement the action plan directly increased her **decisional capital**.

Functional Fluency-based coaching enabled this headteacher to increase her human, social and decisional capital. This resulted in a considerable increase in **professional capital** but, more important, a huge boost in Tina's confidence to lead her school in the authentic manner that brings so many benefits to her, her colleagues and pupils.

The 'as if' principle: acting your way into a new reality

In his book *The As If Principle* (Wiseman, 2012), Professor Richard Wiseman explores William James's contention that 'if you want a quality, act as if you already have it'. This fits very well with the approach of Functional Fluency for a couple of reasons.

Firstly, Functional Fluency is all about behaviour. When a teacher completes a TIFF, they are indicating their likelihood to behave in a certain way. It is not about how they feel or the emotions behind the behaviour – they are likely to explore these in the subsequent feedback meeting. The profile itself is all about what we actually do: our behaviour. It is our behaviour that other people experience – the emotion behind our anger is generally neither here nor there for someone on the wrong end of it; all they experience is the anger. The focus of the action-planning phase with a teacher is all about how they want to change the balance of this behaviour and this results, if it is successful, in our teacher's colleagues, pupils, friends and family experiencing them behaving in ways that are more effective and more likely to enable both themselves and others to thrive.

Wiseman (2012) explores the wide range of psychological experiments that have gone on over the last century or so to investigate whether there is any truth in James's contention. And what he finds is that there is. He cites work completed by Hohmann in the 1960s with US Army veterans with varying degrees of injury-induced paralysis. What Hohmann discovers is that 'the higher the spinal damage, the less able they were to move around and the less likely they were to experience emotions' (Wiseman, 2012).

He also cites several other studies that show that, contrary to our general view that emotions drive behaviour, in fact behaviour to a very large degree drives emotions. If we are unable to behave physically in a wide range of different ways due to paralysis, Hohmann found that we are unable to experience a wide range of emotions too. This suggests that Functional Fluency's focus on behaviour is a very appropriate one. If we change the way we are behaving, James suggests, supported by Hohmann's practical research, that this has a direct impact on our underlying emotions and feelings. This should have a further beneficial effect of reducing our impulse to react in less effective ways as we get caught up in this virtuous circle of increasing Functional Fluency. So, if a colleague's behaviour makes us feel angry, rather than releasing this by engaging in some form of argument, Wiseman contends that it would be better to engage in some focused Accounting. This adaptation of the expected pattern of behaviour has a corresponding impact on the pattern of emotions, reducing the level of anger and making it easier to engage constructively with the colleague on professional matters.

Wiseman's (2012) section on the power of calm resonates particularly clearly with the central Functional Fluency concept of Accounting. He references the work of Bushman, who demonstrated, in a series of experiments, that the best way to dissipate negative or violent feelings is not to act them out by, for example, punching an effigy of the person who has upset you. Instead, it is far more effective simply to spend some time in quiet contemplation. 'To calm down, act like a calm person.' Functional Fluency explicitly builds this calming break into one's behaviour by encouraging Accounting prior to embarking on a course of action. In so doing, it is ensuring that our behavioural choices are far more likely to be thoughtful, calm and rational and lead to positive outcomes for ourselves and those we are engaging with, rather than the impulsive choice that a less Functionally Fluent person might make.

The positive implications of this for teachers are obvious. Repeatedly during an average day, colleagues and pupils give teachers reasons to react negatively, by shouting or being sarcastic or otherwise rash. The key is to pause first, consider the situation in the round, think about the available options for Structuring, Nurturing, Cooperative and Spontaneous responses and then choose a blend of these that is appropriate and enables you and the pupils or colleagues concerned to benefit. In this way, the teacher is modelling a Functionally Fluent response that may well avoid a range of difficult issues in the future that often result from a less Functionally Fluent reaction.

The practical benefits of applying Functional Fluency, such as the deliberate behavioural choices the 'as if' principle advocates, are clearly demonstrated in the work of practitioners including Hilary Desousa, who uses the model to shape her leadership and teaching.

Functional Fluency in Action

Hilary Desousa

In my interview with Hilary Desousa of Cornwall College, she is very explicit about the dual nature of her use of Functional Fluency within her work: as an influence on her approach to leadership and as a key component of the courses she creates and teaches. Both aspects of this work have a strong focus on improving the nature of relationships with and between colleagues.

Firstly, she uses the model internally to help to establish effective working relationships with her colleagues. The Business Development team that she leads works across the county and beyond, delivering a wide range of courses. They have been using a flexible working model for many years prior to Covid and don't follow the normal term dates, unlike the rest of the College. This inevitably means that they are spread very widely and rarely see each other; consequently, the effectiveness of the team is highly dependent on trust and professionalism. Hilary, as a trained Functional Fluency professional since 2010, knows the Functional Fluency model well, and the flexibility and balance that lie at its heart are manifest in the way she leads her team. She models Functionally Fluent behaviour to her colleagues, and the consequence is a team that is trusted to get on with the tasks that need to happen in ways that best suit the needs of the clients, without placing undue burdens on the staff. This results in high levels of motivation and low rates of staff turnover and explains her own continuance, in what was initially a temporary job, for over 20 years. This flexibility is something that schools find particularly difficult to replicate but, given the rise of digital nomadism post-Covid, is something the sector will need to grapple with in the coming years if the staffing crisis is not to become even worse.

Secondly, and more explicitly, Hilary uses Functional Fluency as part of the courses she delivers to businesses around the county. The two main types of course where Hilary uses Functional Fluency are coaching and leadership courses. She introduces Functional Fluency as a model, alongside other models and, in some cases, after some light-touch coverage of Transactional Analysis (TA). This work may focus on the discussion and analysis of motivation styles or learning styles. For example, in a coaching course Hilary may well use the Functional Fluency model as a way into discussion about relationships, rapport-building and maintaining appropriate boundaries within a coaching relationship. In all this work, there is a strong focus on leaders and managers needing to know themselves better and using the model as a means to achieve this. TIFF is often offered to those on the training, and is explicitly built into the level 5 coaching courses that Cornwall College run. TIFF has also been used as part of the college's level 5 Management Apprenticeship course.

When she is using TIFF as part of a course, Hilary firstly introduces the cohort to the Functional Fluency model. She then explains in a one-to-one session with each learner how the TIFF works. Then, assuming they raise no objections, she sends them the link to their own TIFF and, once they have completed it, schedules their personal feedback session. Sometimes Hilary finds that teams opt for a psychometric instead of TIFF and this is perhaps because they are seduced by the way these other tools divide the workforce into groups, suggesting that they will provide a clear and relatively simple way to identify issues. What tends to happen in these cases is that the individuals complete the psychometric and it creates an initial buzz, but fails to translate into changes in the culture of the group or the nature of the relationships between its members. In contrast, Functional Fluency and TIFF do not categorise people and therefore perhaps appear to have limited short-term impact. What they do, though, is to place focus on the nature of our behavioural choices, and this has long-term benefits, particularly if the language of Functional Fluency becomes embedded in the organisation's ways of discussing its work.

Hilary now works three days per week for Cornwall College and does private work on the other days. One contract she is about to start is with the University of Sunderland, teaching a coaching course; the Functional Fluency model will be part of this work.

Following Hilary Desousa's insights into applying Functional Fluency within college and business-training contexts, we now turn to Giles Barrow, whose work demonstrates its application across a diverse range of educational settings, often with a focus on TA.

Functional Fluency in Action

Giles Barrow

Giles Barrow is an educator with experience across formal and informal educational contexts involving children, young people and adults. Much of his career has involved working with adolescents at the margins of mainstream education and subsequently with educators, figuring out how best to create educational cultures that are inclusive, radically holistic and creatively subversive. Giles is a teaching and supervising transactional analyst in the field of education. He works in both indoor and outside spaces, having an eye for the ecological and the existential dimensions of education, as well as a keen ear for a good story. Giles has written on educational themes and completed a doctoral study on a philosophy focused on soil, soul and society in the educational encounter. A Londoner by birth and upbringing, he now finds himself living on a smallholding in Suffolk. He has written several books on learning, teaching, education and TA and co-edited *Educational Transactional Analysis* (2016) with Trudi Newton.

Giles was working with Susannah Temple at the time of the formation of the ideas around Functional Fluency and TIFF, and started using these ideas immediately. Over several years, Giles has worked using Functional Fluency with a wide range of schools, and these have included residential special schools in the south of the UK, a cluster of schools in the north west, a network of alternative provision in Suffolk and a major city-hospital school. Giles has also worked with a couple of schools in Bangalore, India, through the TA network, which have begun to show an interest in Functional Fluency since Covid. These schools have come across Giles through his work in TA (he is one of a growing number of people in the UK who are qualified in the educational field and can deliver the TA training to school teams). Several of the existing Functional Fluency professionals came across Functional Fluency and TIFF through working with Giles on his TA training programmes, and he can see that there is a growing interest in Functional Fluency and that schools have started to use it for staff to be trained and sufficiently confident in the use of the model to develop the work themselves. This has been mirrored by an increase in the number of people from an educational background coming to work as Functional Fluency professionals.

Giles has delivered hundreds of TA101 courses, and he teaches Functional Fluency as a way of elaborating Functional Ego States. He delivers this training to pastoral teams and leadership teams. Giles feels that a significant benefit of Functional Fluency is that it can be taught to people as a leadership model without them knowing anything about ego states or the more technical aspects of TA. He also introduces Functional Fluency when he is working individually with clients, but more commonly when working with groups, though the model is often in the back of his mind when he is working with individuals.

Within a local alternative-provision setting, Giles is working with adults to upskill them in Functional Fluency so that they, in turn, can introduce the pupils in key stages 3 and 4 (11 to 16-year-olds) to the model. He is also working with behaviour mentors across a multi-academy trust (MAT) in the north west to introduce them to the model so that they too can use it with pupils. Typically, one of the issues with Functional Fluency is that teachers have reservations about using it with pupils until they have developed considerable confidence in the model themselves, and Giles sees his role as providing the training and support that develops this confidence in the relevant adults.

Giles is clear that the efficacy of Functional Fluency does not have to be proved through research, and this response to the question of research is part of a wider problem he sees with the current obsession with evidence-based practice. His concern is that, where there is a preoccupation with professional competence, this can be at the expense of cultivating professional wisdom and judgement. In his view, this risks diminishing our educational work; we need something more than only empirical evidence. What is far more important are the values upon which Functional Fluency is based (see the earlier sections on values and professional capital).

Giles appreciates that many schools would not entertain working with him, as the general move towards managerialism makes his work on Functional Fluency seem relatively counter-cultural. Schools need to step into this work, knowingly, intentionally to ensure they don't fall into the trap of spinning out a superficial version that simplifies the complexity behind Functional Fluency. In light of this, Giles is very enthusiastic about the Certified Functional Fluency Teacher Programme (see the Appendix for details), as this will ensure that the depth of thinking and support required to implement these ideas effectively will be present and that the school will then be linked into a wider group of professionals who can provide additional support and enable them to bring Functional Fluency into reality in a school.

In terms of outcomes, Giles is clear that the evidence that the work has been successful is in the creation of a more effective relational culture within the school. He recognises that this is inherently challenging to measure, but that that doesn't make it anything other than vitally important.

Giles has also used the model as a basis for lesson observation, and he feels that there is an opportunity to develop a suite of resources that could be used to help schools to use Functional Fluency in practical ways (see Chapter 3 for some initial thoughts on what this might look like).

Giles Barrow's emphasis on creating a more effective relational culture through Functional Fluency is particularly relevant when considering how schools can support all learners, including those who are neurodivergent. The model's focus on understanding behaviour provides a valuable framework in this context.

Creating an inclusive staffroom: a guide to neurodiversity and your colleagues

Suzanne O'Sullivan, in an article in *The Guardian* entitled 'The number of people with chronic conditions is soaring. Are we less healthy than we used to be – or overdiagnosing illness?' (O'Sullivan, 2025) writes about the school experiences of a woman she calls Anna who now works as a nurse.

At school, Anna developed exclusive friendships with one person after another and describes herself as an immature people-pleaser. On her first day at a new school, two girls befriended her. In the dining hall they encouraged Anna to misbehave, which Anna did. Later she felt very guilty, and feels this experience had a negative impact on her remaining time at school.

The types of behaviour Anna uses fit easily into the Functional Fluency model; she was keen to make friends (Cooperative) but was easily persuaded to do silly things (Immature). As an adult, Anna is diagnosed with ADHD and prescribed Ritalin. To an extent, this helps Anna to understand some of the issues that she has faced during her life. However, it does not enable her to recover and, in fact, in the article she is described as not being able to go to work and that she does not see this situation changing. O'Sullivan's general argument is that diagnosis, far from helping people to be cured, seems to make recovery more difficult, as sufferers tend to see themselves as having chronic disease that is not susceptible to self or community healing.

If we see the behaviour patterns that Anna exhibits as having many similarities with those of other (undiagnosed) pupils, we emphasise the potential for alternative, more effective patterns of behaviour to be utilised. The possibility of remediation and greater thriving by Anna and those she comes across is clear as there is no pathologising diagnosis that needs to be overcome; simply a pattern of behaviour that could and should be adjusted so that everyone involved can live happier lives.

An analysis of Anna's behaviour using the Functional Fluency model might look something like this: At first, she is utilising effective Cooperative behaviour but this soon turns to Immature behaviour and this in turn becomes Compliant; see Figure 13.

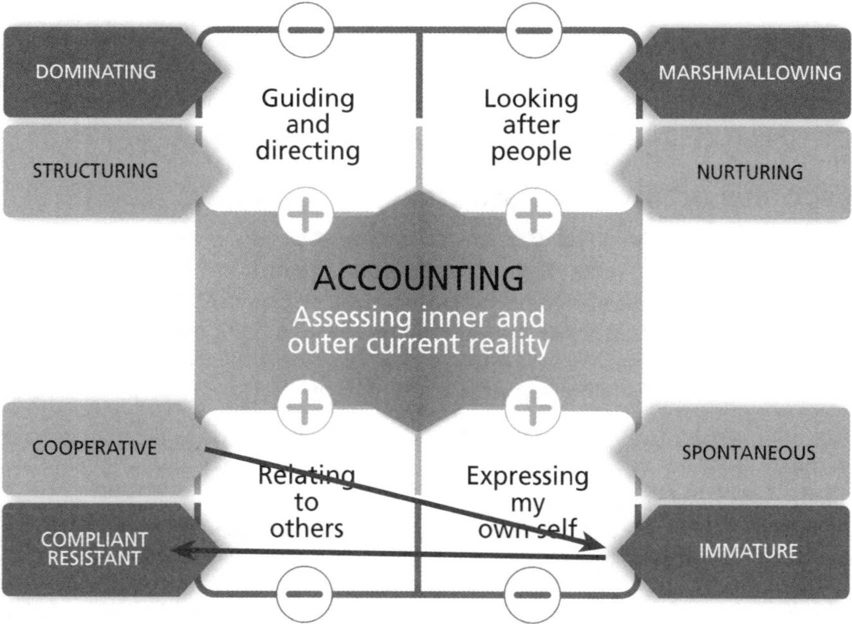

Figure 13 An analysis of Anna's behaviour using the Functional Fluency model

An alternative effective behaviour pattern would have started using Cooperative behaviour, but then would utilise the *rational, aware* behaviour of the Accounting mode to choose effective, Spontaneous responses to the situation, which would have allowed everyone to thrive; see Figure 14.

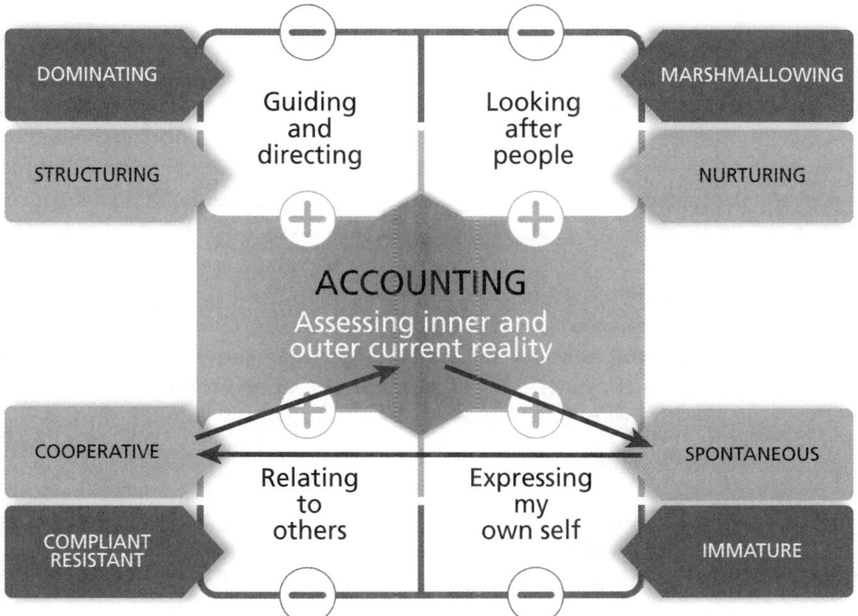

Figure 14 An alternative effective behaviour pattern

This is not to undermine the concept of neurodiversity in any way. It is very clear that there are many young people in our school systems who experience the world in ways that are very different from the experiences of the neurotypical majority. But by using the Functional Fluency model to name and categorise the behaviours that people manifest, we can see that all sorts of people, whether neurodiverse or neurotypical, behave in more effective and less effective ways every day. We all make poor behaviour choices. Functional Fluency enables us to address these choices and the impact that they have for ourselves and for others, without getting bogged down in a reductive, binary distinction that can, if anything, reinforce notions of lack of self-determination and responsibility in ways that can be damaging to our sense of self.

Schools have become much more aware of neurodiversity in recent years. As a society, we are gradually gaining understanding that we do not all think in the same ways and that there are in fact fundamental differences in the way people perceive the world. This is not the place for a detailed analysis of this issue or of the ideal pedagogical provision for neurodivergent pupils.

However, Functional Fluency does have several benefits that help schools more adequately meet the needs of all their pupils, including those who are neurodivergent. It also increases the understanding of neurodiverse pupils and their view of the world by teachers and pupils who identify as neurotypical. An increasing number of adults are realising – sometimes through the diagnoses of their children – that they themselves are also neurodiverse. For neurodiverse teachers, the benefits of Functional Fluency can be helpful in building increased levels of understanding and empathy between colleagues, thus boosting collaboration and reducing the stress and anxiety caused by misunderstanding.

To summarise the benefits of Functional Fluency for neurodiversity:

1. The main advantage of Functional Fluency is that it provides schools with a stable, agreed and shared vocabulary to talk about behaviour. This language can be taught to pupils, staff and parents. This has the benefit of reducing misunderstanding and confusion and helping pupils who might otherwise struggle to put a name to certain types of behaviour.

2. By providing an external model for behaviour to be talked and thought about, Functional Fluency depersonalises behaviour. This allows behaviour to be discussed in a more open, less judgemental manner.

3. This increased ability to talk about behaviour should lead to the uncovering and greater understanding of motivations behind particular behaviours, which should result in increased empathy within the school as people begin properly to understand the thought processes that motivate these ways of being.

Example 8 works through how this might play out.

An inclusive culture extends to the staffroom. Creating an environment where neurodivergent colleagues can thrive requires the Functionally Fluent principles of empathy, clear communication and thoughtful Accounting.

Example 8 Understanding a neurodiverse colleague

A colleague's behaviour has upset you. She responded to a suggestion you made in a recent staff meeting in a very direct way that you found rude.

Your colleague's behaviour has made you feel uncomfortable and reluctant to make further suggestions (*submissive*).

Pause: choice

Using the Functional Fluency model to assess the situation, you realise that your colleague's concerns about your suggestion were logical (Accounting). You begin to understand that you perceived the responses as being *judgemental* (Dominating) when it may have simply been *firm* (Structuring). Your colleague has a very direct way of expressing herself that is due to her neurodiversity, not any antipathy towards you or your ideas.

You:

Functionally Fluent response

You explain to your colleague in a quiet moment how their response made you feel. You acknowledge that you both see the world differently and that the important thing is for you both to gain greater understanding of each other (*empathy*).

You:

Key learning

It is always worth trying to understand situations from the other person's point of view. We don't all have the same values or ways of thinking about issues.

This deep level of interpersonal understanding, so crucial when working with neurodiverse colleagues, is also essential for navigating other common professional challenges. Applying the same principles of empathy and perspective-taking can transform how teachers respond to systemic pressures, such as managing an overwhelming workload.

What are the main school-related drains on your available time and energy? Compare them with Example 9, and think about what a Functionally Fluent response to this situation might look like and how this could result in a situation where both you and others benefit.

Example 9 Tackling teacher workload: moving from overwhelmed to in control

Situation

A week before half-term, your head of department (HoD) tells you that you need to replan the Year 8 unit on *A Midsummer Night's Dream* by the end of half-term. Your HoD probably considers that she is Structuring things so that the whole department can thrive but, from your point of view, this comes across as Dominating behaviour.

HoD:

▼

Immediate thoughts and feelings

You feel annoyed that you have been given little warning. You have plans for half-term, and this means you won't be able to relax and recuperate (*anxious*). Your colleagues don't seem to have to do as much planning as you. Completing this task on this timeline will result in poor-quality work and will potentially cause you to burn out. Your annoyance and anxiety could cause you to have a Compliant / Resistant reaction.

You:

▼

Pause: choice

You recognise that the unit of work does need rethinking and the HoD has perhaps chosen you because your dissertation was on Shakespeare. However, you do need a decent break over half-term if you are going to get through the next seven weeks of teaching (*aware, grounded*).

You:

▼

Functionally Fluent response

You go back to the HoD and explain that you understand the need to rewrite the unit but also that you need a break (Cooperative, *understanding, assertive*). You suggest that you would be happy to draft a new long-term plan and to write the draft lesson outlines for the first two weeks, but suggest that your colleagues need an opportunity to comment on and contribute to the work (Accounting, *evaluative*). You ask the HoD whether she chose you for this task because of your specialism in Shakespeare and thank her for recognising your expertise (Spontaneous, *curious, friendly*).

You:

HoD:

▼

Key learning

Facing up to situations that seem unfair can have positive consequences if you do it in a thoughtful way.

While Functional Fluency provides a clear framework for managing challenges with those who lead us, as seen in this workload scenario, it is equally powerful when guiding and developing new teachers. The model can be especially effective when mentors use it to support trainees navigating the complexities of the classroom.

The Functional Fluency model can be used by mentors, whether in an official role in the case of a School Centred Initial Teacher Training (SCITT) mentor, or as part of a less formal, school-based arrangement.

The distinction between mentoring and coaching is a complex one that we won't get into here. Suffice it to say that mentoring in education is often a mandated situation over which the mentee has little choice, as in the initial teacher training (ITT) situation. The relationship can be a complex one, and it is the responsibility of the mentor to establish from the outset that the relationship is one of mentor–mentee, not coach–coachee, and to explain that this is because it will entail them providing 'guidance and advice' (Oberholzer and Boyle, 2024) because of their professional experience and status that the trainee, at this point in their development, lacks. As Oberholzer and Boyle (2024) suggest:

> When the needs of the mentee evolve to the point where coaching needs to be considered as a more appropriate approach, mentors need to feel confident to offer alternative support and approaches to continue to support the mentee well.

Oberholzer and Boyle, 2024

Example 10 Mentoring for growth: guiding the next generation of teachers

Situation

In the weekly meeting between a mentor and her mentee, the discussion focuses on a situation that developed during the mentee's teaching of a Year 9 class a couple of days earlier. The mentee, in the role of trainee teacher, when teaching the class gave out factually incorrect information about the topic being taught, then got into an argument (*blaming*) with a pupil that disrupted the last ten minutes of the lesson.

Trainee teacher:

Mentor:

Immediate thoughts and feelings

There is clearly a lot of tension between the mentee and this class, and also with the class teacher, who the mentee feels has not been supportive. The mentor asks the mentee to reflect on these two issues and to Get on the Mat to explore her feelings concerning them.

The mentee looks at the model in a suspicious manner for a while before saying that she doesn't really understand what is expected of her and that she just wants to know what to do with these difficult pupils (Compliant / Resistant).

Trainee teacher:

Mentor:

Pause: choice

The mentor begins by placing a counter in the Compliant / Resistant mode and saying that this represents the mentee and that this feels like where her energy is coming from in this meeting. The mentor then places another figure in the Accounting mode and explains that, because it is a mentoring situation, not coaching, the mentor feels entitled to point out her understanding of the situation. The mentor then explains that she feels that the mentee is perhaps feeling anxious due to not having full understanding of the required subject knowledge. She then explains that the mentee, when challenged by the pupil, reacted from the Dominating mode. The mentor asks the mentee to respond (*curious*).

The mentee is relieved that this is all out in the open and externalised on the mat. She agrees that the subject-knowledge issue is causing anxiety and that this may have been a factor in her Dominating reaction.

Mentor:

Response / Action

With this shared understanding of what happened, the mentor and mentee start exploring possible solutions. The mentor assures the mentee that the subject-knowledge issue is not surprising, as she has never studied this topic before, but that it can be easily remedied by reading one key book and watching a video (*empathic*). Together, they work through the school's behaviour strategy, using the Functional Fluency model to understand how it aims to balance Care and Control.

This leaves the mentee feeling confident to go away and complete the work required to develop her subject knowledge. She also has a better understanding of the fundamentals underlying behaviour management, which will enable her to implement the school's policy in a way that feels authentic in relation to her own ideas and expectations.

Trainee teacher:

Key learning

Teacher-training is a stressful time. Providing sympathetic guidance for trainees on ways to improve their subject knowledge helps them to become confident practitioners.

In addition to formal mentoring relationships, Functional Fluency can be applied to address and redirect well-intentioned but ultimately unhelpful colleague behaviours, such as Marshmallowing.

Example 11 Challenging Marshmallowing

Situation

You have a colleague who means well. He is devoted to the SEND pupils, and this plays out in him doing too much for them (Marshmallowing). He brings in cakes for them, and you frequently discover that he has helped them with their work to the extent of actually doing it for them.

Colleague:

Immediate thoughts and feelings

You know that something is wrong here, but the colleague's motives are so obviously positive that you find it hard to challenge him. The current situation is making you feel both *rebellious* (you want to tell your colleague to sort himself out) and *placating* (you are tempted to allow things to carry on as they are as you know your colleague has good intentions and you don't want to cause upset).

You:

You:

Pause: choice

It is time to make a stand, though this will not be popular. Applying Accounting enables you to understand that this Marshmallowing behaviour is doing no one any good. It is wasting the colleague's time and money, and it is breeding dependence among the pupils.

▼

You and colleague:

Functionally Fluent response

You set up a meeting where you explain the Functional Fluency model to your colleague. You ask him if anything about it resonates. He may well work out that he puts too much time into Marshmallowing but, if he does not, you point it out. You explain the negative aspects of this kind of care, of which the cakes are an almost literal expression. You show the colleague that the situation will be better for everyone if his time and energy goes into Structuring and Nurturing behaviour instead. Together, you make an action plan to help your colleague achieve this (Structuring) and you pledge to help him (Nurturing).

▼

Key learning

The idea that caring is not always a positive thing is a challenging one for some people to accept.

A school's culture is not forged in policies, but in the thousands of daily interactions between its staff. From challenging a colleague's Marshmallowing to building our own professional capital, the journey to a thriving staffroom is both a collective and deeply personal one. As Parker J. Palmer reminds us, 'good teaching comes from the identity and integrity of the teacher' (2007). A staff culture rooted in Functional Fluency doesn't just create a better place to work; it creates better, more authentic educators. It is this collective integrity that provides the essential foundation for the most visible and vital aspect of a school's character: its leadership.

CHAPTER 5
LEADING THE WAY: HOW TO BUILD A FUNCTIONALLY FLUENT SCHOOL CULTURE

Another day at Meadowbank Middle School is getting started. Headteacher Pat Harrison stands at the main entrance, greeting each child with a warm smile and a 'Good morning, Maya! Ready for a great day?' (Nurturing). As a new Year 5 pupil, Liam, tries to dart past, Mrs Harrison gently but firmly reminds him, 'Liam, please remember to walk in the corridors. We keep everyone safe that way' (Structuring). Clem Watson, science teacher, is also on duty at the gate. Pat was pleased to appoint a physicist, but had begun to wonder in recent weeks whether he really had the strength of character needed to be a success in the classroom. As she is pondering the wisdom of her appointment, she hears Clem, previously so hesitant, echoing her words. 'Hello, Ranjit. Ready for a great day?' Ranjit, who's always seemed a bit of a loner, beams and high-fives Clem. Suddenly, the power of senior leadership to set the culture of the whole school becomes clearer for Pat Harrison than ever before.

*Meanwhile, Chris Andrews is in the staff room, reviewing the daily bulletin. It outlines the day's schedule and any behavioural focus, and reminds staff about the new online system for logging pupil achievements. Chris realises that **detailed expectation** is now a hallmark of Meadowbank, and that this has become much more systematic and structured since the introduction of Functional Fluency. In the recent unit on weather, he had to deal with a lot of disruptive behaviour from his Year 8 class. Thinking about it now, Chris realises that his attempt to be firm and inspiring was heavy-handed and interpreted by the class as bossy and fault-finding behaviour. He makes a mental note to ensure that his expectations of his Year 8 pupils in the unit on plate tectonics are clear from the start, balancing authoritative and compassionate behaviour. He vows to report to the rest of his department on the impact this has on the learning and outcomes of the class.*

Culture starts at the top: the leader's role in setting the tone

Often within an organisation, the leadership that leaders provide their staff mimics the leadership that they themselves are receiving from their leaders, either now or in the past. This is one reason senior leadership is so important. If an appropriate leadership tone is set from those with most authority within the organisation, there is a good chance that the overall leadership culture will be a positive one that encourages all workers to grow and thrive. However, the contrary is also true. If those at the top of the organisational structure model a Dominating or Marshmallowing style of leadership, then there is a very good chance that leaders lower down will model this form of ineffective behaviour, stifling growth and development for both individuals and the organisation, and having a seriously negative impact on outcomes and job satisfaction.

There are many competing models that have been created to help us understand effective leadership. This chapter examines some of them to show that Functional Fluency can underpin all thoughtful leadership models and thus support the claim that it can provide schools with a bedrock model on which to base all their leadership planning and initiatives. Lekha Sharma, in her book *Building Culture* (Sharma, 2023), references Tom Bennett's Creating a Culture model. Table 8 takes each stage in this model and relates it to Functional Fluency.

Table 8 Bennett's Creating a Culture model and Functional Fluency

Feature	Functional Fluency elements
Visible leaders	Leaders realise, through Accounting, that they need to be seen around the school. Leaders understand stroke theory and, while out and about, engage positively with pupils (Nurturing), while also reminding some of issues and rules as necessary (Structuring).
Detailed expectations	Leaders understand the importance of effective communication, and lay out what is expected of all involved in the life of the school in a clear and detailed manner (Structuring).
Clarity of culture	Leaders explain how the school's vision is underpinned by Functional Fluency; Functional Fluency approaches are exemplified frequently so that all staff know how to address issues when they arise.
High staff support	Functional Fluency is clearly linked with the school's Continuing Professional Development (CPD) model so that all staff understand that their learning is prioritised. Links between Functional Fluency and professional capital are made explicit. Supporting and Nurturing of colleagues are explicitly balanced.

Feature	Functional Fluency elements
All pupils matter	The high standards that are expected of all pupils are made clear through Functional Fluency teaching and staff training. All pupils are encouraged to take responsibility for their own behaviour choices.
Attention to detail	The use of a clear system to underpin decision-making, in the form of Functional Fluency, encourages all staff to follow through with issues in a consistent manner.
Staff engagement	The Functional Fluency model explicitly encourages and fosters Cooperation and Spontaneity and provides a clear structure for this engagement.
Consistent practices	Functional Fluency, a consistent model, provides support for practices that encourage consistency. When new issues emerge, the model provides a trusted bedrock on which to base appropriate responses (Accounting).

This clearly demonstrates how Functional Fluency can play a role in establishing a strong and effective leadership culture in any school, as it is fundamental to each of these eight constituent elements of a strong culture.

The foundation of such a strong school culture often lies in the authenticity of its leaders. Andrew Morrish's Authentic Leader model (2022) provides a complementary perspective, showing how Functional Fluency can underpin a leader's journey towards authenticity and purpose.

The Authentic Leader: a four-part model for purposeful leadership

In his book *The Authentic Leader* (Morrish, 2022), Andrew Morrish proposes a model for leadership development that is very much in tune with Functional Fluency. Indeed, I have discussed Functional Fluency in a recording with Andrew for Myatt and Co, and he has lamented not knowing about the model when he was writing the book.

Table 9 is an outline of a Functional Fluency support plan for new school leaders with, on the right, an explanation of how the stages map against those of Morrish's four-part Authentic Leader model.

Table 9 The Authentic Leader and Functional Fluency: a draft plan to support new school leaders

Functional Fluency school leader support	The Authentic Leader model	Commentary
The school leader completes a TIFF and has a feedback discussion with a TIFF provider	*Construct* quadrant: discovering and articulating my purpose: 1. Mission 2. Vision 3. Beliefs	The discussion focuses on the effective behaviours that the school leader believes are central to the school's mission and their own personal vision. TIFF is very much about what we want to become and helps school leaders to develop the self-knowledge required to set an authentic vision for their school.
Feedback meeting resulting in an action plan	*Connect* quadrant: collaborating with others to empower them to work together: 4. Relationships 5. Trust 6. Motivation	Functional Fluency is all about optimising our behavioural choices. The action-planning process involves the school leader working with a TIFF provider to identify the behaviours that they would like to change and then converting these into specific actions to manifest in the leader's work and life in general. Setting out the actions in this way should have the impact of improving relationships, as effective behaviour patterns are reinforced and less effective ones are minimised. This, in turn, helps to build trust within the organisation. The process of co-creating the action plan with the provider and then meeting regularly with them to record progress is highly motivating for the leader.
Get on the Mat sessions to explore issues as they arise	*Commit* quadrant: unlocking potential and increasing capacity to bring about change: 7. Strategy 8. Capacity 9. Growth	School life is never straightforward. Using Get on the Mat sessions to explore situations, examining motivation and considering alternative solutions provides school leaders with clear strategies to enable them to accomplish their action plans successfully, build leadership capacity and to develop their understanding of leadership.

Functional Fluency school leader support	The Authentic Leader model	Commentary
Sharing action-plan outcomes Possible retaking of TIFF	*Create* quadrant: adding value to the community: 10. Impact	By being open and sharing their successes, leaders encourage other leaders to take up the opportunity to use Functional Fluency to build their leadership capacity, thus creating impact across the wider community. The leader can also, at this point, create a revised action plan, possibly as a result of retaking TIFF and reflecting with their provider on the changes and progress that this new set of results reveals.

The development of such authentic Functionally Fluent leaders is the critical first step, but the impact cannot remain isolated to a single office. For true transformation to occur, this individual integrity must be scaled across the entire organisation. This raises a crucial question: how does Functional Fluency provide the foundational toolkit for these broader school-improvement efforts, regardless of the specific administrative structures, such as multi-academy trusts (MAT), in which they operate?

Functional Fluency coaching and authentic leadership

To examine the ways in which Functional Fluency-based coaching can support the development of the authentic leadership that Morrish's model proposes, let's look at the coaching relationship I am developing with Graham (not his real name), a headteacher in a MAT.

During the feedback session with Graham, one of the topics that came up was the need to develop structures to ensure that he was better prepared for the school day. Graham's high scores for *grounded, alert* and *aware* behaviour are symptomatic of the level of self-awareness and honesty required to recognise and admit this. But Graham's scores for *enquiring* and *rational* were a little lower and he wanted to address this head on by consciously Structuring his school day to ensure greater personal effectiveness. This plan fits well with the **Construct** element of the Authentic Leader model.

The **Connect** element of the plan was addressed by consciously Accounting for the impact that this change in behaviour could have on colleagues. Graham acknowledged that being more organised would give him more time and energy to engage with other members of the leadership team. This process should also deliver the increased clarity of communication and sense of purpose that are characteristics of the **Commit** phase.

The **Create** quadrant of the Authentic Leader model is all about adding value and sharing success. Graham was hopeful that his new approach would be clear to his colleagues and that it would boost their confidence in him and in the institution. He hoped that his behaviour would act as a model for others, further boosting positivity. As Morrish states, when writing about impact, any initiative should be 'driven by authentic accountability' (2022). It is interesting that he should choose to use this word, which Graham's candour and openness exhibited so clearly.

Graham's coaching resulted in the co-creation of two further action points. One related to improving pupil and parent voice and the other was about increasing understanding of intersectionality. In both cases, the **Construct** element of the plan involves conscious Accounting. Graham was very clear about the need to be *grounded* to understand fully the nature of the 'hidden' curriculum that was operating within his school so that this could be challenged if necessary. He also wanted to use Accounting behaviour as a starting point for increasing his *curiosity* about the lives of others as a conscious effort to boost his empathy for others to act as a model, facilitating others to **Connect** more effectively with each other in this generally non-diverse area.

The **Commit** phase of these actions would be characterised by a broadening awareness across the school community that the school is authentically interested in the lives of its young people and a deepening understanding that everyone is valued equally. The **Create** phase of these plans would be realised when pupils started to use the language of Functional Fluency independently to de-escalate situations, and staff members across the school community initiated their own projects that celebrated or boosted diversity.

Just a few months into the coaching process, Graham was able to report a series of positive impacts, including successful student-leadership team hustings; improved school-to-home communications resulting in positive feedback; and the effective implementation of teaching and police visits to address racism and hate crime – all signs that the coaching was bearing fruit.

This example demonstrates how coaching based around Functional Fluency fits in with Morrish's model – the two are wholly compatible.

The missing piece of the puzzle: Functional Fluency as the navigation system for school improvement

The landscape of school improvement in England has changed greatly in the last two decades. Gone are the days of local-authority school-improvement teams – the environment in which I first came across Functional Fluency. In their place, we now have MATs. These vary in size, structure and approach to school improvement, and the details of this are not relevant to those outside England. However, I believe that Functional Fluency can provide a beneficial underlying structure to support school improvement across all these different types of MATs and that, by extension, this demonstrates its universal value within the wide variety of educational administrative structures across the world.

Functional Fluency is about helping people to **thrive** as opposed to just **surviving**. The model provides a map and a menu of ways of using time and energy that school leaders, teachers and pupils can all employ to increase the effectiveness and mutual benefit of their work together. Functional Fluency is a practical methodology that we can apply that helps us to act in accordance with the values of our organisation, achieve its vision and thus thrive as individuals and as an institution.

Many MATs have devised their own approaches to teaching and learning in an effort to create a shared vocabulary and institute a common approach to pedagogy across several schools. These likely focus on teaching routines that they expect all teachers to use so that there is a uniformity of experience between classrooms and sites. Often, these are pedagogical approaches that educational consultants have devised, such as the Walkthrus work created by Tom Sherrington and Oliver Caviglioli (Sherrington and Caviglioli, 2020). What these provide is clarity about how common tasks, such as questioning or retrieval practice, should be conducted. They are based on sound educational research, and are broken down into clear, illustrated steps to make training and application as easy as possible.

The five modes of behaviour that are at the core of the Functional Fluency model relate closely to and are necessary for the effective application of pedagogical models such as Walkthrus. Looking through the Contents page of the first Walkthrus book, it is striking how clear the links are with Functional Fluency, for example in the section on Behaviour and Relationships. The five-stage Walkthru on positive relationships is a great example.

Table 10 Walkthrus and Functional Fluency

Positive relationships Walkthru	Functional Fluency
1. Establish norms around clear roles and boundaries	This is *firm* and *assertive* behaviour from the Structuring mode…
2. Communicate kindness	… balanced by Nurturing, as Functional Fluency suggests is required for people to thrive.
3. Learn names and use them	This is a blend of Cooperative and Structuring mode behaviour.
4. Combine assertiveness and warmth	Again, this is very much the combination of Structuring and Nurturing behaviour that Functional Fluency suggests is the ideal way to put time and energy into developing others.
5. Always be the adult	The language here is very much that of Transactional Analysis (TA), in this encouragement of teachers (who are by definition adults) always to stay in their adult ego state and not to be drawn into either parent or child ego states, whatever the provocation. Functional Fluency builds on TA, as explained in earlier chapters.

Other Walkthrus can also be analysed in terms of their use of the effective modes of Functional Fluency behaviour. For example, the sequence 'process questions' encourages teachers to use Accounting and Spontaneous mode behaviours so that their own thinking is clearly modelled to the pupils, who then have opportunities to explain their own thinking. This sequence thus encourages teachers to blend the effective behaviour modes and to provide circumstances that make it likely that pupils will respond using effective modes of behaviour too: the Structuring, Nurturing and Accounting behaviours that we saw earlier in the learning feedback loop.

Functional Fluency can thus be visualised as a tool that could be used within a MAT or other form of school administrative structure, alongside their values and pedagogical models, to help them achieve their vision by providing a framework that empowers the development of the authentic and genuine relationships that we all need if we are to fulfil our learning potential.

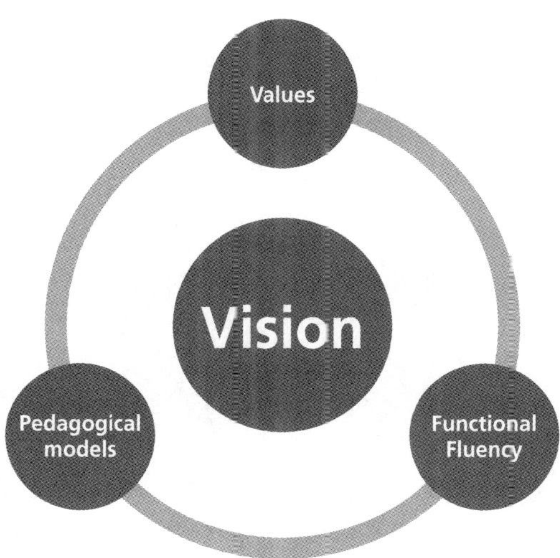

Figure 15 School vision and: Functional Fluency, values and pedagogical models

An alternate conceptualisation would put Functional Fluency – given that it is about fundamental human behaviour – at the centre, empowering the achievement of the administration's vision and values, improving teaching and learning and developing leadership and management, so that all can flourish.

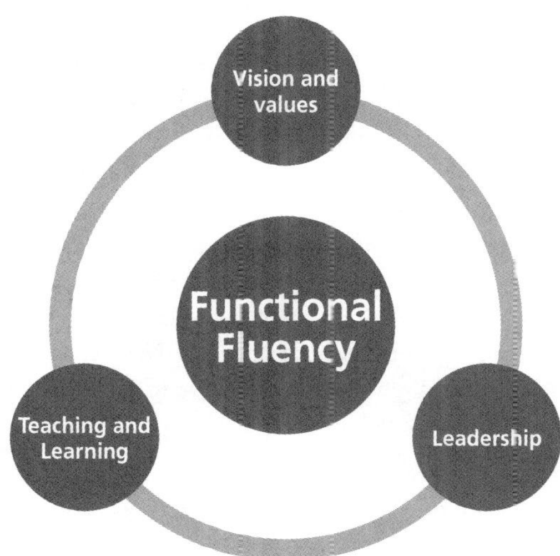

Figure 16 Functional Fluency and: vision and values; leadership; and teaching and learning

Figure 17 demonstrates the potential for Functional Fluency to contribute to school improvement across all the areas identified for judgements in the Ofsted Inspection Framework 2025.

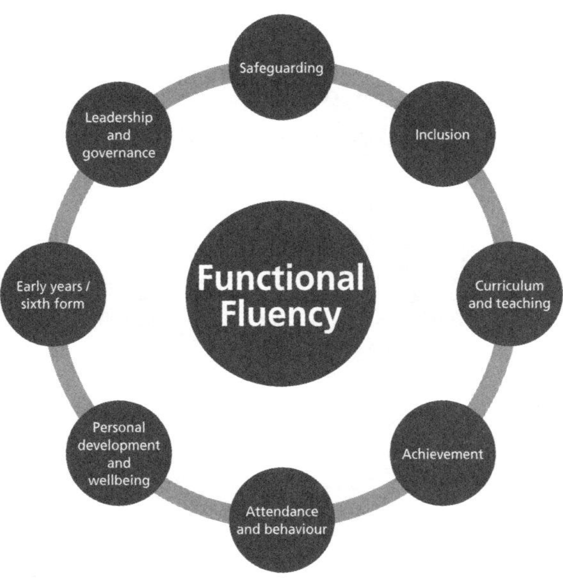

Figure 17 Functional Fluency and the 2025 Ofsted Framework

The relevance of Functional Fluency to most of these areas is evident. The only area where it is not central is perhaps 'curriculum', though the inclusion with the Certified Functional Fluency Teacher Programme of a structure and set of lesson outlines to teach Functional Fluency points to relevance here too. Similarly, conducting yourself in a Functionally Fluent manner, whether as an educator or a pupil, has a beneficial impact on achievement also, as you guide and direct others or yourself in ways that effectively keep the goals of learning and academic performance in mind while balancing this with fairness and self-care to avoid burnout or undue anxiety. Other areas, such as 'attendance and behaviour', 'personal development and wellbeing' and 'inclusion' are covered more explicitly elsewhere in this book, demonstrating their clear links with Functional Fluency.

It is perhaps worth pointing out that, just because Functional Fluency is relevant to these judgement areas, does not mean that they are aspects of school life that should be judged in this way. There is a strong body of opinion that this approach to school accountability is highly damaging, and I would refer readers who wish to know more to Andrew Morrish's excellent book *Beyond Belief* (2025), which includes a short contribution by me about Functional Fluency and accountability.

Within the multifaceted endeavour of school improvement, curriculum leadership stands out as a critical area where a school's values are enacted. Functional Fluency, with its emphasis on thoughtful Accounting, is particularly pertinent here.

Functional Fluency: the bedrock of an inclusive culture

Throughout this book, a key theme that I hope is clear is that Functional Fluency is directly linked to inclusion. The focus on improving relationships between everyone in the school community is about helping all pupils and staff to feel included so that they can thrive and fulfi their potential. Functionally Fluent interactions, day in, day out, are what build this type of community, where all feel psychologically safe. These interactions are so much more secure if they are based on the shared vocabulary of Functional Fluency, the empathy-building practices of Get on the Mat activities and the robust truth-seeking structure of the Accounting Framework.

By explicitly equipping teachers and staff with a structure that encourages them to balance high expectations (Structuring) with the deep, individualised support (Nurturing) that every pupil, particularly those with additional needs or from marginalised groups, requires to succeed, Functional Fluency can be a cornerstone of the inclusive teaching and culture our pupils need.

Your leadership journey: practical steps to becoming a Functionally Fluent leader

In recognising the value that Functional Fluency brings to such crucial areas as the curriculum, the practical question for leaders becomes: how can we cultivate this approach? While the Certified Functional Fluency Teacher Programme (CFFTP) offers a clear path for teachers, what are the equivalent steps for leadership development?

The first and most obvious is shared with the CFFTP: engage a qualified TIFF provider, complete your TIFF profile and have a feedback session with them. This will give you useful insights into your current behavioural choices. Through discussion with your provider, you will identify developmental action points that will help you move towards the more effective choices that will enable you to use your finite time and energy more effectively so that you and those you lead can thrive. Ideally, this would lead into regular coaching sessions in which you revisit your TIFF profile and your resulting action plan to ensure that you are maintaining your focus and making the behavioural changes that have been identified. Coaching sessions provide the opportunity to reflect on challenges and gains you have made and to identify the benefits to you and to others that these changes are bringing. This will be highly motivational – noting the gains you are making will encourage you to maintain the coaching and your plans to become more Functionally Fluent. Gaining positive feedback from colleagues and others about the benefits they are perceiving will further enhance this sense of progress.

Having successfully used Functional Fluency coaching to improve your own leadership, you may decide to bring in colleagues, encouraging them to make use of Functional Fluency-based coaching. This will contribute to increased use of the terminology of the model across the school as it begins to be embedded in the processes of the institution. This will itself further reinforce the perceived value of the approach. Individuals within the organisation could further escalate the involvement by taking on training to become TIFF providers or Get on the Mat facilitators, so that the school is no longer reliant on external provision and instead can begin to build up its own in-house capacity. (See the Functional Fluency International website for details.)

Given the economic realities of school life, engaging external coaches is not always possible, but this should not put off school leaders from starting to work with Functional Fluency. One way is to work through a copy of *The Fluent Leader* (Fawcett, 2023), making notes on ideas that come up that are applicable in your work context. You could perhaps set up a monthly book group with colleagues, where you all read a chosen chapter in preparation and then discuss how you can use the ideas within it.

A self-evaluation exercise that school leaders could do involves carefully considering their own behaviour in the light of the nine modes of behaviour identified in the Functional Fluency model. Taking 100% to represent the sum of all your time and energy, and thinking realistically about your behaviour choices over the previous month, allocate a number to each of the nine modes. Ensure that each mode has a number (no zeros allowed) and that the total adds up to 100. It is useful to write a sentence for each mode to justify your score and to capture your thinking process. This gives you a basis for considering how you could adapt your behaviour choices in the coming month so that the totals in the golden (lightly shaded) modes increase and those of the purple (darkly shaded) modes decrease.

In Table 11, the school leader has worked up an action for each of the golden modes to guide their behaviour choices for the coming month.

Table 11 Functional Fluency self-evaluation

Dominating 10%	Marshmallowing 7%
Structuring 13% • Try to focus on possible solutions rather than blaming colleagues for problems.	Nurturing 12% • I know I am good at delegating. I need to continue to trust colleagues to take responsibility.
Accounting 16% • I am highly evaluative in my work, but I need to ensure this does not lead to a lack of decisiveness.	
Cooperative 14% • A focus for my leadership this month will be encouraging colleagues to engage positively with challenges and not to be placating or submissive. I will aim to model this myself.	Spontaneous 12% • I would benefit from focusing more of my time on activities that I really enjoy.
Compliant / Resistant 9%	Immature 7%

After a month, you could review the situation and create a new set of figures and some new action points to improve the balance between golden and purple modes. In this way, a self-evaluation and improvement cycle develops as you strive to use Functional Fluency as a practical tool to improve your leadership.

If you are looking for an approach that is less costly than one-to-one Functional Fluency coaching but more motivating than this self-evaluation method, the Functionally Fluent School Leaders Programme might be the answer. This involves a TIFF questionnaire and individual feedback session followed by five monthly group sessions, each focused on a different golden mode. In this way, a group of up to 12 school leaders, who may or may not know each other in advance, explore the Functional Fluency model in detail; consider scenarios using the Get on the Mat methodology; and receive feedback on their progress towards their Action Plan targets from the programme leader and their fellow school leaders. Go to either the Functional Fluency International website (https://functionalfluency.com) or my own website (www.swillshawconsulting.co.uk and follow the link to 'coaching programmes') for more details.

Unlocking your team's potential: the five keys to thriving

As leaders develop their own Functional Fluency, a natural extension is to foster this within their teams. Sam Croome (2023) has written a detailed and insightful book about the role of teams in school leadership. He identifies five key elements that characterise high-performing, thriving teams in schools. Each of these elements interacts or correlates with aspects of Functional Fluency in ways I think will resonate with readers.

Table 12 Croome's model

Croome's model	Description	Interaction with Functional Fluency
Team Belonging	'Once a team's belonging, identity and safety have been established, the team can immerse itself in its core work.'	Knowing the Functional Fluency model and having a shared language with which to talk about behaviour can increase psychological safety and the team's sense of collective identity.
Team Alignment	'Together, the team will agree upon why it is here and what it aims to do, with team goals to work on together.'	By working with Functional Fluency to clarify the school's vision and values and using the model to think about what kinds of behaviour these translate into, the team's alignment can strengthen.
Team Operations	'Operational areas of team life may provide fewer inspirational soundbites, but their impact is high leverage; this is the engine room of team process and performance.'	Developing Functionally Fluent approaches to key operations, such as team meetings and communications, can hugely enhance the clarity of all aspects of the team's work.
Team Dynamics	'It's important that the team and its leader are aware of motivation theory and have an understanding of needs models such as self-determination theory.'	By focusing on the effective use of time and energy, Functional Fluency can directly benefit team dynamics, ensuring improved understanding of individuals' motivations and how these can contribute to team endeavours.
Team Development	'Constructive team debriefs add a huge amount to a team's development, because a high-performing team considers one of its core remits to be the capacity to learn and improve.'	The team's ongoing use of the Functional Fluency model in activities such as Get on the Mat sessions ensures that the focus remains on co-constructed learning.

It is reassuring to note the connectedness between Croome's model (2023) and Functionally Fluent behaviour and the ways in which Functional Fluency can help a leader to develop the various elements of Croome's model within the team they lead.

Croome also writes interestingly about the factors that lead individuals within a team to be motivated to work hard and accomplish their goals. The model he relies on most to help understand this issue is self-determination theory (SDT), which stems from the work of Deci and Ryan (1985). This proposes that the fundamental psychological needs that we all have if we are to function effectively are **autonomy, relatedness** and **competence**.

It is worth reflecting on each of these in the light of Functional Fluency:

- Functional Fluency has a strong focus on the personal **autonomy** of the individual. The model is predicated on the idea that we all have volition and make behavioural choices many times every day. These are not inevitable: we could make different choices. So, an organisational focus on Functional Fluency should result in emphasising to the individuals within it that they have autonomy; SDT suggests that this is motivational.

- The essence of a teacher's role revolves around **relatedness**. We all have a need to interact with, connect to and care for others, and these drives are especially relevant within the teaching context. They are also very much what Functional Fluency is all about – the 'fluency' of the name of the model relates precisely to how we engage and interact with others. It is a model to help us to see when we are relating effectively with others and when this is less effective.

- Functional Fluency also has a dual relationship with the concept of **competence**. We have a drive to do things well; this is what teaching is all about. Teachers exist to help pupils develop ever-greater competence. The role of Functional Fluency here is to help teachers consider the best ways in which they can work with pupils to do this. Just as a teacher who is operating in a Functionally Fluent manner is more effective, so a pupil who approaches the subject of their desired competence, whether that be mathematics, art or geography, has a greater chance of success if they do so in a Functionally Fluent way. This dual or meta impact of Functional Fluency indicates the fundamental way in which the model relates to human motivation, and also the complex and multi-faceted ways in which knowledge of the model helps teachers and leaders to operate in a more effective manner.

To support teams in cultivating these thriving dynamics, a dedicated tool, the Functional Fluency Team Scan, is being developed to build on the principles of individual TIFF.

A mirror for your team: introducing the Functional Fluency Team Scan

Over the last few years, I have been part of a team that has been developing a version of the TIFF questionnaire for use with teams: the Functional Fluency Team Scan. Each member of any team undertaking it will be allocated access to a version of the questionnaire and will answer the questions, not about their own behaviour but about that of the group. The responses will be aggregated, and the team will work with a trained provider to identify effective behaviours they can aim to use more, and ineffective behaviours that they will work to reduce.

This development builds on previous work with teams that Functional Fluency professionals have instigated, using the individual TIFF results of team members. The example that follows is based on work I have developed with teams of people who work together in the same school, including pastoral teams, the administrative team, departmental teams and a team made up of a headteacher and his PA.

The team are all given copies of the scaffolded discussion sheet (Table 13). The provider leads them through the structure at the top of this, working with them to devise answers to these questions. Prompts such as 'We work together on…' appear very straightforward, but it is surprising how often teams have never sat down together to discuss their purpose. This question sometimes elicits valuable information about a lack of any clear understanding of purpose across a team: identifying this at an early stage is vital for making serious progress.

The subsequent prompts are designed to encourage a general discussion about the kinds of behaviour that are likely to result in effective team functioning. Again, this can be highly instructive. It leads on to discussion of how the team, the school's pupils and other relevant groups all benefit if this team makes more effective behaviour choices. This sets the scene helpfully, clarifying the importance of the work the team is engaged in.

The provider then guides the team through a discussion using the prompts in the boxes. These enable the team to consider, in a more precise and structured way than they have probably done before, the ways in which they currently use the effective modes of behaviour as identified in their TIFF, and how they could make even better use of this time and energy in the future. They then look together at the effective modes of behaviour that only some of them utilise. The provider encourages them to think through practical ways in which they can make use of those individuals who already behave in these effective ways and how they can encourage the others to start putting more time and energy into these behaviours. This may involve creating contracts between individuals within the team to encourage or remind each other of particular behaviours they would benefit from using more often.

This may develop into a discussion about the effective modes of behaviour that none of the team currently uses as often as they could and the agreement of collective actions they can take to address this. Finally, the group is led through a discussion of the less effective purple (darkly shaded) pitfall behaviours that they are currently prone to, and the co-construction of plans to help them avoid these behaviours in future.

No single meeting is going to revolutionise team functioning in a permanent way. A series of meetings in which the team work with the provider to discuss, create and reshape plans and evaluate progress is required. The long-term nature of this process helps maximise its chance of effectiveness; it is also why it is so important to establish the potential gains clearly at the start of the process, and for the provider to revisit these regularly.

Table 13 Scaffolded team-development outline

Name of team:
Institution:
Team members:
We work together on:
The Functional Fluency modes of behaviour that we need for us to work together effectively are:
If we were able to be more Functionally Fluent, this would bring the following benefits for: us: our pupils: our colleagues: our community:
The **effective** modes of behaviour that our TIFFs suggest we are **all** likely to use are: The implications of this are:
The **complementary effective** modes of behaviour that **one** of the team is likely to use are: The implications of this are:

<table>
<tr><td>The effective modes of behaviour that we need to work together to use more are:

The advantages if we could do this include:</td></tr>
<tr><td>The ineffective modes of behaviour we need to work together to use less are:

The advantages of putting less of our time and energy into these modes of behaviour are:</td></tr>
<tr><td>Review:

</td></tr>
</table>

The Team Scan is being piloted prior to its launch, but it is already clear that it will represent a major step forward for Functional Fluency, providing a powerful new tool to enable coaches and school teams to work together with increasing insight.

This new tool for enhancing team effectiveness naturally leads to an examination of one of the most critical and time-consuming team activities: the meeting.

What if your meetings actually worked? A blueprint for productive collaboration

School leaders spend a lot of their time in meetings but, from personal experience, I would suggest that these are rarely a useful use of the time of those involved. Because of this, it is worth considering an alternative approach that might free up thinking and result in more considered decisions. The potential gains are huge, as you will realise if you calculate the cost of any meeting by adding up the hourly pay rate of all those involved.

So, what might a Functionally Fluent meeting structure be like?

Here, I am indebted to the work of Nancy Kline on thinking and thinking environments (Kline, 1999) and Liz Wiseman on multipliers (Wiseman, 2017).

Effective meetings start with a clearly defined focus. There is little that is more disconcerting for a school leader than going to a meeting without a clear idea of the main topic of discussion or clarity about what success in that meeting might look and feel like. I have attended many meetings where the topic is sprung on the team at the last minute, or indeed after the meeting has begun, and this results in a feeling of lack of control and unpreparedness. This is often what the type of leaders that Wiseman describes as 'diminishers' choose to do, as it ensures that they control things (because they are the only ones who know what is about to be discussed). It ensures that other leaders cannot contribute properly; thus the existing leader's pre-eminence is maintained. But it results in a shameful waste of time and talent, not to mention money.

Table 14 provides a structure for a Functionally Fluent meeting.

Table 14 A Functionally Fluent meeting structure

Meeting element	Features
Clarity around meeting focus and successful outcome	Parameters of the discussion are agreed, including how much meeting time will be given to the item. This is a contracting session where the team agrees on what a successful outcome of this item will look like. By clarifying the aims of the discussion, everyone involved knows why the item is being given time and what gains will be made by reaching an agreement on actions to be taken. Structuring, Cooperative and Accounting behaviours are prevalent here.
Discussion	The topic owner outlines the topic, then all those present have an opportunity to contribute. As they speak, each person takes a representative counter and places it on the Functional Fluency model to represent the mode of behaviour they feel they are using, and which they are advocating in their response to the topic.
Chair	The chairperson uses Accounting behaviour throughout to work out when contributions need to be extended through judicious questioning and when they need to be curtailed because they are over-long, rambling or off the point. The chair also considers whether it is necessary to request contributions from specific team members who have not spoken. It should be accepted that silence on a topic is a reasonable response – not all team members have relevant experience on all topics and not wasting meeting time by talking needlessly is an acknowledged sign of a successful team and meeting structure. The chair can encourage the team to consider responses to the topic that incorporate any of the effective golden modes of behaviour that have so far not been used. This ensures that all relevant approaches are considered.
Decision	A decision is reached. Whenever possible, this should involve the agreement of all team members, but it must be acknowledged that this is not always possible. Resulting actions are noted, along with the modes of behaviour needed to complete them effectively. The team should work together to ensure that all effective modes of behaviour are included, as this will give the decision the highest chance of success. Attention should be paid to Accounting, with the team carefully considering how they will monitor the actions taken to ensure they are effectively implemented, and that the consequences are those intended.

The theoretical applications of Functional Fluency for teams and leaders come to life through the experiences of practitioners. The following insight from Joanna Williams, a therapist and TIFF provider, offers a compelling case study of these principles in action.

Functional Fluency in Action

Joanna Williams: beyond meetings – a case study of whole-self leadership with Functional Fluency in schools

As a registered British Association for Counselling and Psychotherapy (BACP) psychotherapist, executive coach and leadership consultant, Joanna Williams helps individuals and organisations navigate the challenges of growth, wellbeing and fulfilment in both their professional and personal lives. Combining psychotherapy and coaching, Joanna helps leaders understand how unhelpful patterns such as over-adaptation, perfectionism and people-pleasing impact their wellbeing, relationships and leadership practice.

As a licensed TIFF provider, Joanna uses the Functional Fluency model to help clients explore their behaviour and relationships, especially the crucial relationship with self. This integrated approach is particularly valuable in schools, where culture, accountability pressures and personal wellbeing are deeply connected.

The following scenario is a composite example, inspired by real practice, with details changed to protect confidentiality in line with UK Council for Psychotherapy (UKCP) and BACP guidelines. Any resemblance to an actual individual is entirely coincidental. The practitioner's name is included with full respect for professional transparency and to illustrate real-world application, but no client can be identified from this material.

Leadership isn't just about what happens in the boardroom; it's also about what's happening within the leader.

A senior leader in a multi-school trust sought support from Joanna after experiencing rising stress and an increasing sense of disconnection from their role and themselves. While the presenting concern focused on burnout and performance pressures, it soon became clear that the roots lay deeper:

in longstanding patterns of perfectionism, over-adaptation and people-pleasing – strategies that had once kept them safe but now fuelled anxiety and exhaustion.

Working with Joanna, the leader undertook a process that blended coaching with therapeutic exploration. The TIFF profile offered a clear lens through which to view their day-to-day behaviour patterns – but the real work lay in understanding 'why'.

Together, they revisited fundamental beliefs that had shaped the leader's identity: a need to be useful, a fear of letting others down, a conviction that worth depended on always 'getting it right'. This exploration helped the leader to see how these beliefs led to patterns of micro-management, blurred boundaries and unsustainable self-sacrifice – not only at work, but at home.

The unique strength of using Functional Fluency in this context is its ability to act as a bridge: the model gave the leader a structured, practical way to check in with their behaviour moment to moment, while the therapeutic work addressed the underlying emotional drivers and relational dynamics that fed these behaviours.

As the work progressed, the leader became more able to pause, notice when they were slipping into over-adapting or rescuing and consciously shift towards more balanced modes: using Accounting when assessing what was truly needed; Structuring when setting healthy boundaries; Cooperative when inviting others in, rather than carrying it all alone.

The leader's deepened self-awareness started to transform how they approached meetings and conversations. Instead of using meetings to maintain tight control and achieve unspoken perfectionistic standards, they began to see them as thinking spaces where they could model trust and shared responsibility and even challenge.

However, the process also surfaced systemic realities: the wider culture still rewarded over-functioning and discouraged vulnerability. Part of the leader's growth was recognising that they could not change this alone – and that staying true to their values might mean stepping away from environments that undermined their wellbeing.

In time, they chose to move to a role that allowed them to lead in a more authentic, balanced way, taking with them the tools to keep using the

Functional Fluency model as a check-in – not just for leadership practice, but for their ongoing personal wellbeing.

Joanna's reflection

Working with school leaders means recognising that their professional roles are rarely separate from their personal lives. The pressures of inspection, performance targets and accountability in the UK education system can amplify unhelpful patterns such as perfectionism, over-adaptation and people-pleasing. Many leaders feel they must constantly hold everything together – often at great personal cost.

When coaching or offering therapeutic support in this context, it is vital to contract clearly and maintain robust boundaries, ensuring that work remains safe, ethical and within our competence. Regular supervision and peer reflection are essential when we find ourselves working at the edges of therapy and coaching, especially when power dynamics, organisational cultures and histories of trauma surface.

Sharing this illustrative scenario demonstrates how Functional Fluency can bridge the gap between individual insight and day-to-day leadership practice. In schools, this means more than just running better meetings – it means helping leaders reconnect with themselves, challenge unhelpful patterns and model healthier ways of working for their teams.

By supporting leaders to develop greater self-awareness and behavioural flexibility, we can contribute – even in small ways – to cultures where staff wellbeing and pupil success are not in tension, but part of the same healthy system. Protecting the confidentiality of those we work with is part of this wider responsibility: we honour our clients by safeguarding their stories, while sharing what we learn to benefit the wider sector.

Joanna Williams' account illustrates a profound individual transformation through Functional Fluency therapy and coaching. The principles of Functional Fluency are equally impactful when applied to the dynamics of an entire leadership team, as demonstrated in Leona Bishop's work with a school in the Caribbean.

A Caribbean case study

Organisational and team coach Leona Bishop collaborated closely with a school in the Caribbean to build overall school effectiveness. She writes about this process in a detailed case study (Bishop, 2024), where she explains how she used Functional Fluency to understand the dynamics of the leadership team:

> She [Bishop] makes sense of this complex situation by viewing it through the lens of the Functional Fluency model in order to pinpoint exactly what the problem is.

The senior leadership team of this school is made up of three people: the principal and two deputy directors (DD1 and DD2). Completion of TIFF questionnaires and subsequent feedback meetings revealed the energy drains (ways in which energy was being lost in less effective behaviour) and energy gains (types of more effective behaviour that need more time and energy) shown in Table 15.

Table 15 Energy drains and energy gains

Role	Energy drains	Energy gains
Principal	*Disorganised* Dependent on deputy director 1 to organise things Failing to address issues *Inhibited* *Placating* (Compliant) Frustrated *Bossy* (Dominating) *Blaming* (self)	Needs to put more time and energy into: *Evaluating* (Accounting) *Authoritative* (Structuring) *Expressive* (Spontaneous) *Compassionate* (Nurturing)
Deputy director 1	Bogged down by organisational tasks Spends too much time helping and giving attention to others (Marshmallowing) Others leave things for her to clear up (Immature)	Empowering colleagues (Structuring and Nurturing) Setting firm limits (Structuring) Establishing high expectations (Structuring) Responding more empathically to own needs (Nurturing)
Deputy director 2	Too content to allow colleagues to take over work (Immature) Happy with success of small features but not contributing enough to overall success (Compliant)	Contributing ideas to help solve issues for principal and DD1 (Cooperative and Structuring)

Looking at their work through the lens of Functional Fluency allows the team to realise how they have developed less effective patterns of behaviour and communication. The situation is played out in microcosm in the team's meetings, as shown in Example 12.

Example 12 A Caribbean case study

Situation

Team meetings are unorganised (Immature). The principal tends to think out loud, using DD1 and DD2 as sounding boards.

Principal:

▼

Immediate thoughts and feelings

The principal thinks this approach is Accounting but actually it is self-serving (Immature).
DD1 and DD2 go along with the principal (Compliant / Resistant).
DD1 is increasingly annoyed with the principal (Dominating) but is also annoyed with themselves for not saying anything (Compliant).
DD2 just puts up with it (Compliant) and stops listening (Immature).

Principal:

DD1 and DD2:

▼

Pause: choice

Collectively, the team need to take responsibility (*authoritative, assertive*) for making the meetings more effective to stop wasting their own time and energy and also to provide impetus to the school-improvement ideas.

Team:

▼

Functionally Fluent response

They decide that each meeting should have a clear objective and amount of time allocated to it (Accounting and Structuring). They consider each other's needs (Nurturing).
They each agree to provide constructive criticism to get them back on track when they begin to drift (Cooperative).
They start to express themselves more effectively, make more progress and have more fun (Spontaneous).

Team:

▼

Key learning

A less effective behaviour choice by one member of a team can have negative consequences which lead to further less effective behaviour choices by others. The Functional Fluency model provides teams with the vocabulary and the opportunity to address these issues, without blame. The result should save everyone involved a lot of time and energy.

As Bishop (2024) points out, 'Behaviour in school is inseparable from educational achievement, safety, welfare and wellbeing, and all other aspects of learning. Its correct direction is equally crucial and should be viewed as an issue of the highest strategic importance. Behaviour does not manage itself, except haphazardly'. The behaviour of the adults – those who direct the path that the institution will take, setting the models that the pupils will inevitably follow – is therefore in need of the most careful evaluation.

This example shows how one institution was able to use Functional Fluency to make its meetings more effective and, in the process, recover a lot of time and energy they would otherwise have wasted. Using the Functional Fluency model as a lens through which to view and evaluate the actions of the leadership team provided Bishop with a series of insights that enabled the top layer of the school's decision-making structure to become far more effective. This, in turn, facilitated the development of more Functionally Fluent practices at other levels within the organisation, resulting in a series of radical improvements in the way the institution delivered education, with consequent benefits to the pupils: the true aim of school-improvement work.

Running a meeting

If adopting Functionally Fluent meetings is too big a step for your team, here is an example of how you can use the model to inform your approach and improve the effectiveness of this important team time.

Example 13 Running a meeting

Situation

You must organise a team meeting next Monday evening. You find these meetings difficult. Several of the team members resent (Compliant / Resistant) having to attend, and their body language makes this clear (Immature). Changes are needed in the way the team operates, but these individuals will resist any attempts to bring in new practices.

Team:

▼

Immediate thoughts and feelings

You are using up energy being *anxious* (Compliant / Resistant). Other people's *defiant* behaviour is sucking you into this reaction. Because you do not enjoy running these meetings, you have put off preparing for it until the last minute (Immature). This enables some team members to claim prior engagements (Compliant / Resistant). You are tempted to buy several cakes and packets of biscuits in the hope that this will improve the mood (Marshmallowing). To avoid confrontation, you are likely to resort to placating or submissive behaviour (Marshmallowing), even though you know it is wrong, as you have been appointed to lead (Structure and Nurture) this team. As a way out, you use over-indulgent behaviour (Marshmallowing), wasting your money on cakes and biscuits for the team, which they should not be eating anyway, as a way of buying their favour – but you are then even more upset when it doesn't work.

You:

Team:

Pause: choice

You take some time to think about what these meetings are for (Accounting – *grounded*). You regain clarity, recalling that the focus is all about improving learning opportunities for young people so that they can have the most fulfilling lives possible. You consider each member of the team and realise that they all have the best interests of the young people at heart.

By returning to first principles, you are avoiding the dangers of reacting. You use *alert* and *aware* (Accounting) behaviour to gain a better understanding of your colleagues and their motivation.

You:

You pull together a plan for the meeting and circulate the agenda to the team (Structuring), asking for comments and additional items prior to the meeting. You also think through the items you will need to cover to move the team forward over the rest of the year and you allocate these to the remaining meetings (Accounting and Structuring). You think about each team member in turn and what motivates them to improve. You draft a short but powerful piece to read out at the start of the meeting in which you outline your unhappiness with the current situation, explain your motivation to improve things for the young people and ask your team members for their support. You make an appointment with your line manager to share this statement with her prior to the meeting to ensure she is supportive (Structuring).

You are now responding, using *assertive* behaviour. By planning, you will reduce your *anxiety* and the team will appreciate that you are treating them as adults. You remind everyone why you are all in this job and you can approach the meeting *confident* that you are well prepared and have the support of your senior leaders.

Functionally Fluent response

You:

▼

Key learning

Planning is important, and so is insisting that colleagues take their professional responsibilities seriously. The Accounting toolbox helps you achieve both tasks effectively.

Effectively managing team interactions such as meetings is crucial, as is navigating personal transitions within leadership, such as taking on a new role.

Example 14 Taking on a new role

Situation

You:

You have been promoted to a new post. You applied for it rather optimistically and are now very daunted (*anxious*) that you will actually have to step up and take on the role.

▼

Immediate thoughts and feelings

You are allowing yourself to choose Immature and Compliant / Resistant behaviours. You are also choosing *fault-finding* behaviour from the dominant mode – dominating yourself.

Thinking about a previous team leader you have worked for, you consider setting out a clear plan and insisting that it is carried out to the letter, with penalties for non-compliance. Then you flip to thinking that what you need to do is listen to others and take your lead from them.

You appear to be alternating between Dominating and Compliant / Resistant behaviour. Neither of these is likely to prove effective.

You:

Pause: choice

You take some time to think about your original application; what you said you would do if appointed; and the comments the headteacher made after your appointment. You realise that you have a lot of skills and expertise to bring to this role and that you care a lot about the success of this team (Accounting).

By choosing to use *grounded* behaviour, you are getting a better perspective on your situation.

You are using *aware* behaviour to get a better understanding of your own motivation.

You:

Functionally Fluent response

You spend some time preparing for your new role, thinking carefully about the direction you want to take and how this will be beneficial for the young people, the school, its community and yourself (Accounting).

You realise the need to give your colleagues an opportunity to share their ideas and possible fears about the future so that you can reassure them. You understand that your vision for the role is valid and that you have a responsibility to explain it with clarity and verve (Cooperative, Spontaneous).

You have realised the importance of balancing Structuring and Nurturing if your work in this new role is to be a success.

You:

Key learning

You have been appointed to this role because leaders believe you have the capacity to be successful. Functional Fluency can ensure that you do not let them down.

Stepping into a new leadership position often comes with heightened scrutiny and pressure, akin to the stress experienced during school inspections, particularly in such contexts as the English Ofsted system.

In England, the possibility of a visit from Ofsted can have a negative impact on the professional and personal behaviour of teachers and leaders – in stark contrast to the school improvement that is the intended outcome of such accountability measures. Example 15 shows how the mindful deployment of Functional Fluency can help to alleviate anxiety and support more effective behaviour choices.

Example 15 Inspection stress

Situation

You become increasingly *aware* that many of your actions and much of your work is designed to meet the needs of Ofsted on their next visit, even though this could be at any time in the next two years.

You:

Immediate thoughts and feelings

This is making you a tense and irritable teacher (Compliant / Resistant). It is beginning to have an impact on your home life, as you spend too much time at weekends and in the evenings trying to write policy documents and predict lines of inquiry.

You:

Pause: choice

You spend some time in conscious Accounting. You are *alert* and *aware* of the work you and colleagues are completing every day. You *evaluate* the impact of your work on the school's pupils. You acknowledge there are things that are not perfect, but you also recognise that everyone is working hard for the benefit of the young people.

You:

Functionally Fluent response

You make a conscious decision that this is 'good enough' and, using a blend of Structuring and Nurturing behaviours, plan to stop doing any unnecessary work so that, instead, you can focus on doing what really matters **well**. As a result of this process, you immediately begin to feel calmer. You gain a much tighter focus on what matters in your work, which you are confident will benefit you when Ofsted do arrive, and you become a much more pleasant person to live with (Cooperative).

You:

Key learning

There are many ways in which schools are accountable; inspection is only one of them. If you use the golden-mode behaviours of Functional Fluency, you will be able to maintain a sense of reality that will help you to avoid burnout and be a long-term success.

Beyond managing external pressures and personal anxieties, a key leadership responsibility involves addressing challenges within the team, such as supporting and guiding underperforming colleagues.

When those you lead are not discharging their responsibilities in appropriate ways, there comes a time when, as a leader, you need to take action. In Example 16, some of the deep empathy (Nurturing) for others that Viv Grant (2024a) advocates begins to uncover the root of the problem, enabling a new and more effective type of behaviour to be initiated.

Example 16 Underperforming colleagues

Situation

You notice that a colleague is no longer following the agreed departmental procedure for booking equipment. As a result, things colleagues need for lessons are not available as they should be, and you and a couple of other teachers have recently had to make last-minute adjustments.

Colleague:

▼

Immediate thoughts and feelings

You feel angry (Compliant / Resistant). The colleague knows the agreed procedure well but, through *selfishness* (Immature), is not following it and is *inconsiderately* (Immature) not thinking about the implications.

You:

Colleague:

▼

<table>
<tr>
<td>Pause: choice</td>
<td>Taking the time to think through this situation, you use an enquiring (Accounting) approach to ask yourself why this colleague has started behaving differently. You decide to speak to him, using a curious (Spontaneous) strategy to find out what is going on in his life.</td>
<td>You:

</td>
</tr>
<tr>
<td>Functionally Fluent response</td>
<td>After initially being inhibited (Compliant / Resistant) and apologising for the issue in a rather childish manner (Immature), the colleague begins to respond to your approach. He tells you that he is struggling to cope with the pressures of the job and reveals that there are several issues going on in his private life that are making things difficult. While you are unable to resolve these external issues, it is clear that talking openly about them has been helpful and your colleague agrees that his behaviour has been selfish. Together, you make a plan to review the equipment you will need to book for the following week at lunchtime each Friday – a plan that will help you both have more relaxing weekends in the future (Structuring, Nurturing).</td>
<td>You:

Colleague:

Both:

</td>
</tr>
<tr>
<td>Key learning</td>
<td>Teaching is an intricate and demanding role, and teachers are complex individuals with lots going on in their lives. If something is not right at home, it has an impact on professional performance. Functional Fluency can help identify these issues and suggest ways forward.</td>
<td></td>
</tr>
</table>

Conscious behavioural choices and the effective use of finite time and energy empower leaders to build trust; foster positive school cultures; enhance wellbeing for themselves and their staff; and ultimately contribute to improved student outcomes. Introducing Functional Fluency into a school's leadership practice is a developmental journey. While it requires commitment, the model's inherent flexibility and focus on starting with self-awareness (often through TIFF) allow for gradual integration. The benefits of more effective communication, improved team dynamics and better energy management typically encourage wider adoption, as colleagues experience the positive impact firsthand.

Ultimately, leadership is an act of culture creation. Whether viewed through the frameworks of Tom Bennett, or through Andrew Morrish's journey to authenticity, a leader's primary role is to set the conditions for others to thrive. Functional Fluency is not just another tool for a leader's toolkit; it is the very philosophy that guides the architect. It empowers leaders to move beyond simply running a school to truly building a community – a place where trust is the currency; time and energy are spent wisely; and every individual feels seen. This foundation of trust and shared purpose is what makes the crucial partnership with the families we serve not just possible, but powerful.

CHAPTER 6
BUILDING BRIDGES: PARTNERING WITH PARENTS AND CARERS FOR PUPIL SUCCESS

Pat Harrison, headteacher, is not looking forward to her after-school meeting with Jamie Prentice's dad. He is renowned for being difficult and, though Pat knows that Jamie has been in some minor trouble recently, she doesn't really know why Mr Prentice wants to see her.

When he marches into her office smiling, Pat Harrison starts to relax. It turns out that Mr Prentice has met with several staff members recently, including Chris Andrews, regarding an incident on a humanities trip to a local castle. All the teachers have referenced Functional Fluency in their conversations with him, explaining that Jamie needs to understand the distinction between Spontaneous and Immature behaviour. Mr Prentice has taken a copy of the model home and is using it with all his children. 'They are even starting to use it themselves,' he says, going on: 'I'd just like to congratulate you on this initiative, Mrs Harrison. I don't know where you heard about Functional Fluency, but I can tell you it is making a difference in my house!'

How would a Functionally Fluent teacher relate to parents and carers?

To explore how a Functionally Fluent teacher effectively engages with parents and carers, it's helpful first to consider the principles of a Functionally Fluent family, as articulated by James Hollis.

The goal of a 'good-enough' family: nurturing growth in every member

In his book *Finding Meaning in the Second Half of Life*, James Hollis (2005) outlines some views about the family that are very much in line with Functional Fluency.

> The modern healthy family posits the nurturance of the individual as its highest value – all the individuals in that family. The family, as with

the intimate relationship of the parents is to support the growth and individuation of each of its members, parent and child alike. None is there to serve the narcissistic needs of any other. Each is there to support that growth and feel that support in return. This is not an idealistic view of the family. It is a functional goal, an eminently practical plan that serves the society by presenting it with more mature, evolved citizens.

Hollis, 2005

This focus on the output of upbringing, along with the use of the word 'functional', is a clear link with the thinking and the evolutionary mandate behind Functional Fluency that is outlined in the introduction to this book.

Hollis goes on to make the point that:

The lessons of history reveal over and over that the struggling family will be dominated by its least conscious parent. The parent's first task is personal growth, allied with the conscious assumption of responsibility for the growth of others.

Hollis, 2005

Again, it is notable that Hollis is using the language of Transactional Analysis (TA) and the Functional Fluency descriptors here. Many of the TIFF feedback sessions that I have completed over the last 12 years have demonstrated very clearly that many parents and carers, particularly those in leadership roles, either neglect or are unable to make time for this personal growth. This results in a TIFF profile that lacks balance. Hollis's phrase 'least conscious' could, in Functional Fluency terms, be understood as putting the least amount of time and energy into Accounting. Again, this would result in an unbalanced profile.

This makes clear the links between the use of Functional Fluency to develop better relationships between schools and the families they serve and to improve relationships within the families of their staff. When a school successfully adopts Functional Fluency, this involves committing to explain the model to parents and carers. There are several reasons why this is important:

- If parents and carers understand the school's approach to behaviour, it is possible that they may start to use a similar approach at home. The resulting congruence makes life much easier for the pupils to navigate, as there is a similarity between what is expected of them at home and in school.

- Parents and carers will understand the principles that underpin behaviour policies and decisions made on issues by the school.

- There will be a shared vocabulary used to describe behaviour at school and at home.

- Parents and carers will understand that teachers are human beings with needs and weaknesses, just like them, and that they have a right to privacy and respect.

- Parents, carers and teachers alike will more explicitly understand the shared practical plan for the growth and development of each individual, which should result in an increased sense of shared purpose and a corresponding reduction in time and energy wasted in disputes.

This shared understanding highlights a critical factor in successful home–school partnerships: congruence. A lack of congruence is often a source of friction, as we will now explore.

The power of consistency: why a united front between home and school matters

One of the sources of friction between schools and the pupils' parents and carers is a lack of congruence in their respective responses to the behaviour of the child they collectively have responsibility for bringing up.

Approaches to discipline are often different between a child's two parents or carers, so there are inevitably going to be distinctions between the way some parents and carers of any school community and the school itself respond to behavioural issues. Equally, there are often distinctions between the responses of different teachers to the same behavioural issue within a school, and this can lead to problems that make navigating school life unnecessarily difficult for pupils. The more congruence there is between teachers in terms of how they implement the school's values, as we saw in Chapter 4 ('Beyond the classroom door: creating a thriving staff culture'), the better for all concerned. If this congruence extends to how parents and carers respond to their children before and after school, this will establish a shared understanding of what constitutes appropriate behaviour and help the pupils to understand adult expectations.

This idea of congruence is deepened when we come to consider the TA concept of the 'auxiliary parent'. The teacher's role as an 'auxiliary parent' is most effective when there is congruence between the behavioural expectations of the school and the home.

In TA terms, our experience of how our parents or carers care for and control us shapes our understanding of what parenting is all about. But we also take in ideas about parenting from others who help us to grow and develop: grandparents and older siblings; youth workers; religious or community leaders; and, of course, teachers.

Clearly, we do not live in an ideal world and, very often, for a variety of reasons, our pupils do not have a strong experience of parenting in the home. Whether this is due to mental-health issues affecting parents or carers; parents or carers working long hours in multiple low-paid jobs, causing stress; or the impact of inter-generational trauma, the impact on pupils is detrimental. If this negative cycle is to be broken, it is important that teachers play a strong role in helping to develop an auxiliary model of parenting for pupils. Functional Fluency can play a huge role here.

Teachers who balance effective care for their pupils (which demonstrates *empathy*, appreciation and *understanding*, while avoiding *smothering* and *over-indulgence*) with effective control (providing *firmness*, *inspiration* and *consistency* and avoiding *blaming*, *judgement* and *bossiness*) are providing them with a priceless parenting model that they may be able to draw upon if they become parents or carers themselves.

Teachers may never know the impact that they have had, and pupils may not be conscious of it either. But be assured that every authoritative yet compassionate exchange you have with a pupil will foster many more effective relationships in the future. Through your modelling of the importance of responding rather than reacting to situations, you are demonstrating the effective approach to the development of future generations, which is so vital if our families and communities are to thrive. It is exactly this 'auxiliary parent' role that Chris Andrews fulfils in the scenario at the start of the chapter that so impresses Jamie Prentice's dad. The impact on Jamie and his siblings, who no longer constantly have to switch between different behavioural rules, which saps their energy and undermines their sense of security, is clearly beneficial. There will be many similar examples where your successful modelling of Functionally Fluent approaches to behaviour leads to a reduction in the relational friction that causes so much strife in so many homes.

Understanding the profound impact of the teacher's role as an 'auxiliary parent' provides a powerful impetus for intentionally fostering strong home–school relationships. This is achieved through a systematic approach encompassing communication, training and demonstration. Let's begin by exploring effective Communication.

Putting partnership into practice: a three-step approach

Communication: creating a shared language

Functional Fluency is a term that will need explaining to parents and carers. They will need to read about the concept so that they have some time to think about its implications and supporting principles, and decide whether this is something that they want for their children. A great starting point for schools is to send the link to the Functional Fluency starter pack from the <u>functionalfluency.com</u> website to all existing and prospective parents and carers. It explains the origin and principles behind Functional Fluency, and it is the basis for the 12 lessons on Functional Fluency that have been devised to help teach it to pupils at the start of each key stage (see the Appendix at the end of this book for more details).

On top of this, Functional Fluency needs to be referenced in school communications to parents and carers. So, if a new policy is written to cope with an emerging issue and posted on the school website to inform parents and carers of the school's response, this should incorporate Functional Fluency and the ways in which the model has informed the thinking behind the new approach.

Then, when parents and carers come into school to discuss specific incidents, teachers should reference Functional Fluency as a way of explaining the school's response to the pupil's behaviour and modelling the way it can be used to address issues.

Additionally, it is important that the school's communication embodies Functional Fluency as effectively as possible. Pages on the school website should therefore aim to be *authoritative, well-organised* and *inspiring*, as well as *empathic, encouraging* and *cherishing*. A school that is confident in its Functional Fluency could invite parents, carers and pupils to point out instances where their communication falls into the less effective purple (darkly shaded) pitfall areas. This discussion should help to build trust and transparency, as well as developing an understanding of exactly what Functional Fluency means within a school context. In the post-Covid context, schools are reporting ever-increasing degrees of animosity and defiance in their encounters with parents and carers, which saps energy all round. If embracing Functional Fluency can help to dispel some of this, there will be advantages for all concerned.

While effective communication lays the groundwork, a deeper, more systematic understanding of Functional Fluency for parents and carers often requires dedicated training opportunities.

Training: deepening understanding together

The Functional Fluency model is deceptively simple. It is easy to take in at a glance, and most people can understand how it works very quickly. However, it is also a profound model that repays repeated attention and careful consideration.

For parents and carers to develop a genuine understanding of how the model works and how they can use it to underpin their own care for their children, they need to experience a systematic training opportunity. This should be offered to them as close to the start of their child's time with the school as possible. It should take the form of a series of face-to-face meetings in which teachers and other members of staff from the school explain the model and how it is applied practically within the institution. This could cover how the model reflects the school's values, how it is lived out in the school's rules and how teachers have been trained to use the model in resolving the daily issues that arise.

Parents and carers can be encouraged to think about specific common scenarios that arise with young people and to discuss in small groups how they could use the model, first of all to understand the pupil's behaviour and then to construct a response that is most likely to be effective.

This training needs to be repeated regularly as new parents and carers become part of the school community, to remind them of the principles and give them an opportunity to deepen their understanding and insight into the model and its applications.

Beyond theoretical understanding, experiencing Functional Fluency in action through practical demonstration can significantly deepen parents' and carers' insight. One particularly valuable aspect of this training is the use of Get on the Mat sessions.

Demonstration: making the abstract real with Get on the Mat

Get on the Mat sessions are part of the core training for all Certified Functional Fluency Teachers (see the Appendix), for the simple reason that this activity helps to make the abstract Functional Fluency model into something that can be understood and lived.

The mat itself makes the model both concrete and external. It becomes a space through which we navigate, experiencing the feelings that we and others have felt in the specific circumstances that we choose to discuss. This helps us to empathise with others, enabling us to look at events and situations from their perspectives. We also experience the visceral reactions of our bodies as we occupy and internalise the model: how does it feel to use Marshmallowing behaviour as opposed to using Nurturing? How does it feel to be on the receiving end of Marshmallowing and Nurturing behaviours? We can then explore the motivations behind behavioural choices and consider the impact that these have and how alternative choices could have different outcomes, from which we and others could benefit.

One major advantage of Get on the Mat sessions is the way in which they enable participants to explore and get to know the model better. They experience the freedom of discussing alternative responses in a risk-free situation and begin to uncover some of the motivations behind their behaviour choices, of which they may not have previously been conscious. This training becomes critical in navigating difficult, real-time conversations. Example 17 (at the end of this chapter) provides a step-by-step demonstration of how a teacher can use an Accounting stance to manage a hostile encounter at a parents' / carers' evening.

Taking groups of parents and carers through Get on the Mat activities models for them ways in which they could think about approaching behavioural issues when they occur at home. The mat makes the model a much more familiar resource that they can use to examine motivations and choices within the family situation, with a view to helping all to make more effective choices in the future. The training that parents and carers receive will begin to feel much more real. They will feel a greatly increased understanding of how it is used within school as an approach to improve behaviour and how they, in turn, can mimic this in a way that builds an important level of home–school congruence into the lives of the pupils. This helps pupils to grow up with an improved understanding of how to make behaviour choices from which they and others can all benefit.

The effective completion of the processes outlined here – congruence, communication, training and demonstration – will help the school to move towards the realisation of its plans to become a Functionally Fluent school, the stages of which are outlined in the People and Place frameworks in Chapter 7.

The commitment to congruence, effective communication and robust training and demonstration are not mere theoretical ideals. Indeed, these methods are being successfully applied and yielding transformative results in schools around the world. To illustrate this, we turn first to the experiences of therapist Joaquim Braga in Brazilian schools.

Functional Fluency in Action

Joaquim Braga: using Functional Fluency with parents and carers in Brazilian schools

Joaquim Braga PhD is a trained therapist with over 20 years of experience working with individuals, couples and families. Since 2017, he has also worked with organisations, focusing on leadership and team development, as well as initiatives to promote mental health in the workplace. He now works in Brazil, where he lives with his wife and children, but trained and built up his practice while living in the United States.

Joaquim was keen to start moving away from therapy towards coaching and, to facilitate this, he completed the training to become a Functional Fluency / TIFF provider. His children, who were born in the US, now attend a bilingual Portuguese–English school in Brazil run by the Canadian franchise Maple Bear; the school invited Joaquim to lead some training using Functional Fluency. Maple Bear runs over 200 schools in Brazil alone, and soon some of them were inviting him in to repeat the training for their staff. This work has focused on relationship-building for teachers, focusing on their relationships with their colleagues and, particularly, with parents and carers.

These schools attract high-income, professional-class parents and carers who approach their schools with a sense of entitlement. Joaquim leads workshops with school leaders, teaching them the Functional Fluency model to help them develop the skills to navigate these relational dynamics. The response has been very positive. As Joaquim explains the model, the teachers soon start to understand how it works and to apply it to their work, and the school community begins to see how it resonates. In his own children's school, the leaders have, through their own initiative, printed off copies of the model and placed them by their desks or computers as a mindful reminder to reference them prior to meeting with challenging parents and carers.

The next phase of the plan is to teach the model to the parents and carers of pupils at Joaquim's children's school. This is an approach he has already been asked to use with a group of parents and carers in a school in Sao Paulo, to address a particularly difficult situation that arose, which involved pupils, parents and carers refusing to cooperate with the school. In that school, as soon as Joaquim began to explain the model, the parents and carers quickly used it to understand their own, the school's and their children's behaviour. At the end of the meeting, the group of around 25 parents and carers approached the school to ask Joaquim to teach the model to the pupils, as they could see the immense value of it.

Although Functional Fluency is still in its infancy in Brazil, Joaquim is planning to present the model to the CEO of Maple Bear in Latin America. The potential for the model to facilitate more mindful behavioural choices, improve inter- and intra-personal relationships, while also helping schools to address difficult problems such as bullying and teacher burnout, suggests that knowledge of Functional Fluency in the region could soon be developing exponentially.

Further demonstrating the profound real-world impact of Functional Fluency, particularly in the vital role of the 'auxiliary parent' and the importance of ongoing professional support, we now turn to the supervision work of Sue Ashby.

Functional Fluency in Action

Sue Ashby

Sue Ashby is a Certified Transactional Analyst (CTA) Psychotherapist and a licensed TIFF provider working in Dorset. She met Susannah Temple in 2003 and, shortly afterwards, completed the TIFF Provider Licensing Training (TPLT). Having previously worked as a further-education lecturer and freelance trainer in education, local government and arts organisations, she has always believed in the importance of reflective practice for mental, emotional and physical wellbeing. For 12 years, Sue has been working with two therapeutic youth workers, Jake and Danny of 360 Learning and Skills.

To understand the practical application of Functional Fluency in challenging educational settings, let's consider the supervision work of Sue, Jake and Danny. Supervision offers support by providing a safe place to reflect on practice; it is non-judgemental, collegial, creative and a cornerstone of professional development. This work has a strong focus on the concept of the 'auxiliary parent'.

Jake founded and continues to run the 360 Learning and Skills programme, which provides a high-needs inclusion service in the Dorset, Hampshire and Isle of Wight area. Initially, Jake and Danny's work was directly contracted with the local authority, but now they work two days a week (Jake) and five days a week (Danny) for Bournemouth and Poole College. Sue's role is to meet with them both for monthly supervision sessions.

Jake and Danny's work at the college involves running a transition programme to help vulnerable and high-needs young people transition into adulthood. From September 2026, they are responsible for setting up the Government's Transitioning from School to Further Education initiative. Their approach is built on resilience and never giving up, whatever setbacks they encounter. Their mantra is 'we always come back'.

Jake and Danny's work is highly influenced by Functional Fluency. 360 Learning and Skills has a Philosophy, Principles & Practice statement that sets out their approach to their work. In it, they state:

'Using a range of psychological concepts and models from Transactional Analysis and other disciplines to aid a clear and deep understanding of each child. These guide us in our practice to create an I'm OK, You're OK relationship where mutual respect is the desired outcome and supports each child's self-determination.'

They then specifically reference Functional Fluency as one of their main operational approaches, adding the note:

'Because Functional Fluency is relational at its core we are mindful of always using effective behaviours to relate to students when they react using ineffective behaviours.'

This demonstrates the fundamental nature of the impact that Functional Fluency has on their practice. They take on the role of the 'auxiliary parent', using Functional Fluency approaches along with perseverance and patience to help turn these young people's lives around. By trying to balance Structuring and Nurturing behaviour in their interactions with the young people, Jake and Danny provide a clear example of what effective Care and Control can look like; this is especially valuable if these vital behaviours have previously been missing from parenting.

Jake and Danny are not themselves trained Functional Fluency providers, but their monthly supervision sessions with Sue Ashby have given them a regular context in which to explore and discuss their experiences using Functional Fluency to process and make sense of their work. Having trained as a Functional Fluency provider with Susannah Temple back in 2003, Sue is deeply embedded in this way of thinking. Part of Sue's other work involves running supervision sessions for Functional Fluency professionals on behalf of Functional Fluency International. Because Jake and Danny's work is predicated on building relationships with the young people they work with, it is necessarily taxing and takes up a huge amount of emotional energy. These monthly supervision sessions are vital to the success of their work and for the maintenance of their own mental health.

Jake and Danny's work utilises a humanistic approach with a strong relational basis. It is based on the belief that our wellbeing is directly linked to the quality of our relationships. However, many of the young people:

- do not have a history of strong and sustained bonds

- are in the care system

- may have suffered significant trauma in their lives.

As a result of all these complex factors, this work is especially difficult and emotionally demanding, making the monthly supervision sessions with Sue vital.

Additionally, many of the young people have experienced problematic care. Many carers fall into the category of the 'wounded carer', turning to the profession because of their own personal experience of suffering or trauma. This may make them highly empathic and give them greater insight into young people's needs. But it can have potential downsides, including the possibility of projecting their issues onto the young people, over-identification or burnout. The result in Functional Fluency terms can often be ineffective care or Marshmallowing behaviours, such as over-indulgence, which blurs the line between 'wants' and 'needs'. While this might appear to have benefits for either the carer or the young person, in the long-term it causes confusion and frustration. The Marshmallowing discourages the young person from developing the independence and self-determination their increasingly adult life requires, leaving them feeling inadequate. Simultaneously, the carer probably feels that their hard work and commitment have not been properly valued, and this may well breed resentment.

This form of ineffective behaviour often makes it harder for Jake and Danny to establish effective Functionally Fluent relationships with the young people who may have become used to Marshmallowing. An additional impact of this ineffective behaviour is that it often reduces young people's self-esteem as it locks them into a cycle of dependence on others, which undermines their sense of personal adequacy.

There are two key ways to use this example as a model across the teaching profession. The conscious application of the gold (lightly shaded) modes of Functional Fluency, even when responding to purple (darkly shaded) mode behaviour from pupils and young people, should be the aim of all teachers (see Chapter 1 for an explanation of the gold and purple modes). Whether they are aware of it or not, all teachers form a part of the 'auxiliary parenting' experiences of all the pupils they teach and, as such, should be mindful of the impact that they are having in every encounter – especially those involving young people who may not have experienced very much effective parenting behaviour in their home lives.

Secondly, the provision of supervision for teachers, particularly those working with vulnerable young people, is a great model of the ideal situation that should be available to all teachers. Supervision provides the time and space for Jake and Danny to process the emotions that their work gives rise to; to consider in a strategic way how they can develop their approaches; and an opportunity for their experiences to be externally validated. The high number of teachers leaving the profession before they fulfil their professional potential would perhaps reduce if such a practical response to the pressure and mental-health challenges of the profession were more widely available.

Navigating difficult conversations: a guide to parents' / carers' evenings

Example 17 Parents' / carers' evenings

Situation

A parent or carer is immediately hostile. They disagree with an assessment you have made of their child. They launch into a loud and negative speech in which they question your motives and your professionalism (Compliant / Resistant).

Parent / carer:

▼

Immediate thoughts and feelings

You are taken aback. It is nearing the end of a very long day, and you are tired. The barrage of abuse is unexpected, as the child in question is very low profile and appears to be making reasonable progress. You can feel yourself going red and tears begin to prick your eyes (*childish*, *submissive*).

You:

▼

Pause: choice

Staying *grounded*, you realise that there may be more going on for this parent or carer than you know. You glance around the room (*alert*) and see that your head of year is currently free.

You:

▼

Functionally Fluent response

When the tirade ends, you take several deep breaths. You acknowledge the parent or carer's strong feelings (*aware*) and reassure them that you share their high expectations (*encouraging*). You point out that it is the end of a long day and that you are both tired (Accounting). You suggest that it might be best if the parent or carer speaks to the head of year first to explain the whole situation and say that you will join them shortly to find out how you can help move things forwards. Your use of Accounting energy ensures that you are responding to the situation and not reacting. It also gives the parent or carer a chance to consider their approach and to disrupt the pattern of Compliant / Resistant behaviour that they have adopted.

You:

▼

Key learning

Parents and carers want the best for their child. This can result in unreasonable behaviour. Other situations that are unrelated to school may also trigger inappropriate reactions, and Accounting can help you not to take this personally.

The school gate should not be a boundary, but a bridge. As the work of practitioners from Brazil to the UK makes clear, partnering with parents is about creating a powerful congruence between the worlds a child inhabits. When we share the language and tools of Functional Fluency, we are not just managing behaviour; we are co-creating an ecosystem of support. This united front, built on a shared understanding and purpose, is what enables individual Functionally Fluent classrooms to coalesce into a truly Functionally Fluent school – an institution ready to embed these practices into its very DNA.

CHAPTER 7
FROM INDIVIDUALS TO INSTITUTION: EMBEDDING FUNCTIONAL FLUENCY ACROSS YOUR SCHOOL

Jo, Pat Harrison's PA, rings to say that Tom Perry, headteacher of a local school in a different Trust, is on the phone. Pat picks up, wondering what's up.

'Hi Pat, it's Tom. Now, I won't beat about the bush. What's this Functional Fluency thing I keep hearing about? Is it some fancy new literacy initiative?'

'Oh, good to hear from you, Tom,' says Pat. 'Well, where have you been hearing about that then, Tom?'

'All the parents at our intake evening were on about it – they said Dave and some young geography teacher had given a talk about it at your place. They seemed very impressed.'

Pat sits back in her chair. 'Ah yes, that's Chris Andrews. Well, Tom, it is about much more than literacy; it's about all our behaviour choices and how we can make them more effective.'

'Oh, OK,' says Tom. 'Sounds like I'd better come over and discuss it with you and Dave.'

'Let's do that, Tom – it would be a pleasure to work with you so that we can all benefit. And I'll include Chris in our discussion too,' says Pat, smiling.

What would a Functionally Fluent school be like?

Part 1: The problem and the solution

Avoiding burnout: creating a culture of sustainable success

Teaching can be a lengthy career. If you go straight into teaching after completing your first degree and teacher-training course, you have, potentially, around 40 years ahead of you in the profession. As Hargreaves and Fullan (2012) point out in *Professional Capital*, teachers start to fulfil their potential only after about eight years in the job. So, it is vital that the profession retains teachers until well beyond this point to get the best out of them for the benefit of the pupils.

However, as the rest of your career stretches in front of you, it is easy to become demoralised. While some teachers find the rhythm of the school year reassuring, for others it can soon become stale. If you are promoted, this can bring additional interest as new responsibilities alter the pattern of your year. But there is a limit to the number of job changes that any teacher can take on during their career. Whether you remain in your first role for many years or you are rapidly promoted to headteacher and then must stay in that role for a long time because no further promotion is possible, you are going to have to manage your career to ensure you retain interest in your work. One of the saving graces of education is that, while the job may stay the same, there are always changes, in the form of new specifications or school policies, to keep you on your toes and, more important, a new set of pupils arrives each year with an associated batch of interests and challenges.

The combination of cyclic annual repetition and what can often seem like (or indeed is) continually increasing productivity pressure, can in some cases result in burnout. This is a human tragedy for the teacher concerned, for their family and for the pupils they teach. Most teachers who have been in schools for a few years, whether in inner-city schools or affluent suburbs, will have known colleagues who have had to give up the job because they have burnt out. The years of experience and professional capital that they have accrued is lost from the profession.

Jayne Morris is an expert on burnout and a trained coach and Get on the Mat facilitator. She has written extensively about burnout (Morris, 2015), how to come back from it and how to avoid it in the first place. She writes about the changes that have taken place in our society that contribute to burnout, which have only accelerated since her book was published.

> Neuroscientists increasingly warn us that we are consuming too much information, which causes the brain to function in a continuously hyper alert state.

> **Morris, 2015**

For a wide range of reasons, many of which are addressed elsewhere in this book, teachers report ever-increasing levels of stress as their lives become, in Morris's words 'clogged up' with 'conscious and unconscious thought clutter'. In a phrase very reminiscent of writing on Functional Fluency, Morris suggests:

My guess if you are feeling burnt out is that you are spending more time with what I refer to as 'energy vampires', rather than 'energy radiators'.

These two categories of people (though it could equally apply to activities) are sometimes described by Functional Fluency practitioners as 'energy drains' and 'energy gains', respectively. In terms of the model, the vampires or drains are the people who drag you towards the less effective purple modes rather than the productive golden modes.

This demonstrates the first way in which this approach is potentially useful in helping teachers and others working in schools to avoid burnout. By providing a visual structure and some commonly understood terminology, the model enables those at risk of burnout to name and describe their experiences. This may be enough to alert the at-risk teacher and their colleagues of the potential danger of the situation, allowing the teacher to take the necessary steps to guide them back towards using golden modes of behaviour. This should have the effect of reducing stress and limiting the chance of burnout, with all the negatives that come with it.

By enabling teachers to identify and describe their experiences, Functional Fluency provides a clear pathway to reducing the stress that leads to burnout. However, for this approach to gain traction and be supported by school leadership, its benefits must be demonstrated. If we are to justify the investment of time and resources needed to build a sustainable, healthy culture, we must answer a crucial question: how can the positive impact of this deeply personal work be tracked, measured and proven?

Proving the value: how to measure the impact of your work

By enabling teachers to identify and describe their experiences, Functional Fluency provides a pathway to reducing stress and preventing burnout. However, for this approach to be adopted more widely and supported by school leadership, its positive effects must be more than just anecdotal. This raises a crucial question: How can we track and demonstrate the benefits of Functional Fluency? This section explores tools designed to measure its impact, ensuring accountability and proving a return on investment for the school.

If Functional Fluency is to have any lasting beneficial impact on your life, it needs to be something you return to frequently, hold in your mind and reflect on at regular intervals. We also need to have processes for tracking any benefits that result. This is particularly important for senior leaders, who want to have a clear metric to prove that there is a positive return on the investment from this work.

One of the key issues for coaches is confidentiality. What is discussed between the coach and coachee must remain privy to them only. This makes it particularly difficult to demonstrate the impact that the work is having, even when this is very clear to both parties. Table 16 facilitates this process.

The TIFF story is a mechanism to encourage educators who have completed TIFF to reflect on the impact it has had. Some may want to complete two versions: one for their own personal evaluation and a second they are willing to share more widely. They could be collected and shared with school staff in the form of a booklet, online collection or staffroom wall display as a way of making the impact of the work clear to all. It may encourage others, who have until then been unwilling to get involved with Functional Fluency, to give it a try, when they read about the beneficial impact it has had on their colleagues.

Table 16 Your TIFF story

Your TIFF story
Explain your situation in 10 words or fewer.
Why did you do TIFF?
What did you want or need from TIFF to thrive?
What did you get from TIFF and the feedback meeting?
What measurable effect or impact did this have?
What is your message to others?

Table 17 An example TIFF story

Your TIFF story
Explain your situation in 10 words or fewer. *I am a humanities teacher and Year 8 tutor.*
Why did you do TIFF? *I was stressed, anxious and beginning to get panic attacks.*
What did you want or need from TIFF to thrive? *I needed to realise that I could actually do the work easily and didn't have to fret.*
What did you get from TIFF and the feedback meeting? *I learned from doing TIFF what I have written in the box above.*
What measurable effect or impact did this have? *I stopped over-preparing and imagining disasters, gained courage to believe in my capabilities, booked regular rest / play time, cheered up and the panics ceased.*
What is your message to others? *Find out how TIFF could help you to thrive too.*

A second approach to tracking the impact of this work is the target-setting form explained in Chapter 3 (see Table 6). There, it is linked with lesson observation, but it can also be used in the context of coaching. The final impact-statement section is designed to be shared with line managers and those responsible for demonstrating the impact of Functional Fluency work, and should be agreed between the coach and coachee before it is submitted. In this way, the impact of the work can be centrally collated, and informed judgements about return on investment can be made.

To see how this works in real-world school settings, the following case studies present three practitioners who have implemented Functional Fluency. They provide concrete examples of the challenges, processes and positive outcomes discussed so far. The first is Stephanie Carlin, who is working to embed Functional Fluency at Ladybridge High in Bolton.

Part 2: Stories from the field

Functional Fluency in Action

Stephanie Carlin

Stephanie Carlin is a coach, facilitator and TIFF provider. She works with individuals, schools and organisations to help them communicate effectively, create their vision and reach their goals.

Stephanie's passion for Functional Fluency developed during her teaching career, when she realised its value in helping teachers and leaders to understand interactions ranging from classroom dynamics to leadership conversations.

Stephanie is working with Ladybridge High in Bolton where the headteacher is Paddy Russell. Stephanie previously worked with Paddy in a school in Rochdale. Both have a background in Transactional Analysis (TA); the school had previously worked with Giles Barrow and another Educational Transactional Analyst, and this laid the foundations for their work with Functional Fluency. As Giles expanded the TA work across the Trust that the Rochdale school was part of, Stephanie became an in-house trainer. Listening to Giles talking about Functional Fluency was a lightbulb moment for Stephanie, who thought 'Why aren't we using this?'. She started to deliver Functional Fluency workshops and got to a stage where she needed to choose between carrying on with her teaching and leadership role and retraining in Functional Fluency and as a coach. Inspired to share Functional Fluency after seeing its impact in the classroom, she took the plunge and decided on the latter route.

Paddy was keen to engage an external trainer to make Functional Fluency central to his school's life and so their paths crossed again.

To start off the work, Stephanie ran a two-hour training session with the whole staff – around 70 teachers and teaching assistants. They discussed the background to the model and then had mini Get on the Mat sessions to talk through scenarios that Stephanie provided, spending around 40 minutes working through challenging conversations with a colleague, parent or carer or revisiting a classroom experience. There were 10 teachers with more experience of Functional Fluency, having heard about it from Giles, and they were spread out around the groups. Stephanie used one mat with the model printed on it and copies of the model made up from printed A4 sheets.

As part of Stephanie's Functional Fluency training, Paddy became one of her training clients. He completed a TIFF and immediately decided that he wanted his whole teaching staff to have this experience. Within the first term, 26 teachers completed their TIFF, including the whole English department and the pastoral team.

This work enabled Stephanie to identify some general issues, as well as to work with individuals on a wide range of matters. She met with the heads of the pastoral team to discuss ways to empower team members to make the key decisions needed for the benefit of the pupils, unencumbered by worries about making life-changing decisions on behalf of others. Functional Fluency revealed a tentativeness that held back the team from operating in an optimal way. The model enabled new, more dynamic ways of working to emerge that focus more explicitly on engaging with pupils to solve problems.

Stephanie and Paddy are in discussion about how best to make use of the insights gained from completing all these TIFFs in a way that moves the school forward without compromising any individual's confidentiality. Stephanie ran a session for heads of departments and completed team profiles, aggregating the results of the individuals in each department. Stephanie used these results to devise bespoke approaches, informed by what the results reveal about the needs of each department.

The contracting process evolved over time as the nature of the potentialities of this work became clearer. Two outcomes that have been agreed are:

- Teachers will get protected reflection time to think about their TIFFs and how they can best integrate their findings into their work.

- Team profiles will be created and shared with colleagues who work together. (Team profiles enable providers to work with teams on their shared behavioural tendencies. This is distinct from the Team Scan, where individuals respond to test items that ask about how the team behaves.)

In these ways, this piece of Continuing Professional Development (CPD) moves from a one-off intervention to a continuous piece of multi-phase work, thus meeting Standard 4 of the government's 'standard for teachers' professional development (DfE, 2016): 'Professional development programmes should be sustained over time', which is vital if the intervention is to have lasting impact. Exploring ways in which people who work together can be guided – through a contracting process that allows them to share elements of their profiles – to make the behavioural changes required to move forward as professionals and teams is central to the next phase of this work.

Stephanie is very passionate about the capacity that TIFF has for revealing the positive behaviours that colleagues use daily, without necessarily realising their power. It has enabled her to discuss the importance of *authoritative* behaviour with some teachers, freeing them up to utilise this type of behaviour much more within their school life, clear about the distinction between *authoritative* Structuring behaviours and the less effective Dominating behaviours.

Staff are increasingly comfortable using the language of the model to self-diagnose 'purple' behaviour. Paddy himself talks about situations in the past when he has felt lured towards Dominating behaviour. On one occasion, a pupil he was reprimanding walked away from him and he was tempted to use *punitive* behaviour to take control of the situation. Accounting for this situation now, he realises that this reaction stemmed from his own *anxious* reaction, concerned not to appear weak in front of colleagues and other pupils, rather than from an *empathic* or *curious* concern about why the pupil was feeling so unsafe or challenged in that moment that they were behaving in this way.

Since the start of this work, the school has seen a reduction in the number of behavioural incidents that escalate to a serious level as staff make a conscious effort to avoid Dominating reactions to pupil provocations. For example, one pastoral leader was able to identify when, due to a lack of sufficient Accounting, they were being sucked into Marshmallowing mode behaviour by a situation. Due to this awareness, they were able to adjust their response to lead and nurture in a more effective, sustainable and helpful way.

The result has been a dramatic reduction in permanent exclusions, which, at the time of writing, are now the lowest in Bolton. We know that permanent exclusion comes with a range of negative long-term consequences for pupils, so this is a huge achievement. Additionally, pupils who move into the school having been permanently excluded elsewhere are now succeeding to a much greater degree than before, again resulting in life-changing positive impacts for families.

As the school moves into the third year of this work, Stephanie's coaching linked to the Functional Fluency model continues. As Paddy says, 'Steph's coaching was what we needed, giving staff space to talk and find solutions. The result is ongoing momentum, positive accountability and challenge to allow staff to reflect and go deeper'.

One of the important aspects is staff know their coaching is confidential. Paddy does not want to know the specifics of coaching meetings. Some general feedback and themes are useful for leaders to receive, and heads of departments benefit from seeing the headline overview of their department's strengths and challenges. Staff often speak to Paddy about the benefits of their coaching, and he sees the impact around the school:

'With self-awareness comes control. We're seeing fewer instances where incidents escalate, with adults confidently remaining as the type of adults children need. Lots of pupils don't spend time around adults showing healthy adult behaviour. I see nurture, understanding, and willingness to lead humbly and say sorry when it's right to, winning over our pupils each day. The staff are incredibly positive about their coaching experience. I've no doubt it contributes to the wellbeing, retention and development of my team.'

All the teaching staff at the school and most of the associate staff (teaching assistants and administrative staff) have now completed their TIFF surveys and had a feedback session with Stephanie. She plans to use the Team Scan with the senior leadership team. Paddy is now looking at ways to incorporate Functional Fluency into the curriculum, and is considering using the lesson outlines that are part of the Certified Functional Fluency Teacher Programme. He is convinced that the model is a valuable underpinning to the culture of the school as staff and, increasingly, pupils actively try to use golden mode behaviour as much as possible. Another potential whole-school development revolves around peer observations, using the Functional Fluency model as a guide. (See Chapter 3 for an example of a way in which the model can be used as a starting point for lesson observations.)

The third of the school's three beliefs is 'Honesty promotes learning'. Paddy is convinced that Functional Fluency has played a huge role in making this an authentic feature of the school's culture.

Functional Fluency in Action

David Brown

David Brown was an English teacher and, prior to that, a police officer, before he trained as a TIFF and Functional Fluency provider and left the classroom to set up Future Fixers, the community-interest company he runs in Kendal, Cumbria, with his wife.

When presenting workshops to teachers in schools, David includes a range of personal-effectiveness models, culminating in an explanation of Functional Fluency. David then invites the teachers to find out more by completing their own TIFF and having a one-to-one feedback session with him to explore the curiosities and insights the results provoke.

A sector that David has worked with in this way is primary-school headteachers; a group of people who are often quite isolated in their work (often physically as well as psychologically in rural Cumbria), but who are not often targeted for this kind of personalised support. He set up his coaching on a one-to-one basis in his locality. One of his key takeaways from this work is that, due perhaps to the nature of the headteacher role and the complex pressures involved in it, there is a tendency for the headteachers to put too much of their time and energy into Marshmallowing behaviour. Often, they explain this as a quick fix to a problem, necessary in the circumstances to get results quickly.

However, they often realise, during their coaching, that this isn't a sustainable long-term approach, as it can:

- add to the pressures on the headteacher themselves, increasing the potential for burnout
- build a dependency culture, where staff members could become reluctant to display or take initiative, and
- reduce rather than build capacity.

As a result of this work, several of the headteachers have gone on to set up new systems specifically to address these issues, thus helping all involved to fulfil their potential more effectively.

David is very clear about the huge differences between individual primary schools and the effectiveness of Functional Fluency as a model to absorb this difference and provide useful personalised ways forward for leaders in all these schools, regardless of the specific circumstances.

Completing a Functional Fluency feedback session often leads to ongoing coaching with the headteacher, which David uses to address the various drivers or triggers that may be encouraging the headteacher to use Marshmallowing behaviour. One of these is the driver to hurry up, which is often embedded in many aspects of educational discourse.

David used Functional Fluency in the context of more specific career-change coaching to help a headteacher prepare themselves for an interview for the headship of a larger school. In other situations, the Functional Fluency-related coaching has enabled David to work with headteachers on a range of other issues, including adapting to headship in your fifties and having to adapt to leading people who were previously your colleagues. He has also collaborated with governors, helping them to plan and run more productive meetings, planning more effectively to deal with matters as they arise by beginning to predict potential issues, and dealing with anxiety.

One headteacher he worked with has put a printed copy of the Functional Fluency model on their office wall to function as an aide memoire, encouraging them to remember Functional Fluency and to try to use the effective golden forms of behaviour more often. In this way, Functional Fluency helps school leaders to make the most effective use of their limited budget, whether we are talking about money, time or energy. Investing a small amount of time and money in Functional Fluency coaching with David can reap huge benefits.

Functional Fluency in Action

Steve Russell

Steve Russell has been working with Functional Fluency and TIFF for around 14 years now in his role as a behaviour consultant. His use of Functional Fluency usually takes one of three forms:

- CPD sessions for whole-staff teams, with a focus on how Functional Fluency can help staff with relational issues

- Work with trainee teachers around relationships and wellbeing for the National Education Union (NEU)

- Coaching work using Functional Fluency with identified teachers and in drop-in clinics.

The model that he has developed with many of the primary schools that he works with generally follows this pattern:

1. He starts with a whole-staff training session to introduce everyone to the Functional Fluency model. This involves using the mat to make the model tangible and to begin to introduce everyone to the relevant vocabulary, and working through some scenarios to see how using Functional Fluency can help people to develop solutions to their relational issues. During these sessions, Steve very deliberately models a Functional Fluency approach to building relationships so that staff can witness the model in practice.

2. This session is followed up by a series of drop-in days (generally six per year: one per half term) when Steve is on site and available for any member of staff to book a slot to talk through any issue confidentially. The mat is again present, and Steve uses a coaching approach to work with staff members to help them work towards a solution to whatever problem it is that they bring to the meeting.

3. To augment these activities, Steve uses Functional Fluency as the basis for lesson-observation visits. He carefully contracts these in advance with the relevant staff. He asks them about the golden-mode behaviours that they expect he will notice when he is in their classroom.

Steve then visits the class and makes notes on what he sees, using a simplified version of the model as a prompt sheet. Each member of staff receives individual feedback on the 'golds' that Steve notices during his visit. These often include additional features that the member of staff had not flagged up, and this can be very empowering for them. Occasionally, there may be some 'purples' that Steve notices too, and he shares these if this expectation has been established during the contracting process. He also feeds back to leadership the 'golds' that he notices, with the agreement of the member of staff concerned, along with more general feedback on the nature of staff engagement.

This is all part of a process whereby Steve is training up leaders to use Functional Fluency themselves as the methodological structure of their observations, along with the contracting processes that he has established, which all serve to make this a positive one for all concerned.

4. This process is enhanced by additional top-up sessions on Functional Fluency for new staff who join the school so that the approach becomes increasingly integral to the school's way of doing things.

A learning point here for Functional Fluency International is around the need to develop a Functional Fluency course for school leaders that will equip them to conduct similar work in their own schools, across their multi-academy trust (MAT) or in the form of peer work with other local schools. In an ideal scenario, these Functional Fluency School Leaders would work across phase, linking up primary and secondary schools within the same MATs or localities using shared approaches and vocabulary, so that teachers, pupils and parents get used to the same approaches being used throughout education.

Steve has been involved in the direct use of Functional Fluency with pupils. In one school, this took the form of a series of discussion lessons, looking at the nature of leadership through some key historical leaders and analysing their approaches using Functional Fluency.

Another school asked him to work with a group of pupils to identify what they needed to get the most out of their time in the classroom. Once Steve had taught them the Functional Fluency model and asked them some carefully considered coaching questions, they were able to identify in a surprisingly precise way, using Functional Fluency vocabulary, the ways in which they needed the staff members to behave for everyone in the classroom to thrive. Clearly, this is an advanced use of Functional Fluency, which requires very careful contracting to ensure everyone fully understands and agrees the ground rules, but it is a powerful example of the huge possibilities of the model.

An example of the success of Steve's work is provided by one specific pupil who he first came across in Year 4, when she had a habit of walking out of lessons. He spent some time teaching her the model, which she quickly understood. Later, when a new teaching assistant (TA) started to work with her, the pupil asked to meet with Steve again so that she could explain Functional Fluency to the TA herself. The TA was amazed by the depth of the pupil's understanding of the model and the way in which she used it to explain the nature of the support that would be helpful to her and the type that would hinder her from thriving.

On another occasion when Steve was in the school, this pupil was having an issue and left the school buildings to go to an area of woodland that was part of the school grounds. A teacher followed her out and was attempting to get her back inside. The pupil did not appreciate the approach the teacher was taking, and said 'Stop Marshmallowing me!' This demonstrated the extent to which the vocabulary of the model had permeated the school. It also opened the situation for some real dialogue, and the teacher was able to explain why she was behaving as she was, and why, in her view, it was not Marshmallowing. The incident soon seemed less serious, and the pupil was able to come back into school with a feeling that she had been listened to and an understanding that perspective can make all the difference in relationships.

These insights from Stephanie, David and Steve demonstrate the versatility of Functional Fluency in practice – from whole-staff training and leadership coaching to transformative work with pupils. Having seen these specific examples of its impact, our focus now shifts to strategic implementation. How can a school leader move beyond individual interventions and embed Functional Fluency into the very fabric of the school's development? The following frameworks offer a guide.

Part 3: Implementation frameworks

The behaviour of teachers and leaders is directly linked to a school's distinctive culture, and school leaders are in a highly influential position to shape it. As Bishop (2024) states, 'What they do or do not do, is crucial'. To create a deliberately positive and effective learning community, leaders require clear strategic frameworks. The following sections explore how Functional Fluency can be integrated into two powerful models for managing school development.

Mapping your journey: using the Cycle of Development to embed lasting change

Levin and Landheer's Cycle of Development model, cited in Pratt (2021), is a very helpful one for enabling institutions such as schools to consider their development from a fresh perspective. The model posits that human beings (and, by extension, the organisations that they create) need to go through a series of stages if they are to become fully and properly developed. Major events in a school's life, such as an Ofsted inspection or the change of headteacher, require the cycle to be restarted and all its elements revisited, if development is going to be built on solid foundations. Functional Fluency can be used in each of these stages to help ensure that all the necessary steps are completed and that the school does not become 'stuck'.

At Meadowbank Middle School, Pat Harrison is researching Functional Fluency and comes across Levin and Landheer's Cycle of Development model. The introduction of Functional Fluency into Meadowbank Middle School seems to Pat to represent a new start. She decides to think about how she can ensure that its implementation meets the development needs that the model suggests are necessary if any new start is to be built on a firm foundation. To explain the whole process, Pat decides to write an open letter to parents / carers and staff to share her thinking as widely as possible.

Dear Staff and Parents / Carers,

As you will know, in the last couple of months we have been introducing Functional Fluency to help us improve the quality of relationships within the school. It is my firm belief that effective teaching and learning is built upon strong relationships.

In my reading on this subject, I have come across the Cycle of Development model, proposed by Levin and Landheer. They suggest that, when a person or an organisation enters a new phase of their existence, there is a series of stages they must progress through to ensure that their development is built on solid foundations. The model is not a strict, chronological plan, but a series of steps, each one more empowering than the last.

The introduction of Functional Fluency is a significant moment for the school, and so I want to use the Cycle of Development theory to ensure it is as successful as possible. I want to encourage everyone involved with Meadowbank to embrace Functional Fluency and use it, at their own discretion, to improve their effectiveness. All I ask is that we are open about our progress and any problems we encounter.

Stage 1, which Levin and Landheer call Being, is about making sure everyone understands that we all matter. It equates to the first few months of a newborn's life, when we need to demonstrate that we are pleased they are here and that their needs are important. In terms of the introduction of Functional Fluency, this is why I have spoken about this development in assemblies and why I am writing this letter to you now: to demonstrate that everyone is part of this initiative. I am very keen that you all understand what the school is doing, feel involved in the process and know that we are going to use Functional Fluency to help meet all your needs.

The second stage in the cycle is Doing. Now that we have held our introductory assemblies and are starting on the lessons that will teach Functional Fluency to the pupils, we are entering this phase, which is about trusting each other to explore what it can do to improve our relationships with each other. We will introduce Get on the Mat sessions, where pupils and staff can explore scenarios in a safe environment to become confident in using the model as a tool to help them work things out and improve their relationships.

In the Thinking phase, which will start straight after half term, key staff will complete additional Functional Fluency training, which will enable them to start using the model in their interactions with pupils and families. My hope is that the training and subsequent opportunities to use the model will show that, as a school, we trust pupils, families and staff to use this tool to think for themselves.

The fourth stage is all about Identity and Power. This is when we will start to run workshops about the five golden modes of behaviour in the model. We will discuss how we can all use them to help us to assert our individuality in appropriate ways. The emphasis here will be on reacting less and responding more, so that we use our power in effective ways.

Skills and Structure is the name of stage 5. This will be when we start to gather evidence of the ways in which our work with Functional Fluency have been successful, and also of the mistakes we have made. We will use the model to organise our meetings and thinking as we assess the progress we have made and the steps we still need to take.

The sixth and final stage is Integration. Here, we will aim to incorporate and synthesise all the feedback that we have received over the first year of our Functional Fluency journey. Staff will share evidence of their progress in the form of their TIFF Stories, which will be published in the school magazine. We will share with you success stories relating to issues that Functional Fluency has helped to solve. We will encourage groups of pupils to share their thoughts on the ways in which Functional Fluency has helped them through the year, and we will produce guidelines and examples to enable us to embed this work even more effectively next year.

This is not a passing fad or a project that will soon be replaced. It is too important for that. It is about the relationships we all have with each other. The combined strength of those relationships will be what determines whether this school is successful. If our pupils understand that forming strong and positive relationships with each other, with staff and, above all, with their families is what really matters in life, then we will have achieved our aim. They will be equipped with a vital skill to enable them to have a happy and worthwhile life. A great year awaits us.

Best wishes,

Pat Harrison

Headteacher, Meadowbank Middle School

Pat's letter outlines the vision for Meadowbank's Functional Fluency journey. Table 18 provides a more detailed, strategic look at the specific actions and benefits at each stage of development.

Table 18 Cycle of Development and Functional Fluency

Cycle of development	School development needs	Functional Fluency options	Benefits for pupils and staff
Being	To use Functional Fluency to make it clear to pupils, their families and members of staff that they matter, and we are glad they are here	• Reference Functional Fluency in briefings and speeches • Thought pieces: short articles about the use of Functional Fluency written for the school newsletter and website • Add references to Functional Fluency to resources, leaflets and other publicity materials • Incorporate Functional Fluency into the induction programme, including TIFF for all new starters	All stakeholders understand that their needs will be met
Doing	To use Functional Fluency to give pupils, families and staff the understanding that they are trusted to explore and experiment	Develop Functionally Fluent Meetings training package, drawing on Nancy Kline's thinking-environments material (1999) and train leaders (see Chapter 5)	All stakeholders experience Functional Fluency and the trust and licence that it brings

Cycle of development	School development needs	Functional Fluency options	Benefits for pupils and staff
Thinking	To use Functional Fluency to make clear that pupils, families and staff can think for themselves	• Leaders (heads of year and heads of faculty) complete the Introduction to Functional Fluency course, enabling them to introduce Functional Fluency to their teams, which in turn enables team members to utilise Functional Fluency in their interactions with pupils and families • Introduce Get on the Mat training sessions to enable staff to use Functional Fluency (and the interactive-mat tool) when engaging with families or other staff; this is about empowering the use of Functionally Fluent dialogue	All stakeholders benefit from the independence to think for themselves that comes with knowledge of the Functional Fluency model
Identity and power	To use Functional Fluency to clarify that pupils, families and staff can try out different roles and can learn to be powerful	• Run facilitated workshops on how to put more time and energy into the five golden modes (Accounting, Structuring, Nurturing, Cooperation and Spontaneous), as an option for anyone who has completed TIFF feedback • Provide coaching for leaders who have completed TIFF • Facilitate team meetings to discuss team profiles and agree actions to make the collective use of time and energy more effective	All stakeholders begin to learn to react less and respond more and use this power to be more effective

Cycle of development	School development needs	Functional Fluency options	Benefits for pupils and staff
Skills and structure	• Compile an understanding of the engagement with and impact of Functional Fluency using Guskey's Five Levels of Evaluation model (Guskey, 2000) • Celebrate the skills gained and structural progress made	• Produce an annual report on engagement with and embedding of Functional Fluency ideas and practices, possibly written by an independent Functional Fluency professional; share it with stakeholders and use it locally to explain changes to families and to raise the school's profile • Teams use the Functional Fluency Team Scan to gain a better understanding of how they function	All stakeholders have a better understanding of the journey, the skills that have been acquired and the mistakes that have been made
Integration	To use Functional Fluency to be clear that pupils, families and staff can develop their own interests	• Incorporate and synthesise all feedback received, including TIFF stories, and make this available • Produce guidelines and examples of Functionally Fluent engagement in collaboration with school leaders	All stakeholders understand how they have become more fully themselves and how they can continue to grow

Looking at their school's (or department's or Trust's) progress through the lens of Levin and Landheer's cycle (Pratt, 2021) provides leaders with clarity and insight into the actions they need to take. It is a framework that clarifies the functions that Functional Fluency fulfils in the evolution of an organisation as it works its way towards effective, integrated maturity.

While Levin and Landheer's cycle provides the **philosophical map** for an organisation's developmental journey, leaders also need a **practical toolkit** for navigating the specific process of change. This is where a structured change-management framework becomes invaluable. John Kotter's renowned 8-Step Change model (Kotter, 1996) offers a clear, sequential process for implementing significant initiatives. By pairing Kotter's 'how' with Levin and Landheer's 'why', a school can manage change in a way that is both strategic and human-centred.

Your eight-step plan for managing change (Kotter's model)

Table 19 summarises how Functional Fluency can help to deliver Kotter's 8-Step Change model so that change is initiated and sustained in appropriate ways.

Using this approach helps to keep the change process on track and to ensure that the benefits are felt as widely as possible. Change is not in itself a positive, and we have all experienced changes that have been implemented in ways that have caused considerable distress. Table 19 demonstrates an effective way to build Functional Fluency into the school's operational structures.

Table 19 Kotter's 8-Step Change model and Functional Fluency

Kotter's 8-Step Change model	Key Functional Fluency actions	Rationale / desired outcome
1. Create urgency	• Use Accounting transparently to share data on why change is needed and the threats involved in not changing (for example student wellbeing surveys and behaviour incidents). • Use Nurturing to create a safe space for staff to voice concerns about the change.	Staff understand the rationale and emotional case for change, feeling both informed and supported.
2. Form a powerful coalition	• Use Structuring and Cooperative energy to identify and bring together a diverse group of change leaders (not just senior staff). • Model Spontaneous behaviour to foster creativity and build authentic relationships within the coalition.	A powerful and trusted team is built to guide the change process, with broad-based support.
3. Create a vision for change	• Create an *inspiring* and *assertive* statement capturing the vision for change. • Test the vision by *evaluating* the extent to which it *encourages* and reinforces golden-mode behaviour and discourages purple-pitfall behaviour.	The statement makes clear why the change is required and the gains that will result; this galvanises energy to help it become a reality.
4. Communicate the vision	• Actively seek opportunities to communicate the vision. • Use Spontaneous (*zestful, expressive*) and Nurturing (*understanding*) energy to bring the vision to life in all communications.	A range of communication methods ensures that the vision is shared effectively.
5. Remove obstacles	• Use Accounting to analyse potential barriers to change. • Blend the five golden modes of Functional Fluency to create responses to the identified obstacles to change.	Staff can see that strategic forethought has been applied, and this boosts their confidence in using Functional Fluency to address change.

Kotter's 8-Step Change model	Key Functional Fluency actions	Rationale / desired outcome
6. Create short-term wins	• *Evaluate* the costs of implementation (human and financial) and target low-cost actions first. • *Inspire* colleagues to achieve targets.	Staff are aware of the gains and of how rapidly they have been achieved through this strategic approach.
7. Build on the change	• Be *rational* about successes: What went well and why? What could be improved further? • Combine Structuring and Nurturing energy to ensure that momentum is maintained.	All stakeholders can see that progress is taking place and that each step facilitates further change.
8. Anchor the changes in Academy structures	• Use Accounting and Structuring to build the desired changes into systems and structures. • Be *alert* to the ways in which leadership changes could impact on the continued success of the change. • Be *well-organised* in ensuring that the vision continues to be *inspiring*.	The planned changes become an established feature of how the organisation operates, ensuring that benefits gained are long-lasting.

Your people and your place: two frameworks for implementation

Successful implementation of Functional Fluency requires a dual focus: developing the skills of the people within the school and embedding the model into the fabric of the school itself. To help leaders manage this, this section provides two distinct but interconnected frameworks.

The first, the People framework (Table 20), outlines the developmental journey for each individual stakeholder, tracking their progress from Learner to Advocate. It answers the question 'How skilled are our people?'.

The second, the Place framework (Table 21), provides a roadmap for whole-school implementation, assessing the institution's progress from an Emerging to a Strategic state. It answers the question 'How embedded is Functional Fluency in our school's culture and systems?'.

Used together, these tables provide a comprehensive tool for planning, implementing and evaluating the journey to becoming a truly Functionally Fluent school.

Table 20 The People framework: tracking growth from Learner to Advocate

Stages	Learner	Knowledgeable user	Advocate
Pupils...	• recreate the Functional Fluency mode diagram from memory and explain it • participate in the 12 Functional Fluency lessons, completing all relevant tasks • demonstrate basic understanding of Functional Fluency in pupil-voice initiatives.	• apply the model by explaining two instances in which understanding of Functional Fluency has enabled response rather than reaction • provide feedback about the best way to use the model to improve the school.	• plan and implement a small-scale project to increase knowledge and understanding of Functional Fluency approaches • support Functional Fluency teaching with younger pupils • use the model instinctively to regulate disputes, find common ground and improve mutual understanding.
Parents / carers...	• describe the basic principles of the Functional Fluency model used at the school.	• understand the model and use it to improve the nature of their relationship with their children.	• use the model actively to address behaviour issues at home.
Staff...	• understand Functional Fluency and how it can be used to inform teaching and learning.	• understand Functional Fluency and use it to explore the effectiveness of their own and others' teaching and learning • confidently participate in Get on the Mat sessions to refine practice.	• complete the Certified Functional Fluency Teacher Programme • lead Get on the Mat sessions for colleagues, inspiring them to get involved in the programme.

Stages	Learner	Knowledgeable user	Advocate
Middle leaders...	• complete the Introduction to Functional Fluency training course • complete the TIFF questionnaire and, in a feedback meeting with a TIFF provider, develop a Functional Fluency action plan.	• incorporate Functional Fluency into a key leadership activity • confidently use Get on the Mat sessions with their team.	• complete the Functionally Fluent School Leaders Programme (see https://functionalfluency.com/training-programs for details), exploring the use of Functional Fluency within a leadership context.
Senior leaders...	• complete TIFF and, in a feedback meeting with a TIFF provider, develop a Functional Fluency action plan • participate in three Functional Fluency workshops over the course of a year with other leaders, exploring the use of Functional Fluency within a leadership context.	• complete the Functionally Fluent School Leaders Programme, exploring the use of Functional Fluency within a leadership context.	• complete the Functional Fluency Team Scan and take part in a team feedback session, resulting in a detailed action plan • design and articulate a whole-school Functional Fluency development plan.
Governors...	• attend two twilight training sessions at least six weeks apart.	• articulate how Functional Fluency principles should inform the school's strategic plan.	• build understanding of Functional Fluency among school stakeholders.

Table 21 The Place framework: Is your school Emerging, Operational or Strategic?

Stakeholders	Emerging	Operational	Strategic and innovative
Pupils	• The 12 Functional Fluency lessons are part of the PSHE curriculum. • Disadvantaged pupils are offered the Introduction to Functional Fluency training and, on completion, become Functional Fluency Ambassadors.	• Introduction to Functional Fluency training is offered to pupils who, on completion, become Functional Fluency Ambassadors.	• Functional Fluency is regularly incorporated into pupil-voice feedback and is a standing item on the school-council meeting agenda. • Functional Fluency Ambassadors play a full role in the life of the school.
Parents / carers	• Functional Fluency is explained in communications, and displayed at parents' / carers' evenings. • The Introduction to Functional Fluency training course is offered at least once a year.	• The Introduction to Functional Fluency training is incorporated into new parent induction meetings. • Systems to consult with parents about the best ways in which Functional Fluency can be used to improve the school are established.	• Get on the Mat sessions are incorporated into parents' / carers' evenings. • Functional Fluency is referenced regularly in newsletters. • Parents report positively on the impact of Functional Fluency.

Stakeholders	Emerging	Operational	Strategic and innovative
Staff	• The Introduction to Functional Fluency training course is provided for all staff.	• The rollout of TIFF is a key element in the school's CPD offer for staff. • Get on the Mat sessions are systematically used to explore scenarios and help resolve conflicts.	• All teachers complete TIFF and have a personal feedback session with a TIFF provider. • Functional Fluency is embedded in school structures and procedures, such as teacher-observation tools. • The Functional Fluency Team Scan is a key element of the school's approach to team development.
Middle leaders	• Middle leaders understand the school's Functional Fluency goals and can explain the basics to their teams.	• All middle leaders have completed TIFF and are implementing their action plans. • They regularly use Functional Fluency concepts, including Get on the Mat sessions, in team meetings. • Middle leaders are embedding Functional Fluency into their teams, using the Functional Fluency action plans developed from their TIFF feedback (as outlined in Table 6).	• Middle leaders actively contribute to the whole-school Functional Fluency strategy. • A formal Functional Fluency coaching programme, led by middle leaders, is established and accessible to all staff.

Stakeholders	Emerging	Operational	Strategic and innovative
Senior leaders	• Senior leaders understand Functional Fluency and use it to explore the effectiveness of their own and others' teaching and learning.	• Senior leaders have a clear understanding of Functional Fluency and use Get on the Mat sessions to explore the effectiveness of their own and others' contributions to the development of the school community. • TIFF is an established part of the Senior Leader induction process.	• Functional Fluency principles are a standing item on senior-leadership team-meeting agendas. • The senior leadership team models the use of the Functional Fluency Team Scan, sharing insights and resulting actions.
Governors	• Governors use Functional Fluency to explore the effectiveness of the relationships within the school.	• Governors use Get on the Mat sessions and the Functionally Fluent meeting structure to explore the effectiveness of their own and others' contributions to the development of the school community.	• Governors develop their Functional Fluency using the Functional Fluency Team Scan tool. • Functional Fluency is embedded in the governors' action plans.

Embedding Functional Fluency is a journey, not a destination. The People and Place frameworks are not rigid prescriptions, but maps to guide your school's unique path, from Emerging to Strategic. This process is far more than a school-improvement initiative; it is a profound investment in human potential. By systematically cultivating these skills in our people and embedding these values in our place, we do more than create better schools. We begin to forge the building blocks of a better, more thoughtful society, one classroom at a time – a challenge and an opportunity we will explore in our final chapter.

CHAPTER 8
MORE THAN A SCHOOL: CREATING THE SOCIETY WE NEED, ONE CLASSROOM AT A TIME

At the local Innovation Hub run by the university, Pat has been asked to give a presentation. Reflecting, she realises that not planning this until two days before the meeting is a good example of Compliant / Resistant and Immature behaviour. This gets her thinking. Why not base the talk on the school's Functional Fluency journey?

Two days later, Pat is driving back to school after the meeting, giving Chris Andrews a lift. Their presentation has gone well. So well, in fact, that four people, including the Vice Chancellor of the university, came up to them afterwards asking for more information about Functional Fluency. As she turns off the ring road, it occurs to Pat that setting up a meeting at school for all the local stakeholders who are interested would be a great way to take this work forward, to help the whole community thrive.

'Chris,' she says, 'I've just had an idea. How would you feel about setting up a meeting to tell the governors all about Functional Fluency?'

How might Functionally Fluent schools contribute to the creation of a more Functionally Fluent society?

Modern culture, heavily influenced by big tech's drive to minimise human interaction for profit, is contributing to a society increasingly wary of social connection, particularly with strangers. As Rebecca Solnit vividly describes in her *London Review of Books* article 'In the Shadow of Silicon Valley' (Solnit, 2024), this pursuit of profit paints a dystopian picture of people afraid to engage with one another. While this trend presents significant challenges, Functional Fluency offers a powerful model to help us remember and re-establish effective social interactions. Losing this fundamental human capability poses an existential risk to our society.

This retreat from one another is not just a social malaise; it is a skills deficit. We are losing our fluency in the very behaviours that build robust communities. This chapter argues that Functional Fluency provides a learnable language for these interactions, offering a structured way for schools actively to teach the relational competencies that society is at risk of forgetting.

Meanwhile, schools are often overwhelmed by a constant influx of interventions and initiatives; their development plans filled with well-intentioned but frequently disconnected projects. Like many educational texts, I make the claim that this book offers something different. Functional Fluency, rooted in the foundational ideas of Transactional Analysis (TA) developed by Eric Berne in *Transactional Analysis in Psychotherapy* (1961) and *Games People Play* (1964), is not a fleeting trend. It provides a clear and simple explanation of how our behavioural choices fall into effective and less effective patterns.

Functional Fluency offers a system for gradually incorporating more beneficial decision-making into our lives, helping us use our finite time and energy wisely. It describes the behavioural choices essential for thriving – an imperative that has become acutely urgent alongside the deepening climate crisis. Our collective ability to make choices that support widespread thriving is crucial for the survival of our species.

Rather than adding another burden, Functional Fluency serves as a valuable tool for enhancing existing efforts within schools. By guiding individuals towards more effective behavioural choices, it helps conserve energy, avoid time-wasting conflicts and find the capacity needed to pursue other initiatives successfully. Encouraging a shift from reacting to pausing and responding, it allows teachers, leaders and pupils to focus on what truly matters.

Because Functional Fluency has developed from TA and shares much of TA's theoretical basis, it also shares the same theoretical underpinning. Giles Barrow (2016) has written persuasively about the importance of the concept of 'natality', which he describes as the 'act of birth and the subsequent processes of becoming, beginning and belonging'. This fits the purpose of education in the most general sense, but is also a perfect description of the Functional Fluency model, with its focus on personal self-actualisation through the modes of Cooperative and Spontaneous behaviour and helping the self and others to grow and develop through the Structuring and Nurturing modes.

Barrow goes on to suggest that natality is important 'in terms of combating a natural tendency to decline and entropy, which results in death and is ultimately expressed in the concept of mortality' (Barrow, 2016). He states that 'Educational TA is about more than instigating social change; it is in support of the renewing human spirit fulfilling itself beyond what it has so far accomplished' (Barrow, 2016). TA and Functional Fluency are both about helping individuals to fulfil their potential and, in so doing, to replace the capacity that is always being lost from the teaching profession and humanity in general through burnout, career change, retirement and death. Seeing it in this way makes the social and biological imperative behind this work very clear, and lends an urgency and momentum to the work to which this book seeks to contribute.

Furthermore, Functional Fluency provides a template for schools to construct thoughtful, appropriate and effective responses to complex societal challenges, such as increasing sexism, misogyny and racism. It can help cultivate educational communities and curriculum plans that ensure all young people feel valued, regardless of their intersectional identity. In the context of the climate crisis, Functional Fluency brings us back to basics, helping us focus our time and energy on behaviours beneficial to the planet's and species' survival.

Escaping the 'greatness' trap: the radical power of the 'good-enough' school

In his book *The Good-Enough Life*, Avram Alpert (2022) outlines an approach to philosophy, economics and life in general that attempts to switch our focus away from greatness and instead encourages us to pursue a life that is 'good enough'. His thesis is that the relentless pursuit of greatness has had hugely negative impacts on our society, fuelling inequality. He cites the civil-rights movement and its excessive emphasis on the work and achievements of outstanding individuals such as Martin Luther King, to the exclusion and eventual detriment of the wealth and welfare of the unexceptional millions of global majority people whose lives remain hugely disadvantaged. Alpert concludes a section of his book with the following couple of sentences – which read like a powerful endorsement of Functional Fluency as an approach to building more effective relationships and living a better life:

> Developing the abilities to relate to each other and to find what is meaningful and glorious in each other requires a shift in perspective away from greatness and towards our various possibilities – maligned though they have been, oppressed though they are. Aspects of a good-enough life are possible in the midst of a terrible world, and we have an ethical injunction to bear witness to their existence.

Alpert, 2022

This quotation encapsulates a lot of the thinking behind why Functional Fluency could be such a potent force for improvement in all schools, referencing, as it does, the importance of diversity and the climate crisis: two themes that help to provide a contextual underpinning for my ideas about how Functional Fluency can be applied in schools to the benefit of all.

Alpert cites the phrase, associated with John F. Kennedy, 'A rising tide lifts all boats'. This philosophy has run through recent capitalist thinking and the policies of recent UK governments, but evidence that the notion that wealth 'trickles down' to benefit all in society is increasingly disproved by both societal evidence, as we become a more and more unequal society, and by academic and theoretical economics (Kretchmer, 2021). This patronising, paternalist approach is based on the idea of a 'great' few making huge fortunes that, in some vague and ill-defined way, benefit everyone, and the public has somehow been persuaded to support policies that advance this approach.

There are ways in which the policies implemented in the education sector over the last couple of decades mirror this thinking. Schools have been encouraged to compete for the highest results, and this creates chronic 'pains' that cause multiple negative side-effects. This approach drives competition for the best teachers and the least disadvantaged pupils. It is bolstered by an inspectorate that implements a framework that largely equates success with performance in examinations. Most schools and individuals (pupils, teachers and parents) lose out in this system. The curriculum becomes narrow, and choices are driven by self-serving, superficial motives. Schools that do not perform well are judged poor by Ofsted and, in the perverted version of parental choice that we implement, families choose, if they can, to avoid such schools, resulting in their further decline, to the benefit of the supposedly 'great' school down the road. A downward spiral begins that is very difficult to break out of and, in the process, the educational prospects of young people are restricted, and the professional prospects of the teaching staff are reduced. Huge quantities of potential are thus wasted in the name of competition and the pursuit of greatness. These are not trivial 'pains', but ones that are debilitating for families, and that restrict the development of society in fundamental ways.

Imagine instead a context that benefits from the 'gains' that would flow from a situation where schools cooperated with each other for the greater good. Visualise a situation where progress and achievement of schools and individuals is judged on a collective rather than individual level. Picture how things could be different if teachers and school leaders could make decisions in the light of the long-term benefits that would accrue for their pupils and society rather than always seeking quick wins.

Functional Fluency could help us to reframe our approach, so that we move away from these 'pains', and instead move towards the 'gains' that a more equitable system could deliver. Instead of fostering beacons of excellence, the emphasis would be on ensuring that all schools are 'good enough'. This would ensure much greater equity of provision, avoid the 'sink school' scenario, provide better professional opportunities for teachers and enable all pupils' potential to be achieved. But this requires a radical rethinking at both the policy level and the inter-personal level. The policy aspect is beyond the scope of this book, but it is my contention that Functional Fluency could genuinely provide a model that could enable schools to implement this much needed 'good-enough' approach at the inter-personal level. Education is built upon relationships – between teachers and pupils, teachers and teachers, pupils and pupils, teachers and leaders and all these groups and parents This book is an attempt to outline how Functional Fluency could be used to inform thinking about how these relationships can become 'good enough'.

This critique of a society driven by competition and a narrow definition of success leads to a deeper question: with what do we replace these flawed ambitions? For centuries, humanity looked to other systems for its behavioural and moral guidance.

This damaging pursuit of 'greatness' begs a fundamental question: if we can see that a cooperative, 'good-enough' approach would create a more equitable and effective system, why do we continue to perpetuate a model that causes so much harm? The answer lies in a timeless human struggle, a phenomenon the ancient Greeks knew well. They had a word for the frustrating gap between knowing what we *should* do and actually doing it: *akrasia*.

Why we know what's right but do what's wrong (and how to fix it)

Humanity has been aware of this problem for centuries and, for many people and for many years, the answer was religion. Religious teachings, holy books, prayers, collects and hymns constantly reminded us of how we ought to behave. The power and persuasive capacity of this meant that it was always possible to subvert it for nefarious purposes, and thus religions have, over many centuries, been perverted by those with power so that they can use them as mechanisms for maintaining and extending this power rather than for perfecting human existence on Earth. For many years, particularly in the West, our faith in religion has been declining, but it has not been replaced in any systematic way with a code or set of principles that can provide citizens with a similar sense of moral purpose. Superficial solutions such as capitalism have provided temporary answers, but it is all too clear that the behavioural imperatives that they impose upon the public (buy, buy, buy) are not designed to spread equity and social cohesion – quite the opposite.

This seems to me to be a situation where Functional Fluency could be helpful. It provides a non-dogmatic model to help us to decide what is the appropriate or mutually beneficial way to behave. It allows us to reflect on past actions and see where things have gone wrong or where opportunities to deepen relationships have been missed. In a school context, the model provides us with a touchstone against which to judge policies drafted, choices made and rules implemented. When, inevitably, things don't go well, Functional Fluency is a lens through which to examine the errors and identify the causes of the issues. This book focuses on finding ways in which schools can use Functional Fluency to establish a fair, non-doctrinaire approach to behaviour that enables all those in the institution to thrive.

It should also be pointed out that Functional Fluency complements rather than replaces religion. The central emphasis on compassion, which sits at the heart of the great world religions, as Karen Armstrong has identified in her book *The Twelve Steps to a Compassionate Life* (Armstrong, 2011), sits very comfortably with Functional Fluency. This means that the model can be used within schools of all faiths and none to add clarity and potentially to overcome difficulties caused by contested religious language when all parties do not share the same beliefs. Functional Fluency International works with adherents of a wide range of religions, as well as those with no faith, and all can use the model to gain greater understanding of their own and others' behaviour.

While the loss of a shared moral framework explains the deep-seated 'why' of our societal challenges, the 'how' is expressed in the very texture of our daily interactions, which have been fundamentally reshaped by modern media and technology.

Now let's look at a book that is very clear about the importance of developing classrooms where relationships are paramount.

High challenge, low threat

Skim-reading the contents page of Mary Myatt's important book on school leadership, *High Challenge, Low Threat* (2016), it is easy to spot the connections with Functional Fluency. The second chapter is entitled 'Human beings first, professionals second'; a concept that aligns directly with the belief in the dignity and importance of individuals that lies at the heart of Functional Fluency. Myatt describes top school leaders as demonstrating 'a combination of warmth and tough love', which sounds very similar to the blend of Structuring and Nurturing behaviour that Functional Fluency suggests is necessary to help yourself and others to grow and develop effectively. She identifies the way effective leaders support their colleagues by making thoughtful enquiries that show that they are taking an interest in them as individuals: a manifestation of the strokes we have seen are vital to effective functioning. But Myatt shows that strong school leaders also provide clear and honest advice that doesn't sugarcoat things (Marshmallowing) in the following chapter, which borrows Kim Scott's phrase 'radical candor' (First Round Review, 2015; Scott, 2019) to encapsulate this approach.

Several chapters reference leadership behaviour that could be described as Accounting. In the chapter 'Everyone has a voice', Myatt focuses on the universal need to 'have our voices heard', and how this can be realised for both staff and pupils. The *alert, aware, grounded* and *evaluative* behaviours that constitute Accounting need to be to the fore to make this a success. Myatt takes this further in her chapter 'The power of noticing', which describes the Accounting that classroom teachers need to develop if they are to be successful. 'They notice what is significant, what children are saying, their body language and the quality of their work' (Myatt, 2016).

The chapter 'The paradox of fun' describes the Spontaneous behaviour that a Functionally Fluent teacher needs. Myatt explains how effective teachers and leaders know their classes and colleagues so well that they take pleasure with them in the small, everyday wins; and share the satisfactions of difficult work done well, the enjoyment of being together, 'the quiet pleasure rather than rah-rah fun and games' that characterise Immature behaviour (Myatt, 2016).

In an important chapter, Myatt writes about the leadership of inclusion. Here, she proposes an approach to leadership that ensures that **all** pupils get appropriate provision – not just the more able ones who are likely to achieve the results that will improve the school's data. Inclusive leaders 'give them [the pupils] the richest, deepest possible curriculum. They don't dumb down. They offer difficult, challenging stuff and help them to access it with the right support. They put high challenge, low threat into action. They deploy staff that have the greatest skills in unpacking a curriculum to work with these pupils. And they expect everyone to learn from them' (Myatt, 2016).

This is where Functional Fluency can offer a new vision of how schools should operate, to the benefit of our society. As Myatt points out, the provision should start with and be constantly informed by evidence and ideas gathered through active, planned Accounting. This is what enables schools to identify accurately what the pupils need and how best to address these needs.

This should be followed by Structuring, which provides opportunities and frameworks within which pupils and teachers flourish. This must be balanced by Nurturing, so that the individuals who make up the school community feel recognised and valued for their individuality.

These approaches provide the conditions in which the Cooperative and Spontaneous responses, which are the signifiers of effective teaching and learning, can thrive. They signal a move away from leadership driven by narrow definitions of success based on creating winners and losers, to a more mature vision of a society predicated on trust. As Myatt writes in the final chapter, 'Organisations that develop trust have a recruiting advantage, retention advantage and productivity advantage. Externally, trust means that an organisation is authentic, and robust enough to withstand media scrutiny. People realize that you will do the right thing. Trust buys you grace' (Myatt, 2016).

And the mechanism schools can use to develop this trust is Functional Fluency.

Responding, not reacting: staying human in the age of outrage

The ancient problem of *akrasia* – the gap between knowledge and action – has been supercharged by what William Davies calls the 'reaction economy' (2023). Modern technology has not just failed to solve the problem of *akrasia*; it has monetised it. By designing platforms that reward instant, unthinking reactions over considered responses, the digital world actively encourages us to bypass our better judgement. Schools, therefore, are not just contending with a timeless human weakness, but with a modern economic system designed to exploit it.

In a wide-ranging and fascinating article in the *London Review of Books*, William Davies writes about the growth of what he calls 'the reaction economy' (Davies, 2023). Citing a wide range of examples, from culture wars on social media and the obsessively detailed examination of the video footage of the Will Smith slap of Chris Rock following his insulting comment about Smith's wife, to the emails that online companies send following a purchase, Davies argues that our culture has become dominated by a desire to provoke, capture and analyse reactions.

'Seasoned characters such as Piers Morgan are cynically aware that what will keep them in the spotlight is the force, distinctiveness and watch-ability of their knee-jerk responses, which are essentially designed to ignite reaction chains' (Davies, 2023). The problem with this is that it is completely at odds with the culture that we generally want to establish in schools. Pastoral managers spend much of their time dealing with the fallout from reactions, whether that is something that a pupil has said to another pupil, a physical reaction to a provocation or an online comment that has developed into a family vendetta. If this focus on the moment, which results in, at one extreme, deeply offensive trolling and, at the other, touching proposal videos, has become so pervasive across our society, how can schools be expected to develop something so profoundly different in the form of a caring, thoughtful, compassionate community where people think before they act?

The Functional Fluency model can help to provide an answer. The centrality of Accounting to this approach to behaviour is a great asset here. This thoughtful, restrained, considered type of behaviour takes up a symbolic central position in the model, suggestive of its huge importance in this new conception of how we should regulate our behavioural responses to stimuli.

School leaders will, I think, recognise the applicability of the following sentence, which Davies wrote about culture in general, to the specific culture of schools:

> Anger and humour are parallel reactions to a world that appears to have lost the capacity to recognise genuine injustice and has become fixated instead on phoney injustices – a world that is ostensibly diverted by petty offences at the expense of real harms.

Davies, 2023

And the problem in schools is often that there is very little distance between the humorous and the angry reaction to any given situation. Many incidents that blow up in schools are excused by their perpetrator as 'banter', which they feel is harmless but the victim experiences as cruel. The reactions then quickly descend into anger for both parties, and the school has a difficult situation to untangle. This scenario is at the heart of many incidents involving racism and sexism, with the desire for ever more extreme reactions driven by reactionary politicians and online commentators alike.

Towards the end of his article, Davies specifically invokes the situations of schools within this reaction-based situation:

> Children today may not submit to Victorian moral authorities (though the behavioural agenda in many English schools may suggest otherwise), but they are undoubtedly cowed by the authority of reactions. We can blame Instagram, WhatsApp and the possibilities for cyber-bullying afforded by life online, but we should also consider the ways technologies of feedback and reward have become embedded in every moment of a child's school day, thanks especially to the widespread implementation of EdTech. Spontaneity and action become impossible when they are already overtaken by the range of possible reactions that might ensue, not just from

teachers, but from the numerous systems that track a child – or an adult for that matter – throughout the day.

Davies, 2023

Lesson observations and learning walks demonstrate that school leaders have implemented an approach to teaching that requires teachers to provide pupils with constant feedback on their progress, through low-stakes quizzes, mini-whiteboard exercises and starter activities. The result is that pupils are being judged all day long, encouraged to provide answers (stimuli) to which teachers can react. All too often, these reactions do not give any useful information about progress, and can be glibly optimistic and not thought out.

So how can schools use Functional Fluency to address this toxic mess of issues? Davies' article concludes by suggesting that forgiveness is 'unique in being a reaction which breaks the chain, making a fresh start possible' (Davies, 2023). I propose instead that Functional Fluency, with its emphasis first and foremost on Accounting, provides a more coherent and systematic route out of the cycle of reactions. Indeed, it is interesting that, even as Davies describes forgiveness as a solution, he nevertheless labels it too as a 'reaction' – the very thing we are trying to move away from. Leona Bishop, CEO of Functional Fluency International, provides a clear and helpful description of Accounting and how it can help teachers and pupils to move beyond reaction in her record of working with a secondary school in the Caribbean:

> People who understand the Functional Fluency Model and know how to use it are better equipped to respond, rather than react in all kinds of situations. In challenging, uncertain and chaotic times, they use their ability to do complex accounting: the capacity of humans to reflect, consider, imagine and problem solve. Important accounting functions include *assessing* what is relevant in a situation, *working out* what is significant in the circumstances, *imagining* possible implications and *considering* what needs to be decided. Then comes the choosing of options and necessary conditions for action to take place. All of this uses energy internally, 'head, heart and gut', which is why we say that accounting works like an internal 'mode of behaviour' i.e. it is not observable. Accounting, therefore, is what a person does internally in order to choose what to do or say next. It is an internal activity that allows you to act in an emotionally intelligent way, and to be effective in your relationships with others. It means:
>
> - Taking into account what you are experiencing in the here and now, of what you are thinking, what you are feeling, and what you need.

- Taking into account what others are experiencing. By putting yourself in their position, you are able to assess what they think, feel, and need.
- Taking into account what is happening in the context, in the world around you, and of what is relevant and significant.

It embraces what you need to do, and when, to act in line with what is called for by the situation. Accounting is an internal mechanism for managing yourself effectively. By doing Accounting, you are taking stock of the situation, taking into account all relevant aspects to do with self, others, and the here-and-now situation. Effective Accounting helps you decide which blend of the four other golden modes of behaviour to use.

Bishop, 2024

By building understanding of Functional Fluency across a whole school community, there is a chance for teachers and leaders to establish a culture and mode of behaviour within the community that goes against the norm and focuses on empathy, consideration and thoughtfulness. The words I have italicised in the passage above indicate the internal processes that Accounting encourages that teachers need to support and that put a break on reactions, fostering instead a more productive, thoughtful response. This gradually moves those within the community away from instant and potentially hurtful reactions and towards more considered responses from which everyone can learn and grow. Growth of self and others that enables everyone to thrive is central to Functional Fluency and to effective education.

This culture of instant reaction, which prioritises momentary engagement over thoughtful response, is a symptom of a deeper societal issue: we are often measuring and valuing the wrong things. Just as our social discourse has become shallow, so too have our metrics for success, both for a nation and for the schools within it.

If we're measuring the wrong things, can we ever succeed?

Joseph Stiglitz and Amartya Sen, Nobel prize-winning economists, and French economist Jean-Paul Fitoussi (2010) in *Mismeasuring Our Lives*, suggest that, by focusing our analysis on the success of countries on the growth, or lack of growth, of their GDP, we are missing the point. They argue for a much broader and more inclusive set of measures to be used to assess the success of a society, including measurements of happiness.

Just as economists including Stiglitz argue that GDP is a crude and misleading measure of a nation's health, so too are league tables and exam results a mismeasurement of a school's success. Both prioritise simple, quantifiable outputs over complex indicators of genuine wellbeing and thriving.

We need to be thinking about the kind of people that our schools are producing. What skills, aptitudes and levels of resilience do our young people have when they leave? The Covid epidemic put even more emphasis on this way of looking at things as we begin to reap the results of a system focused entirely on academic results at the expense of wellbeing. Example 18 shows how Functional Fluency can be used to provide this broader, alternative viewpoint.

Example 18 Mismeasuring our lives

Parents:

Situation

At a parents' / carers' evening, you talk to a Year 11 pupil and his parents about his A-level choices. It is clear that the parents are against the idea of their son studying the arts subject that you teach as they do not feel it will provide him with the economic prospects that science training will.

▼

You:

Immediate thoughts and feelings

The parents' casual dismissal of the idea that the arts can be the basis of a satisfying career annoys you and you feel tempted to react negatively to them (*defiant*).

▼

You:

Pause: choice

You take the time to be *curious* about their views and ask the parents to explain their thinking in more detail. You want to ask the pupil for his feelings, but you are alert to how he appears uncomfortable with this discussion.

▼

Functionally Fluent response

So, instead, you cite some research that you are aware of about the value of the arts to the UK economy and the number of jobs that the sector supports. You also reference the job satisfaction and mental-health benefits of working in a job that is personally satisfying.

By responding to the situation rather than reacting, you have opened the issue to proper debate. You ask the parents about their own employment history and encourage them to consider whether they are attempting to pursue their own agendas through their son (Dominating).

Finally, you sense (*alert*) that the pupil is now ready to speak, and you ask him for his feelings. He explains that he feels supported by you and the points you have made, and that he had been getting depressed at the thought of studying only science A-levels. Together, you arrive at the idea of combining both science and arts A-levels into a programme that feels satisfactory for all parties.

Key learning

Parents do not always understand their children as well as they think they do, and Functional Fluency can help you to address complex issues from an unbiased perspective.

If we are to move beyond these narrow and damaging metrics, we must fundamentally reconsider the purpose of education itself. The answer lies, not in optimising for test scores, but in designing a curriculum that prepares young people to address the very societal challenges we have discussed.

Curriculum as a societal project

Curriculum planning is a key locus for values-based thinking. The content that you find the time for becomes the teaching that you value; it is important that this is not solely driven by pragmatism and that it will enable pupils to pursue careers. As Hollis writes:

> I strongly advocate the study of the liberal arts curriculum for all persons, because we can always learn the tools of a trade on the job, and in this era of constant change we may practice many trades before we're done. Making a living is the easy part, but far more critical is what liberates us from the limits of our family and cultural history. What values, what ways of critical thinking and discerning evaluation do we possess to enrich

our lives? What understandings of history allow us to escape its binding repetitions ... These rich, intrapsychic companions will seldom if ever be served by the constricted aims of careerism and vocational narrowing. The liberal arts, however, contribute to the liberating arts of a more considered, more thoughtful, more variegated sensibility, which in the end is necessary for more free choice.

Hollis, 2005

The Accounting emphasis of Functional Fluency encourages school leaders to think deeply about their values, and to evaluate the needs of their pupils, the community and wider society, which they will contribute to and live in. Accounting enables school leaders to make the sagacious judgements required to deliver these subtle yet vital outcomes.

Governments, particularly when they are new, often launch a curriculum-review process. These often promise major improvements. However, there is a danger that what emerges, after much consultation, is a new curriculum document that tinkers with curriculum reform, removing a bit of content here and adding in some new material there. The radical reform that encourages schools to start addressing the real issues that 21st-century society needs to start finding answers to is unlikely to come out of this process.

So, what role can Functional Fluency play in this? How can it help us to avoid getting dragged into a futile argument between those who think that improved basic skills are the answer and their opponents who feel that what employers of the future will need are workers with advanced collaborative and creative capacities?

Clearly, it is my belief that Functional Fluency should be an integral part of any new and revised curriculum. Valerie Hannon, in her visionary book *Thrive*, outlines the goals of education in the future:

> The previous chapter discussed how thriving at a societal level is undermined by increased income inequality, with every indication that this will become exacerbated by future trends. To successfully tackle inequality, schools need to engage with two future-focussed purposes: to prepare learners to navigate a disrupted landscape of work, and to reinvent a more participative democracy.

Hannon, 2017

The years that have passed since Hannon wrote this have proved her first sentence to be sadly prophetic. But it remains my firm belief that Functional Fluency can contribute to the achievement of both purposes she outlines. Gaining increased understanding of themselves and their behavioural choices can certainly enable our young people to navigate the increasingly complex world of employment in ways that enable them to thrive, by helping them to understand the need for Accounting to make sense of the demands placed on them by the ever-evolving employment context and also by demonstrating to them the need to balance their use of time and energy across the more effective golden modes of the Functional Fluency model. Additionally, the model helps to pinpoint the placating and submissive behaviour that diminishes participative democracy and encourages the assertive, resilient and firm behaviour that helps it to flourish.

It is often said that it is not worthwhile focusing on skills in education as they are not as transferable as we tend to think. But with its focus not so much on skills as on identifying and improving behaviour patterns, the Functional Fluency model could provide a vital map to help our young people navigate their way through this 'era of constant change' in productive and society-enhancing ways. This is why it deserves a place in any review of the curriculum and, indeed, why Functionally Fluent thinking should underpin the revision processes themselves.

In the *Curriculum and Assessment Review* (DFE, 2025), the results of polling on features that parents and pupils would like to see more time spent on in education between Years 7 and 11 revealed that the following areas are popular with both groups:

1. Finance and budgeting

2. Digital skills or computing

3. Creative-thinking and problem-solving projects

4. Employment and interview skills

5. Academic subjects (for example maths, science, history)

6. Communication (for example debating, public speaking)

Functional Fluency could directly contribute to items 3, 4 and 6; indirectly (through improved teacher–pupil relationships) to 5; and (through the emphasis on Accounting) to 1. This provides a clear mandate for putting time and effort into developing a Functional Fluency approach, as it aligns with several of the top priorities of both parents and pupils.

A curriculum with this sense of societal purpose provides the foundation. The next step is to apply its principles to the most complex and ingrained societal issues that manifest daily within our school communities, such as prejudice and bullying. Functional Fluency provides the paradigm to do just that.

Pedagogical Accounting: a tool to challenge systemic expectations

A stark illustration of these ingrained societal issues can be found in the research of educational sociologist Derron Wallace. In a series of four recordings that I made with him about his book *The Culture Trap* (Wallace, 2023), the importance of pedagogical Accounting became apparent. Here, I am using Accounting in the metaphorical sense of taking 'account' of the whole child, their background and the cultural biases and systemic expectations that impact on them.

In the second recording, we address the issue of ability grouping. A number of researchers, including Wallace, have found that black Caribbean pupils are disproportionately assigned to bottom sets in UK schools. These bottom sets are often allocated less experienced teachers. The result is depressed outcomes for these pupils.

Wallace's research has found that schools' unconscious biases often place different expectations on black African pupils, who they anticipate will be hard-working and high-achieving. These schools often have much lower expectations of black Caribbean pupils. However, they see the success of the black African pupils as evidence of the effectiveness of their anti-racist approach. The result is that the low expectations placed on black Caribbean pupils result in unfulfilled potential and reduced outcomes for these pupils, with all the long term socio-economic and psychological issues that this brings. These unexamined biases are a prime example of the 'reaction economy' operating within our own schools, where ingrained assumptions substitute for the thoughtful, individualised response that every child deserves. Pedagogical Accounting is the tool that allows us to interrupt this reactive cycle.

Pedagogical Accounting requires the systematic assessment of a range of qualitative data on who is in which set, which pupils teachers interact with, who they praise (positive strokes), whose achievements they celebrate and the nature of the feedback they give. Through this type of detailed analysis, schools begin to identify unconscious limiting biases and damaging assumptions that are at play in their practice. This pedagogical Accounting, supported by sensitive pupil-voice initiatives to find out about the pupils' own pedagogical reality, reveals important insights into the unconscious practices that are restricting the progress of so many groups of pupils: not just black Caribbean pupils, but also girls, white working-class boys and disadvantaged pupils, for example.

But Accounting alone is not enough. To make an impact, this use of the tools must be followed by determined action to change systemic expectations. This might involve *authoritative* explanations of the negative impact of some current pedagogical practices and the *firm* endorsement of more equitable alternatives. It might involve *empathic* support for professional development as new approaches that aim to undo the limiting consequences of previous, well-meaning practices are discussed. It entails a willingness to engage in Spontaneous and Cooperative discussion about the complexity of the situation, the nuance of the potential solutions and the vital requirement for change if all pupils are to fulfil their potential. Pedagogical Accounting is not easy, but it is necessary, vital and life-changing for many pupils and, as such, there is a moral imperative for schools to get involved in this Functionally Fluent effort.

This concept of pedagogical Accounting illustrates how Functional Fluency is not just about interpersonal harmony; it is a critical tool for social justice and building a truly inclusive and equitable school system.

A language for equity: using Functional Fluency to tackle bullying and discrimination

The Functional Fluency model provides a paradigm to enable teachers to demonstrate why all forms of prejudice are wrong. Whether the issue is sexism, racism or another form of prejudice or discrimination, it is easy to create a Functional Fluency profile for this combination of behaviours that demonstrates its origin in the purple modes.

To demonstrate how this might work, here are six different types of sexism, as outlined on the website *Medical News Today* (2023), analysed using the Functional Fluency model. The same process could be carried out for racism or other forms of prejudice.

1. The first is **hostile** sexism. This is characterised by deceitful and manipulative behaviour and, while it is hopefully not common in schools, it is certainly not unheard of. It usually involves elements of *blaming*, *fault-finding* and *judgemental* behaviour from the Dominating mode, alongside *egocentric* and *inconsiderate* behaviour from the Immature mode, in conjunction with *defiant* and *rebellious* elements of Compliant / Resistant behaviour.

2. The second form of sexism is classified as **benevolent** sexism, though this is a problematic term as no form of discrimination can ever be seen as

benevolent. It involves a conception of females as innocent and requiring protection. This is a clear demonstration of the *over-protective* and *smothering* aspects of Marshmallowing behaviour, blended with *knows-better* from the Dominating mode.

3. The third mode of sexism is classified as **ambivalent** sexism, and this is essentially a mix of or alternating between 'hostile' and 'benevolent' sexism. The perpetrator alternates between the two sets of purple-mode behaviours indicated above, adding in a dose of Compliant / Resistant behaviour in the form of either *submissive* or *rebellious* behaviour, as their distorted motives dictate.

4. The fourth mode of sexism is **institutional** sexism. This may include elements of Marshmallowing, such as *inconsistent* or *over-protective* behaviour. It could also, in the form of a failure to take the needs of women properly into consideration, involve elements of Immature behaviour, such as *inconsiderate* and *unorganised* responses that fail to cater for women's needs. When women point out their needs, these could be met by *placating* behaviour from the Compliant / Resistant mode or *knows-better* or, worse, *punitive* behaviour from the Dominating mode.

5. **Interpersonal** sexism, the fifth mode, can take the form of any of the purple modes of behaviour. It is worth pointing out here that this form of discriminatory behaviour can never be the result of golden-mode behaviour. It is important that pupils understand this. So, for example, it is easy to imagine a partner *cherishing* a woman in a way that is limiting. This should be seen not as true cherishing, which is inherently positive and affirming, but as a form of *over-protective* or *smothering* behaviour from the Marshmallowing mode. In this way, the Functional Fluency model provides a set of terms with which young people can talk about their experiences of the behaviour of others and explore their understanding of a prejudice in nuanced ways that should, if carefully handled, help to build understanding and genuine communication.

6. The final mode of sexism identified in the article is **internalised** sexism. This is the set of limiting beliefs that a woman may have about herself and her sex because of her experiences and upbringing. Again, the Functional Fluency model helps individuals to explore this by providing a constructive vocabulary. For example, a female pupil may have internalised the idea, from her family and her female role models, that it is reasonable for women to be *inhibited* or *bossy* or *egocentric* or *over-indulgent*, to take one example from each of the purple modes. This is a limiting view of how women should behave, and it is only by recognising this that the damaging implications, whether that be self-harming, lack of ambition or excessive concern about appearance, can be challenged.

This analysis focuses on sexism, but hopefully it is clear how the Functional Fluency model can be used to explore and illuminate the misguided thinking at the heart of any form of discrimination or prejudice. The intention is to provide teachers with a guide to ways in which they can construct a dialogue with which to address issues relating to diversity that will develop rather than shut down communication and foster **response** rather than **reaction**.

Functional Fluency and fundamentalism

Functional Fluency can help us to consider, understand and ultimately (and hopefully) to overcome the shortcomings of fundamentalism, of whatever form. I am drawn back to Hollis's (2009) description of nuanced acceptance of the underlying ambiguity of life: 'the putative fixity of definitions of race, gender, sexual preference or orientation, Western hegemony, trust in government probity, and many other presumptive truisms have been challenged, and largely overthrown, although many millions cling to the slope side of history in service to their psychological security. As a species we ill tolerate ambiguity, contradiction, or whatever proves uncomfortable, and that is what makes the anxiety-fuelled fundamentalism in each of us take over from time to time'. The Functional Fluency model, with its complexity and its simplicity, with Accounting at its heart, enables us to view life with the subtlety to avoid these pitfalls.

What follows are some examples of how these theoretical ideas can be made practical, to the benefit of pupils and young people in a variety of contexts.

Bullying

One of the issues that can ruin school life for pupils is bullying. In the best-run schools, there are still incidents where pupils pick on other pupils, making their lives miserable or even intolerable.

Empowering pupils to better understand and talk about human behaviour by teaching them the Functional Fluency model could potentially reduce the long-term psychological damage that bullying causes. If pupils understand the model, they are at least more likely to question themselves and their peers when bullying is on the cards.

Functional Fluency and racial equity

While writing this book, an issue arose on social media related to a ban that one school imposed on pupils practising their daily Islamic prayer rituals. Apparently, it was difficult to find enough staff to supervise this every day, and it was also becoming divisive, with some pupils accusing others of not being sufficiently Muslim as, in their eyes, they were not praying often enough.

The following day, a teacher posted a thread that explained in detail how his school had addressed exactly this issue. It seemed to me to exemplify a Functionally Fluent approach that the school had worked out for themselves. I will explain three specific examples that demonstrate how Functionally Fluent behaviour choices have enabled his school to navigate these complex issues.

Example 19 Prayer rooms

Situation

70% of the school's pupils are Muslim. This is quite unusual in the city, where schools are generally either 100% or 0%. The Muslim pupils want a place to pray on Fridays.

Pupils:

Immediate thoughts and feelings

The school is keen to try to meet the pupils' needs for a prayer space if it can (*empathic*). But there is concern about potential problems, including the increase in teacher workload that the supervision will involve and *anxiety* about the potential for a backlash in the local press.

School:

Pause: choice

The school takes time to consider all the issues and to consult with pupils, parents and community groups (Accounting).

School:

Functionally Fluent response

The school makes the theatre space available to pupils for Friday prayers and provides staff supervision to ensure everyone is safe (Structuring / Nurturing). A member of staff leads the prayers. On other days, a smaller space is provided where pupils can pray (Structuring / Nurturing). Pupils are sometimes late for lessons after prayers but supervising staff work hard to try to avoid this. This process combines effective behaviours from Functional Fluency and provides the circumstances for pupils to take responsibility for themselves and for others and to grow as people. Pupils late for lessons due to prayers are reprimanded or punished in the same way they would be if they were late for any other reason (Structuring).

School:

Key learning

Functional Fluency can help find solutions to complex issues, including those involving polarising concepts such as religion.

Example 20 Lights out

Situation

During a residential trip, a large group of key stage 4 boys want to pray after lights out. Some are quite rude and aggressive in the way they demand this.

Pupils:

▼

Immediate thoughts and feelings

The staff feel they are in a quandary and are not sure how to react. They are annoyed by the boys' rudeness (*defiant*) but do not want to turn down what seems to be a genuine request (*adaptable*).

Pupils:

▼

Pause: choice

The staff think the situation through. Allowing some pupils to ignore the lights-out rule could send a signal to the other pupils that all rules on this trip could be broken (*aware*).

Teachers:

▼

Functionally Fluent response

It is clear that the rudeness and aggression are unacceptable and that these pupils need to be punished for this (Structuring: *firm, assertive*). A compromise is reached (Cooperative, Nurturing) whereby the prayers are allowed to go ahead, but the rest of the group understand that this is an exceptional arrangement (Structuring) and the rudeness is dealt with in line with the school's usual response to rudeness to staff.

Teachers:

▼

Key learning

Religion can sometimes confuse issues. Functional Fluency can help us to see through the confusion and devise responses that are fair and equitable.

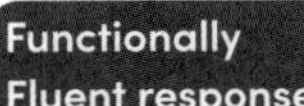

Example 21 Religious bullying

Situation

Some pupils accuse others of being insufficiently Muslim. Sometimes this comes in the form of accusing them of not praying often enough. At other times, it is directed at girls who some other pupils feel are dressing in too Western a fashion. A small number of cases involve homophobic bullying with a religious overtone.

Pupils:

Immediate thoughts and feelings

There are a lot of strong feelings involved in these issues, and staff, particularly non-Muslim teachers, feel concerned that they might get dragged into an exceedingly difficult and compromising situation for which they do not have adequate training (*alert*).

Teachers:

Pause: choice

Thinking the situation through (Accounting), the staff realise that what they are dealing with here is bullying. It is just as inappropriate to bully another pupil about their religious observance as it is about their weight or hair colour.

Teachers:

Functionally Fluent response

Appropriate punishments are given, in line with the school's response to other forms of bullying (Structuring). A programme of education (assemblies, communication with parents) is set up to ensure that everyone understands the situation and knows how it is being dealt with (Structuring and Nurturing).

Teachers:

Key learning

Again, Functional Fluency is a robust model that can help us to come to solutions that benefit everyone.

The teacher is very clear that banning prayer is not an option for him. His priority is that the school clearly represents and reflects its community and that the Muslim faith of the majority is very much in tune with the school's outlook, and with academic success and social acceptance more generally. Whatever problems or issues are experienced are dealt with in appropriate ways that maintain the opportunity to pray while punishing those who misuse this opportunity. Throughout the process, the teacher maintains a clear focus on his and his school's priorities; this is very much the approach outlined in the section on vision and values in Chapter 5. Functional Fluency could certainly help a school to do this, providing a clear steer through these potentially difficult waters, while also saving everyone valuable time and energy and helping the school to come to principled decisions that benefit everyone.

Ultimately, the Functionally Fluent teacher understands that the classroom does not exist in a vacuum. It is a microcosm of society, reflecting its pressures, its prejudices and its potential. By consciously applying the principles of Functional Fluency – moving from reaction to response, fostering genuine connection and building a shared language for behaviour – educators can do more than just manage a classroom. They can create pockets of a healthier, more thoughtful and more equitable society, empowering the next generation not only to navigate the world as it is, but to begin building the world as it ought to be.

When 'thinking' goes wrong: understanding distorted Accounting and toxic masculinity

As we have seen, Accounting in Functional Fluency terms is an effective behaviour. It falls clearly into the golden zone. However, it is also clear that people are sometimes capable of devoting considerable amounts of time and energy to Accounting and yet still make ineffective behavioural decisions.

More concerning are the people whose Accounting results in negative behaviour choices. I am thinking here about people who evaluate their situation and conclude that their interests are best served by supporting extreme, nationalist politicians, or men who employ their *alert* and *aware* behaviour to conclude that they should focus their energy on developing a harem of subservient women with whom they can satisfy their alpha-male desires.

So, what is going on when Accounting results in behaviour that is racist, sexist or generally denies the value and equal humanity of others?

In Functional Fluency terms, this pattern of behaviour is shown in Figure 18.

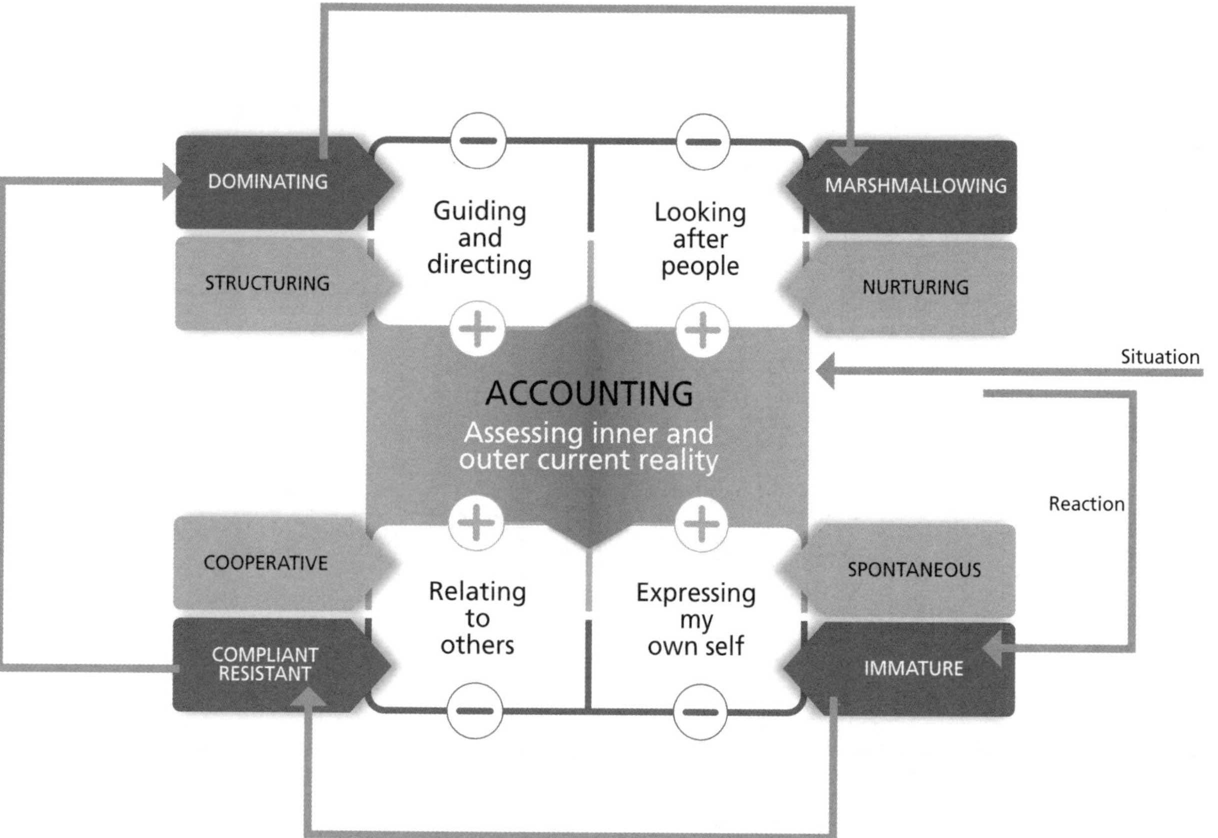

Figure 18 Distorted Accounting

To clarify the situation, we could call this distorted Accounting, where perceived threats short-circuit the golden (lightly shaded) modes of behaviour, pushing people into destructive purple (darkly shaded) behaviours. An example of this behaviour pattern, which is causing huge problems in schools currently, is toxic masculinity. Driven by hugely popular social-media influencers, male pupils are increasingly focusing their time and energy on 'improving' their physical appearance while also developing damagingly negative views about women and highly dysfunctional understandings of the nature of relationships.

How can Functional Fluency counter these powerful trends? How can we demonstrate that Functional Fluency has an evolutionary mandate that is in direct opposition to the myopic approaches of these influencers that have such a negative impact on the outlooks and preoccupations of our young people?

A representation of the behaviour choices that the perpetrator of a racist incident made might be instructive here.

The perpetrator is largely driven to make reactive behaviour choices, informed by their 'understanding' of identity politics. This 'understanding' has been formed by the media, family and friends or a specific incident. The distorted Accounting that is carried out results in the perception by the perpetrator of a threat to their existing status or power. It is important to recognise the role of power in this situation. Racism, sexism and general bullying are all carried out by people who have a dominant position in society but perceive this position to be under threat. This perception of threat is often a direct consequence of a society fixated on greatness and competition. When worth is defined by a dominant position in a hierarchy, any challenge to that position feels existential, triggering the very defensive, reactive behaviours that distorted Accounting describes.

This threat can come in the form of women or ethnic or LGBTQ+ groups or individuals that the perpetrator opposes. And it is this perceived threat that results in the distorted Accounting as the perpetrator bypasses the more empathetic and cooperative modes and defaults to reactive, defensive behaviours. But the people who are perceived as threatening are always in socially less powerful situations than the perpetrator, even if the perpetrator may not be willing or able to recognise this. The result of this distorted Accounting is discriminatory behaviour, which could take the form of Dominating (shouting racial abuse), Marshmallowing (patronising sexism), Compliant / Resistant (rebellious refusal) or Immature behaviour (*reckless*).

Seen in this way, it is clear that Functional Fluency can demonstrate how distorted Accounting leads to a range of negative outcomes. Reaction rather than response, driven by an incomplete understanding of the power dynamics in society, is the result.

Talking through these situations using this language could radically reduce such incidents. It is hard, difficult work, but the rewards will be worth the effort. By clarifying what is going on and providing a shared language to describe behaviour, the Functional Fluency model constitutes a route out of these difficult territories. They will remain difficult and contested, but the model shows clear alternatives in the form of the Structuring, Nurturing, Cooperative and Spontaneous behaviour that thriving societies require.

A call to action: your role in a more Functionally Fluent future

We are at a critical juncture. The rapid rise of artificial intelligence (AI) is no longer a future prospect; it is the central, driving force of change in our world and, along with the escalating climate crisis, will define the next century. Both demand more from us than technological solutions or policy changes; they demand a fundamental evolution in how we think, relate and act. As Valerie Hannon (2017) persuasively argues, the educational paradigms of the past are insufficient for the challenges of the present and the future. If education is to be part of the solution and not the problem, it must be reimagined. This new reality, dominated by the promises and perils of AI and the complex threats resulting from global warming, require us to redefine the very purpose of learning. In this vital process, Functional Fluency offers a profound and practical path forward.

AI presents a paradox. On the one hand, it offers unprecedented opportunities for personalised learning. On the other, it accelerates the 'disintermediation' (Hannon, 2017) that has already reshaped so many parts of our lives. We can book a holiday without a travel agent, and soon a student may be able to access a bespoke curriculum without the daily guidance of a teacher. The risk is that, in our rush to embrace technological efficiency, we strip away the essential human interactions where Nurturing, Structuring and Cooperative behaviours are modelled and learned. An education mediated primarily by algorithms risks producing individuals skilled in isolation but deficient in the relational competencies needed for a thriving, cohesive society.

More profoundly, AI operates as a 'black box', delivering answers without revealing its reasoning. This threatens to erode the critical-thinking and evaluative skills that are fundamental to human progress. If we don't know **how** we know, we risk losing the ability to chart our own course.

This is where Functional Fluency provides a critical framework, especially through the Accounting mode. Functional Fluency is about how we use our time and energy – and AI will greatly multiply the amount of energy at our disposal. It is therefore all the more important that we effectively harness this energy to direct it into the golden modes from which we can all benefit.

The climate crisis presents a different, yet related, challenge. It is a crisis of consequence, demanding that we act now to avert a future catastrophe. It requires a profound shift, from short-term thinking to long-term stewardship. Here, again, Functional Fluency is key.

To manage these challenges effectively, we must cultivate our ability to:

- evaluate and scrutinise, using Accounting to understand complex systems and to understand the consequences of our actions, and to make difficult, evidence-based decisions for sustainabil ty

- make ethical judgements, using Cooperative mode behaviour to foster the global collaboration required to address these borderless problems, moving beyond individual or national interests towards collective action

- weigh consequences and foster empathy using Nurturing mode behaviour to go beyond the immediate answer and consider the long-term impact of decisions on our communities and our world.

Accounting is the essential 'human in the loop', ensuring that technology serves our collective purpose rather than defining it for us. The tools in the Accounting toolbox are the mechanisms by wh ch we maintain our agency. Furthermore, the 'golden mode' behaviours – empathy, understanding, firmness and clear authority – provide the relational wisdom that AI cannot replicate. These human-to-human skills are what build the trust and community necessary for us to face complex challenges together.

A redefined purpose for education

Therefore, the redefined purpose of education is not simply to cultivate Functionally Fluent citizens but to create Functionally Fluent interactions and relationships. Individuals can leverage AI as a powerful tool, but governing it with the wisdom and ethical clarity that comes from well-developed Accounting requires Functionally Fluent relationships. And the collaborative spirit needed to build ethical AI is also needed to forge global climate consensus and drive action.

Functionally Fluent citizens are able to build equitable relationships through skilled Nurturing and Structuring, and engage in creative, collaborative problem-solving through Spontaneous and Cooperative mode behaviour. These are the skills that the pupils of Meadowbank Middle School need as they move into the world of jobs and families.

In this vision, schools become more important than ever. They are the primary arenas where pupils come together to practise these essential human interactions. As Hannon (2017) suggests, they are one of the last places where we can consciously create community and practise the human interactions – the debate, empathy, collaboration and critical inquiry – without which we can solve neither AI nor the climate crisis.

The challenge is significant, but the path forwards is not to add more initiatives to overburdened schools. Instead, it is to offer a unifying language and a shared model for the most fundamental aspect of education: effective human interaction. Functional Fluency is not another programme to implement; it is a way of being for us to cultivate. By embedding its principles, we empower our schools to become workshops for a thriving, humane and 'good-enough' society – equitable, resilient and focused on collective thriving rather than individual 'greatness' – one thoughtful, future-conscious interaction at a time.

It is July and Pat Harrison is thinking about what she is going to say to the staff and pupils of Meadowbank Middle School at the final school assembly of the year in a few days' time. She already knows that the focus will be Functional Fluency. Since her almost apologetic introduction of this concept back in September, the impact has been far greater than she could ever have hoped. Every day now, she hears both pupils and staff using the language of the model in their daily conversations, pointing out when others are using Compliant / Resistant or Marshmallowing behaviour. Perhaps most important of all, she hears them referring to the Accounting Framework, and the reduction in incidents due to pupils learning to respond rather than react has been nothing short of astounding. Pat smiles to herself as she realises that this planning she is doing is a form of Accounting in itself – better than the last-minute panic she had with that talk to the Innovation Hub!

Getting Chris Andrews involved in that was a brilliant idea, she realises. The impact of Functional Fluency on him has clearly been profound – and that governors meeting he ran was truly impressive. He is clearly a future headteacher, something Pat would never have imagined a year ago.

Pat pauses for a moment and catches site of the various cups and certificates that have been gathering in her office in recent days, which she will award at the assembly. These have always given her great pleasure in previous years, but she realises that this year they aren't the main thing at all. It suddenly becomes clear to Pat that what she wants to emphasise most in her talk – the thing that has given her most pleasure during the year and that has been the most rewarding thing she's done in her career – is the introduction of Functional Fluency. People in the school are getting on with each other better as a result and those who leave this summer are better equipped to have happy and successful lives than any who have left before. The school leaders, the staff, the pupils and their families have done this, and Functional Fluency has made it possible. Pat smiles to herself as she starts to write notes for her speech. 'How can I revise the school motto to include the word "thrive"?' she muses.

APPENDIX: THE CERTIFIED FUNCTIONAL FLUENCY TEACHER PROGRAMME

This book introduces Functional Fluency for your personal and professional growth. The Certified Functional Fluency Teacher Programme (CFFTP) trains you to teach Functional Fluency to others, including colleagues, pupils and parents.

Teachers who complete all five elements of the programme become more reflective, self-managing practitioners. They learn how to use their time and energy more effectively, thus gaining capacity. The training and support elements of the programme ensure that they can use Functional Fluency confidently to enhance their professional lives. Additionally, the programme aims to have a long-term beneficial systemic impact across schools. The repeated cycles of teaching of Functional Fluency embed learning and enable pupils to take more and more responsibility for themselves and others as they grow and mature. The extended nature of the programme, with ongoing support opportunities, gives the programme and the teachers who engage with it the best possible chance of success. Plans are in place to have the programme certified by the CPD Standards Office so that teachers who complete it can log their continuing professional development (CPD) hours.

CFFTP1: The Temple Index of Functional Fluency (TIFF)

What is it?

Susannah Temple created the Temple Index of Functional Fluency (TIFF) around the year 2000, using her PhD research to prove the reliability and validity of the concept. The tool provides users with a snapshot of the current patterns in their use of their time and energy.

Why is it important?

See the explanation of TIFF in Chapter 1.

What is involved?

The TIFF provider, a person from a professional background who has completed Functional Fluency International's TIFF Provider Licensing Training, provides the client with access to the questionnaire through a secure website and unique code. Once the client has completed their responses, the provider shares the results report with the client in a feedback session (of around 90 minutes). Here, the provider:

- explains the Functional Fluency model

- talks through the results with the client

- asks questions to help the client explore the ramifications of the results

- works with the client to help them identify an action plan of changes that they would like to make, in light of the results.

This is a holistic process. The feedback discussion may focus on substantive aspects of the client's teaching work, but equally it may not. TIFF explores all aspects of the client's behaviour, with a view to finding any aspects that can potentially become more effective. The nature of teaching is such that a poor relationship outside school can have a serious negative impact on performance in the classroom.

CFFTP2: Introduction to Functional Fluency training course

What is it?

The Introduction to Functional Fluency course is a half-day training course that has been devised by a group of Functional Fluency providers to give a clear explanation of the model and how individuals can use it to help improve their interactions with others.

Why is it important?

This course enables participants to think about how they can use the Functional Fluency model in their life and work. It enhances the understanding of the model that they began to develop during their TIFF feedback session.

What is involved?

This training is a three-hour online course. The Functional Fluency model is explained, and there are opportunities to ask questions and to use the model interactively. A certified trainer from the Functional Fluency International network facilitates the course.

CFFTP3: Get on the Mat

What is it?

The Get on the Mat workshop offers an opportunity to experience Functional Fluency in action.

Why is it important?

The explorative nature of Get on the Mat sessions makes this element of the Functional Fluency teacher-training concept a particularly powerful one for use in schools.

In a school situation, the benefits of this element for the emotional and behavioural learning of young people can hardly be overstated. The vital emphasis that this work places on the importance of Accounting has benefits in a school context long after the Mat has been packed away or the computer turned off.

What is involved?

Using either the physical mat that groups of pupils can stand around and walk on, or the virtual mat with its representative figures, groups investigate issues and situations. They gain insight into an understanding of their feelings and behaviours and those of others. They also experiment with alternative responses and play out different ways of behaving to find more effective solutions. For example, a group might explore the issues surrounding a difficult conversation by having members stand on modes such as Marshmallowing or Compliant / Resistant physically to experience an ineffective dynamic, and then experiment with moving to more effective modes such as Structuring and Cooperative.

CFFTP4: Functional Fluency lesson outlines

What is it?

This element introduces the series of 12 lesson outlines that have been written to enable colleagues to teach Functional Fluency to pupils of all ages and in all contexts.

Why is it important?

The aim behind the set of draft lesson outlines is to provide a structure to introduce pupils to and reinforce their understanding of Functional Fluency through teaching sequences repeated at key transition points: the start of Years 7, 10 and 12. The lessons can be adapted to match pupils' developing sophistication, with the expectation that they will build upon prior learning with each iteration.

The 12-lesson approach was devised to make it easy for schools to fit them into their existing curriculum without having to create a new lesson on the timetable. The lessons could be taught over the first 12 weeks of the academic year in PSHE, or they could be taught in a more concentrated block of three or four lessons per week over four or three weeks in one or a range of subjects. In this way, across the whole of the school community, there is a steady input of teaching and thinking relating to Functional Fluency, gradually building this way of establishing more effective relationships into the very essence of the institution.

What is involved?

The initial session involves an explanation of how to use the lesson outlines and an opportunity to work with colleagues to consider how to adapt these draft plans to meet the needs of pupils in their school. This is fol owed by voluntary online drop-in meetings for teachers on the Certified Functional Fluency Teacher Programme. Here, ideas about how to make best use of the outline lessons are shared, to help teachers prepare to teach them.

CFFTP5: Learning to question

What is it?

This advanced training module utilises the **Accounting Framework** to empower teachers with the skills to interrogate information critically and to teach these skills to pupils. It bridges the gap between psychological fluency and academic rigour, providing a structured approcch to evaluate the veracity of information and ascertain what further context is needed to verify its trustworthiness. The module has been devised by Chdel Cooke (Functional Fluency professional and qualified therapist) and Steve Willshaw.

Why is it important?

We live in an age of increasing information exchange, where it is difficult to distinguish between reliable sources and those designed to exploit us. This course module introduces the Accounting Framework, a structure for teaching to pupils to help them interrogate the information they are presented with, both in the classroom and in the digital world.

What is involved?

Through discussion-based sessions, participants apply the framework to topical events and reflect on how to use these questioning techniques to refine their own teaching practice.

For more information on how to access any or all elements of this programme, visit www.functionalfluency.com or contact the author directly via www.swillshawconsulting.co.uk and click on 'contact'.

REFERENCES

Alpert, A. (2022) *The good-enough life*. Princeton, NJ: Princeton University Press.

Armstrong, K. (2011) *Twelve steps to a compassionate life*. London: The Bodley Head.

Barrow, G. (2016) 'Educational Transactional Analysis: underpinning assumptions, principles and philosophy' in Barrow, G. and Newton, T. (eds.) *Educational Transactional Analysis: an international guide to theory and practice*. Abingdon: Routledge, pp.12–19.

Barrow, G. and Newton, T. (eds.) (2016) *Educational Transactional Analysis: an international guide to theory and practice*. Abingdon: Routledge.

Berne, E. (1961) *Transactional Analysis in psychotherapy*. New York: Grove Press.

Berne, E. (1964) *Games people play*. New York: Grove Press.

Bishop, L. and van den Blink, M. (2023) 'Embracing Challenging Relationships for Effective Leadership: Three Perspectives' in Fawcett, V. (ed.) (2023) *The fluent leader: Functional Fluency and effective leadership inspired by Transactional Analysis*. Abingdon: Routledge.

Bishop, L. (2024) *Building school effectiveness with Functional Fluency: 'there's a whole new school on the block'* [online] Available at https://functionalfluency.com/uploads/files/downloads/building-school-effectiveness-with-ff-case-study-6(1).pdf (Accessed: 22 January 2024).

Blakemore, S.-J. (2018) *Inventing ourselves: the secret life of the teenage brain*. London: Penguin Random House.

Bloom, B.S. (ed.) (1956) *Taxonomy of educational objectives: The classification of educational goals. Handbook I: Cognitive domain*. David McKay Company.

Croome, S. (2023) *The power of teams: how to create and lead thriving school teams*. Melton: John Catt Educational Ltd.

Dana, D. (2018) *The polyvagal theory in therapy: engaging the rhythm of regulation*. New York: W.W. Norton & Company.

Davies, W. (2023) 'The reaction economy', *London Review of Books*, 45(5).

de Botton, A. (2012) *Religion for atheists*. London: Penguin.

Deci, E. and Ryan, R. (1985) *Intrinsic motivation and self-determination in human behavior*. New York: Plenum.

Department for Education (2016) 'Standard for teachers' professional development' [online] Available at: https://assets.publishing.service.gov.uk/media/5a819db8ed915d74e6233385/160712_-_PD_standard.pdf (Accessed: 8 November 2024).

Department for Education (2025) *Curriculum and assessment review: interim report* [online] Available at https://assets.publishing.service.gov.uk/media/67d9617b594182179fe08778/Curriculum_and_Assessment_Review_interim_report.pdf (Accessed: 24 March 2025).

Drew, C. (2023) *79 examples of school vision statements* [online] Helpful Professor. Available at: https://helpfulprofessor.com/school-vision-and-mission-statements (Accessed: 12 September 2025).

Duckworth, A. (2016) *Grit: The power of passion and perseverance.* New York: Scribner / Simon & Schuster.

Ebbinghaus, H. (1913) *Memory: a contribution to experimental psychology.* Translated by H. Ruger and C. Bussenius. New York: Teachers College, Columbia University.

Fawcett, V. (ed.) (2023) *The fluent leader: Functional Fluency and effective leadership inspired by Transactional Analysis.* Abingdon: Routledge.

First Round Review (2015) 'Radical Candor — The Surprising Secret to Being a Good Boss' [online] Available at: https://review.firstround.com/radical-candor-the-surprising-secret-to-being-a-good-boss/ (Accessed: 9 March 2026).

Functional Fluency International (2022) *The Functional Fluency starter pack* [online] Available at: https://functionalfluencyint.activehosted.com/f/1 (Accessed: 11 September 2025).

Grant, V. (2024a) 'New perspectives on leadership and wellness', Myatt and Co recording [online] Available at: https://films.myattandco.com/programs/ssn-new-perspectives-on-leadership-and-wellness-diversity (subscription required) (Accessed: 11 September 2025).

Grant, V. (2024b) 'Wellbeing and resilience blog', Integrity Coaching [online] Available at: www.integritycoaching.co.uk/blog (Accessed: 10 April 2024).

Guskey, T.R. (2000) *Evaluating Professional Development.* Thousand Oaks, CA: Corwin Press.

Hannon, V. with Peterson, A. (2017) *Thrive: schools reinvented for the real challenges we face.* London: Innovation Unit Press.

Hargreaves, A. and Fullan, M. (2012) *Professional capital: transforming teaching in every school.* Abingdon: Routledge.

Hollis, J. (2005) *Finding meaning in the second half of life.* New York: Gotham Books.

Hollis, J. (2009) *What matters most: living a more considered life.* New York: Gotham Books.

Jubilee Centre and University of Birmingham (2022) *Jubilee Centre framework for character education in schools.* 3rd edn. [online] Available at www.jubileecentre.ac.uk/character-education-/the-jubilee-centre-framework-for-character-education-in-schools (Accessed: 31 January 2024).

Kline, N. (1999) *Time to think: listening to ignite the human mind.* London: Cassell.

Kotter, J.P. (1996) *Leading change.* Boston, MA: Harvard Business School Press.

Kretchmer, H. (2021) '"Trickle-down" tax cuts don't work, study says', World Economic Forum [online] 11 January. Available at: www.weforum.org/stories/2021/01/tax-cuts-for-wealthy-impact-lse-study/#:~:text=A%20study%20claims%20that%20taxing,lead%20to%20higher%20income%20inequality%E2%80%9D (Accessed: 17 June 2025).

Lemov, D., Lewis, H., Williams, D. and Frazier, D. (2023) *Reconnect: building school culture for meaning, purpose, and belonging.* Hoboken, NJ: Jossey-Bass.

Medical News Today (2023) '6 types of sexism, examples, and their impact' [online] Available at www.medicalnewstoday.com/articles/types-of-sexism#hostile (Accessed: 13 January 2026).

Menakem, R. (2017) *My grandmother's hands: racialized trauma and the pathway to mending our hearts and bodies*. Las Vegas: Central Recovery Press.

Moore-Anderson, C. (2024) *Difference maker: enacting systems theory in biology teaching* [self-published].

Morris, J. (2015) *Burnout to brilliance: strategies for sustainable success*. Winchester: Change Makers Books.

Morrish, A. (2022) *The authentic leader*. London: Bloomsbury Education.

Morrish, A. (2025) *Beyond belief: why school accountability is broken and how to fix it*. London: Hachette Learning.

Myatt, M. (2016) *High challenge, low threat: finding the balance*. Woodbridge: John Catt Educational Ltd.

O'Sullivan, S. (2025) 'The number of people with chronic conditions is soaring. Are we less healthy than we used to be – or overdiagnosing illness?' *The Guardian*, 1 March [online] Available at: www.theguardian.com/society/2025/mar/01/the-number-of-people-with-chronic-conditions-is-soaring-are-we-less-healthy-than-we-used-to-be-or-overdiagnosing-illness (Accessed: 11 September 2025).

Oberholzer, L. and Boyle, D. (2024) *Mentoring and coaching in education: a guide to coaching and mentoring teachers in every stage of their careers*. London: Bloomsbury Academic.

Ofsted (2012) 'Moving English forward: action to raise standards in English' [online] Available at: www.ofsted.gov.uk/resources/110118 (Accessed: 11 September 2025).

Palmer, P.J. (2007) *The courage to teach: guide for reflection & renewal*. 10th Anniversary edn. San Francisco: Jossey Bass.

Porges, S.W. and Porges, S. (2023) *Our polyvagal world: how safety and trauma change us*. New York: W.W. Norton & Company.

Pratt, K. (2021) *Transactional Analysis coaching*. Abingdon: Routledge.

Priestley, J.B. (1945). *An Inspector Calls*. London: Heinemann.

Rosenshine, B. (2012) 'Principles of instruction: research-based strategies that all teachers should know', *American Educator*, 36(1), pp.12–39.

Scott, K. (2019). *Radical candor: Be a kick-ass boss without losing your humanity*. Fully rev. & updated edn. London: Pan Books.

Sendak, Maurice (1963) *Where The Wild Things Are*. New York: Harper & Row.

Sharma, L. (2023) *Building culture: a handbook to harnessing human nature to create strong school teams*. Woodbridge: John Catt Educational Ltd.

Sherrington, T. (2019) *Rosenshine's Principles in action*. Melton: John Catt Educational Ltd.

Sherrington, T. and Caviglioli, O. (2020) *Teaching Walkthrus: five-step guides to instructional coaching*. Woodbridge: John Catt Educational Ltd.

Sinclair, D. (2024) 'Engaging leadership', Myatt and Co. [online] Available at: https://films.myattandco.com/programs/ssn-engaging-leadership-oracy (subscription required) (Accessed: 15 February 2024).

Solnit, R. (2024) 'In the shadow of Silicon Valley', *London Review of Books*, 46(3).

Steinberg, L. (2014) *Age of opportunity. lessons from the new science of adolescence.* Boston: Eamon Dolan / Houghton Mifflin Harcourt.

Stiglitz, J.E., Sen, A. and Fitoussi, J. (2010) *Mismeasuring our lives: why GDP doesn't add up.* New York: New Press.

Temple, S. (2004) 'Building Self-awareness', *Emotional Literacy Update*, Feb 2004 Issue 4.

Temple, S. (2015) 'Celebrating Functional Fluency and its contribution to Transactional Analysis theory', *Transactional Analysis Journal*, 45(1) pp.10–22.

Temple, S. (2016) 'Becoming a teacher' in Barrow, G. and Newton, T. (eds.) *Educational Transactional Analysis: an international guide to theory and practice.* Abingdon: Routledge.

'Transactional Analysis' podcast (2024) Series 8, Episode 9 [online] Available at: www.buzzsprout.com/2423019/episodes/16037317-s8-e9-functional-fluency-panel-discussion-with-beatrijs-dijkman-layo-seriki-liz-jackson-and-valerie-cionca (Accessed: 16 January 2025).

van der Kolk, B. (2014) *The body keeps the score.* London: Penguin Random House.

Wallace, D. (2023) *The culture trap: ethnic expectations and unequal schooling for black youth.* New York: Oxford University Press.

Warren, S. and Bigger, S. (2017) *Living contradiction: a teacher's examination of tension and disruption in schools, in classrooms and in self.* Carmarthen: Crown House.

Whitaker, D. (2021) *The kindness principle.* Carmarthen: Independent Thinking Press.

Wiseman, L. (2017) *Multipliers: how the best leaders make everyone smarter.* New York: HarperBusiness.

Wiseman, R. (2012) *The as if principle: the radically new approach to changing your life.* New York: Free Press.

Yeager, D. and Duckworth, A. (2024) *The science of motivating young people* [video] Available at www.youtube.com/watch?v=YyX6hf8Q9So (Accessed: 16 January 2026).

ACKNOWLEDGEMENTS

The Publishers would like to thank the following for permission to reproduce copyright material.

p.1–2 Extract from 'Building Self-awareness' in *Emotional Literacy Update*, Feb 2004, Issue 4. Published by Functional Fluency International. Reproduced by permission of Susannah Temple; **pp.2, 16, 33, 52, 80, 104, 105 & 208** Diagrams of The Functional Fluency Model. Reproduced by permission of Functional Fluency International; **p.3** Diagram of behaviour modes. Reproduced by permission of Functional Fluency International; **p.13** Diagram 'The Power of Choice' from *The Fluent Leader: Functional Fluency and Effective Leadership inspired by Transactional Analysis* edited by Valerie Fawcett. Reproduced by permission of Functional Fluency International and Susannah Temple; **pp.13 & 19** Extracts used with permission of Taylor and Francis (Books) Limited UK, from *The Fluent Leader: Functional Fluency and Effective Leadership inspired by Transactional Analysis* by Valerie Fawcett, 2023. Permission conveyed through Copyright Clearance Center, Inc.; **pp.18–19 & 203** Extracts from *What Matters Most: Living a More Considered Life* by James Hollis. Published by Gotham, 2009. Reproduced by permission of Dr James Hollis, Ph.D.; **p.20–1** Extract from *The Kindness Principle* by D. Whitaker, published by Independent Thinking Press, 2021. Reproduced by permission of Crown House Publishing; **p.22 & 28** Extracts from *The Functional Fluency Starter Pack*, 2022. Reproduced by permission of Functional Fluency International; **pp.26–7 & 53** Extracts from 'Celebrating Functional Fluency and its contribution to Transactional Analysis theory' by Susannah Temple (2015) in *Transactional Analysis Journal*, 45(1) copyright © 2017 International Transactional Analysis Association, reprinted by permission of Informa UK Limited, trading as Taylor & Francis Group, www.tandfonline.com on behalf of International Transactional Analysis Association and reproduced by permission of Susannah Temple; **p.31** Artwork reproduced by permission of Viv Grant; **p.46** Artwork reproduced by permission of Simphiwe Mahlanyana; **pp.49–50** Artwork and quote reproduced by permission of Liz Jackson; **pp.64–5** Diagrams of Functionally Fluent teaching and learning feedback loops reproduced by permission of Functional Fluency International; **p.71** Functional Fluency lesson observation form reproduced by permission of Functional Fluency International; **p.76** Artwork reproduced by permission of Sean Warren; **p.78** Artwork reproduced by permission of Martian Slagter; **pp.84–5** Extract from 'Moving English Forward: Action to Raise Standards in English', Ofsted (2012). Available at: www.ofsted.gov.uk/resources/110118. Contains public sector information licensed under the Open Government Licence v3.0. https://www.nationalarchives.gov.uk/doc/open-government-licence/version/3/; **pp.92–3** Extracts used with permission of James Wiley & Sons Inc., from *The Courage to Teach: Guide for Reflection & Renewal* by P.J. Palmer, 2007. Permission conveyed through Copyright Clearance Center, Inc.; **pp.94–5** Extracts from *Professional Capital: Transforming Teaching in Every School* by A. Hargreaves and M. Fullan, 2012. Published by Routledge and Teachers College Press. Reproduced by permission of Teachers College Press; **p.99** Artwork reproduced by permission of Hilary Desousa; **p.101** Artwork reproduced by permission of Giles Barrow; **p.132** Artwork reproduced by permission of Joanna Williams; **pp.135, 137, 171 & 194–5** Extracts from *Building school effectiveness with Functional Fluency: 'there's a whole new school on the block'* by Leona Bishop, 2024. Published by Functional Fluency International. Reproduced with permission of Functional Fluency International; **p.152** Artwork reproduced by permission of Joaquim Braga; **p.153** Artwork reproduced by permission of Sue Ashby; **p.163** Artwork reproduced by permission of Stephanie Carlin; **p.167** Artwork reproduced by permission of David Brown; **p.169** Artwork reproduced by permission of Steve Russell; **pp.192–4** Extract from 'The reaction economy' by William Davies in *London Review of Books*, 45(5), 2023. Reproduced by permission of London Review of Books; **pp.197–8** Extracts from *Finding Meaning in the Second Half of Life* by James Hollis. Published by Gotham, 2005. Reproduced by permission of Dr James Hollis, Ph.D.

TIFF and GOTM are protected intellectual property of Functional Fluency International and are used with permission.